LIFE ON THE RUN

This is the story of one athlete of the 20th century and a record of the changing world of athletics during that period. I have written this because of the vast changes in sport, and athletics in particular, over a period of fifty or more years. There have been many changes but very few have brought about higher standards.

LIFE ON THE RUN

Stan Eldon

Stan Eldon M.B.E

ARTHUR H. STOCKWELL LTD.
Elms Court Ilfracombe Devon
Established 1898

British Library Cataloguing-in-Publication Data.
A catalogue record for this book is available from the British Library.

The book is dedicated to my parents, my wife of forty-four years Marion, my family and those women in my life I have mentioned in this book.

Acknowledgements

My thanks to the following for the use of photographs, newpaper extracts and cartoons used in this book.

E. D. Lacey, photographer; *The Times; The Sunday Times; Daily Express; Sunday Express; The Telegraph; News of the World; London Evening News; Reading Evening Post; Reading Chronicle; Windsor Express; Athletics Weekly;* Len Runyard; Keystone Press Agency.

Thanks also to all those who have helped to make my sporting life so interesting and full, and who have directly or indirectly helped me to put this book together.

ISBN 0 7223 3409-5
Printed in Great Britain by
Arthur H. Stockwell Ltd.
Elms Court Ilfracombe
Devon

Contents

Foreword

By Len Runyard, formerly Hon. Secretary, Eton AC, Windsor and Eton AC, and Windsor, Slough and Eton AC.

I have much pleasure in writing this foreword to, *'Life on the Run'*. When I joined the Eton AC, over fifty years ago, there was a small band of very enthusiastic young athletes who coped extremely well despite a complete lack of facilities. One of these was the fourteen years old Stan Eldon, a pupil from the Windsor Boys' Grammar School. Even at this stage of his athletic career, his potential was obviously outstanding, while apart from this, his enthusiasm and dedication to athletics was boundless. Essentially, I remember him as a cooperative, keen and loyal club member and a very generous natured and nice person; he hasn't changed in the interim!

In 1952 the club moved to Windsor and became Windsor and Eton AC, it was under this name that Stan gained his great athletic reputation. In 1954 he was called up for two years' National Service in the Army. Each week, whether it be track, road or cross-country races, Army duties allowing, Stan would travel considerable distances to represent the club. It is worth remembering that in those days, athletes were completely amateur and paid their own expenses! With increasing fame, Stan was pursued by several leading athletic clubs, but he always refused the offer, and remained completely loyal to his small town club (happily no longer small, and now one of the major clubs in the country). After leaving the Army in 1956, he joined the police force, which because of the long working hours, made training difficult, but somehow Stan coped and continued to run his way to the top.

It is impossible for me to list all his many achievements, so I will restrict myself to picking out one special success which was winning the Southern Counties Three Mile Championship, which was held at the Hurlingham track in London, in June 1957. Unable to obtain the necessary time off, he was on traffic duty at the Royal Ascot races on an extremely hot day. As a concession he was allowed to leave an hour early at 1 p.m., after which he had to rush back home to wash, have a meal, and then get to Hurlingham track ready for a 4.30 p.m. start. I was waiting for him by the entrance, and getting more and more anxious as the minutes ticked away. Suddenly, at 4.10 p.m., he came rushing up asking "Am I too late?" He barely had time to do no more than just jog up the track, plus a few bursts of speed before being called to the start. Taking the lead immediately, he raced away to easily win the title, well ahead of the second runner, and breaking the six mile championship record by over a minute!

The year 1958 was special for Stan, for after brilliantly winning the International Cross-Country Championship, at the age of twenty-one years, he had a series of major wins on the track, including the AAA three mile and six mile titles. However 1959 was his special season (if only the Olympic Games had been held in that year, for in 1960 he was plagued by illness). After winning many of the major distance races in Europe, he was later honoured by being selected as the World Athlete of the Year by the prestigious Society of USA Athletic Statisticians. Only three other British athletes have been so chosen; Roger Bannister, Seb Coe and Jonathan Edwards.

The rest of his athletic career is now part of athletic history. Stan, indeed, has devoted his life to the furtherance of athletics and he is still actively coaching and advising today; he was (and still is) the Best in British athletics!

Chapter One

The Early Years

I was born on 1st May 1936 in Windsor. My father was a retired soldier and had been stationed in Combermere Barracks, Windsor, the home of the Household Cavalry, and that is how I ended up being born in the Royal Borough. My mother, Flora Ivy Tremaine Marshall, had left her home in Tisbury, Wiltshire, where she was one of fifteen children and went to Windsor as parlour maid to the then Dean of Windsor in Windsor Castle at the age of fourteen years. My parents were married in Tisbury on 25th August 1934, when she was twenty-eight, and described on the marriage certificate as a cook; and he was forty-seven years old and listed as a salesman. Their respective fathers, Uriah Marshall, retired insurance agent, and Francis Howard Eldon, retired drayman.

My father, William Frank Eldon, was born at Eton on 18th October 1886 and had enlisted in the Army at the age of fourteen years (he should have been fifteen) in 1900 during the Boer War in South Africa. His father was wounded serving there and his wife took advantage of the free passages for the wives of wounded soldiers, and Dad signed up as a bugle boy so that he could go out as well. As he falsified his birth date, he had two birthdays for the rest of his life. His family also had various spellings of the surname, and when he was born, his birth certificate had his name as ALDEN, but the family had generally accepted ELDON or ELDEN, and when he joined up, he had to select one permanent name, so he settled on ELDON, although his brother and sister kept with ELDEN. Uncertain spellings of surnames were apparently quite common at this time. After he returned from that war, he signed up for the 'real' Army in 1903. He joined the Royal Field Artillery, probably because he had grown up with horses working with his father on the brewers' drays, and horses were still very much in use to pull the guns by the artillery in the early part of the Great War. He went to India and was a sergeant car driver for King George V and Queen Mary on their Coronation Tour of the country in 1911, for which he was awarded a specially engraved Coronation Medal. While in India, he was a British Army Boxing Champion. He then went off to fight in the First World War and was wounded in 1915 and returned to Windsor, where he helped to train the Household Cavalry in horsemanship.

According to his Army discharge papers, he was a 3rd Class Gymnast; obviously not very good, and something that I must have inherited, as gymnastics was never one of my strong activities, but he was a 1st Class Equestrian. He left the Army in 1918 when he had completed fifteen years' service; twelve years with the Colours and three years in the Army Reserve, and settled in Windsor. He kept up his interest in boxing and often went to the Star and Garter Gym in Peascod Street, Windsor, where all the great champions trained right up to Sugar Ray Robinson in 1952. My father was a strange mixture; brought up as a Wesleyan or Methodist, he never touched alcohol and in spite of his years in the Army as a sergeant, I never heard him swear; and I mean never. On the other hand, he had been a smoker from the age of about ten, starting off on Woodbines and progressing to Players, and about twenty a day. He smoked all his life until his death age eighty-eight years in 1974. Because he smoked, none of his children have ever smoked and I have never even tried a drag behind the bike sheds.

I was the first of my father's second family. By his first marriage he had a daughter and two sons, and his wife died when the youngest one, my half-brother Bernard, was seven years old, in 1933. He remarried in 1934 to my mother Ivy, and I came first in 1936, followed by two sisters; one in the year before the war, 1938, and one as peace came in Europe in 1945. I was born in the end terrace house at 25 Elm Road, Windsor, which backed on to Combermere Barracks, which was literally just a few feet away; so I grew up to the sound of bugles playing 'reveille' and 'lights out'. There was no electricity and only gaslights in three rooms; two downstairs, and one upstairs in my parents' bedroom. In the bedrooms of us children, there was a single torch light bulb attached to a picture frame above the bed, that worked from a small battery, or there was a small night-light candle. There was no bathroom and the toilet was outside, although it was within the main structure of the house and not in an outbuilding as many were in those days. I remember the squares of newspaper torn up and tied with string — the substitute for toilet paper. Bath night was a tin bath with hot water heated up by the 'copper' in the kitchen (or was it the scullery?). I seem to remember it was youngest first and oldest last, so the younger you were, the cleaner the water.

I have always liked fresh-baked bread, and the smell of the bakery on the corner of Elm Road, can still be remembered. The little bakehouse at the back of the corner shop, run by the North family, was opposite our local, but as my parents did not drink, my only visit there was at Christmas time to buy a bottle of stout for the Christmas puddings. I did make frequent visits to the bakery, where I would watch the rolls come out of the giant oven and then run the few yards home with them before covering them with butter and eating them while they were still very warm. They cost a halfpenny each and I have never tasted better bread in my life. I cannot remember very much from before the war; I was only three when war broke out, but I do remember my sister Janet Athol being born on 18th December 1938. I remember because there was a lot of snow on the ground and my mother was in the front bedroom overlooking our little road with my new sister. Dad built a huge *Queen Mary* out of snow, and we spent Christmas that year in the small bedroom at the front of the house.

The Sunday that war was declared, I was apparently in All Saints' Church, Windsor with my parents, although strangely enough I do not remember the details. I do however have memories of the war years. My father was in Dad's Army; he had previously served in the Boer War and the Great War, and he used to leave home at night with his rifle and go off to the ack-ack guns in Windsor Great Park, which were presumably there to protect Windsor Castle. My mother and elder brother went off, on the nights my father was not on duty, to man the stirrup pumps at our church and the laundry where Dad worked. I often wondered what the little flow of water that came from the pump, would do in the face of a real fire. At home when the siren went, it was under the stairs where we had a supply of food and other essentials. If there were too many in the house at the time, then the dining-room table was the protection for some.

My early school days were at Spital Infants' School in Windsor, where I started in 1940. My memories there are of Miss Meanwell the headmistress; the introduction of school dinners at five pence a day (2p); and the smell of cabbage. Towards the end of my time there, I remember how we used to be kept informed by the headmistress on the progress of the war. I only remember one occasion when the school was informed about the death of a father of one of the pupils. This was strange really, as Windsor was a garrison town and the barracks were opposite the school. I remember well my last year at Spital School, where we were graded by our arithmetic achievements. I could recite up to about my fourteen times tables.

At the start of the war, we were all supplied with gas masks. I had a Micky Mouse one with a large tongue, but my sister, who was two years younger, had a large one that she could fit inside for the first part of the war, before switching to the Micky Mouse model. These of course had to be carried to school each day in case of the expected gas attack.

Each day when the siren went, we all trooped down to the underground shelter, which was damp and open to the sky at the far end; I presume to let in fresh air.

Windsor was reasonably spared in the war as far as bombs were concerned, except for a few accidental bombs. One major incident was when the railway was bombed and some cottages near the Great Western Station were wiped out.

The biggest disaster was one Saturday afternoon towards the end of the war. I was at home with my father listening to a football match on the radio and my mother had gone shopping in the town. There was a huge explosion that shook the house and we later found out that a V-2 had hit the destructor chimney about a mile from home and destroyed a number of homes in the Dedworth area of Windsor. Not knowing what had happened, I remember waiting for my mother to arrive home. She did come home safely and knew much more than we did about the bomb. News travelled fast by word of mouth in the town.

My brother Bernard, attended the Windsor County Boys' School, first of all at its old premises in Trinity Place, Windsor, and later at the new school which opened in 1938. He looked after the nature hut at the school, where fish, mice and other creatures were kept. He came home one day after a bombing raid very upset, as all the glass containers had been shattered by the blast and all the pets were dead.

Other memories of the war concerned the wounded soldiers from the military hospital who were allowed into town when they were recovering and they were all dressed in bright blue suits. Then there was the death of a friend's father who was a policeman. He was stabbed by drunken Canadian soldiers in a fight in the town.

In 1943, I had joined the choir of All Saints' Church in Windsor, where my brother had preceded me. He had a wonderful voice and had been compared to Ernest Lush of "Oh for the Wings of a Dove" fame. It is always a problem when one member of a family has to follow someone with a great talent, and I suppose that was a problem that my own children eventually had, keeping up with my athletic talent.

I was actually introduced to the choirmaster on St John's Day at the Parish Church in Windsor, St John the Baptist. I went along to the next choir practise and duly got taken into the choir and started to earn my shilling (5p) a month by attending three practise sessions a week and two services on a Sunday.

To start with I spent time in the organ loft watching the service and learning about the procedures. I always enjoyed this and was fascinated by the organ, its four keyboards and all the stops; sometimes I was allowed to pull out a stop to assist the organist.

There were some strange initiations for choirboys in those days. The process at All Saints' where I had joined, was supposed to involve a dead cat being hung around the neck of the 'victim' but it never happened in my time.

I did not have the voice of an angel or the voice of my brother, but I did progress and eventually became senior chorister with the improved pay of five shillings (25p) a month. Funerals and weddings could boost this as we received two shillings and sixpence for each of these extra duties.

One of the most enjoyable events of the year, was singing carols at the King Edward VII Hospital in Windsor at Christmas time. We would visit all the wards, including maternity, and I would often have to sing solo on these visits. I wonder how many premature births resulted. Other highlights of my years in the choir were the trips to London. At least once every year, the priest in charge at my church, the Reverend Sidney Smith, would take a group from the choir to London for sightseeing, which was always enjoyable, especially when it came to eating, as we always ate both lunch and tea in one of the Lyons Corner Houses. The knickerbocker glories were fantastic and I developed a liking for ice cream, which has never gone away.

It was on some of these outings that I experienced London theatre for the first time. The first show I ever saw was 'Oklahoma', but 'Carousel' and many others followed, either on these choir outings or later with the Church Youth Club.

In the early 1940s while at the infant and junior school, I always had a party on my birthday, which was the 1st May. The weather must have been a lot warmer than now, as every year the party would be in our small back yard and I would have school friends of both sexes attending. We always had a large bath of water to play in and we did not bother with costumes. In fact it was frequently so hot, that Dad used to tie a sheet or blanket over the garden to keep us from the hot sun. I do not remember a bad 1st May from those early days. I no longer strip off in the garden on my birthday; fortunately for the neighbours.

I moved on in 1944 and went to the Royal Free School in the centre of Windsor for the next three years. The headmaster here was a Colonel Frome who ruled the school with his swagger stick and did not mind using it on girls as well as boys.

My memories from this stage of my life were of the large number of Dr Barnardo boys in their uniform; black boots and navy-blue clothes.

By the time I reached the middle of the school, which would have been the last year of the war, there must have been a terrible shortage of teachers; the classes were large and I remember that for days on end there was not a teacher in our class and the head would sit me at the front of the class on a high stool at the teacher's desk and tell me to keep an eye on the class of around forty. I think it was because I was one of the tallest in the class and was less likely to be bullied, even though I was only nine or at the most ten years old.

Even during the war, we made the journey to my mother's old home in Wiltshire, and on one trip down there, my Aunt Mary who was a sergeant in the ATS, was on leave and took me by train to Salisbury just fourteen miles away. It was a very eventful day as bombs were dropping on the old city that day, and while I was outside Woolworth, a stray German plane machine-gunned the street. We made our way back to the station, only to find a number of bombs had fallen on or near the railway track. After a long delay, we caught a train, and as we pulled out of the station, I remember seeing a large crater in a back garden only a few yards from the line. We eventually arrived back in Tisbury very late, and to the great relief of my parents, complete with a box of day-old bantam chicks I had bought in Salisbury Market.

These were the first livestock I owned, and when I got home, I did get into trouble, when I tried to see if bantams could swim. The little chick was rescued by my mother, wrapped up to keep it warm, and it survived. These bantams were my first pets and I had them for some years; providing their special little eggs. Later I had pet black mice, racing pigeons, rabbits, and when I was married, a large number of chickens and two very special black Labrador dogs, Simon and Berry; one before we had children and one after.

Our family had many holidays in the little cottage that my mother grew up in with her fourteen brothers and sisters. This was one of a row of five cottages, stone built with two rooms on the ground floor, two bedrooms on the next floor and one attic room that had to be accessed via what was not much more than a ladder. The children slept three up and three down in a double bed. There was no gas, electricity or water in the cottage, and of course no bathroom or other facilities. About thirty feet from the back door, there was a long corrugated shed which spread behind all the whole row. Each of the homes had part of this and in it was a copper (for the washing) and a toilet which needed frequent emptying. My grandfather would carry the slop bucket up to his allotment and he grew some marvellous vegetables and fruit! The water supply was one tap shared by all the occupants of the five cottages. The only hot water came from the range or a Primus stove, that seemed to be forever on the go. The atmosphere in this lovely old cottage was great and I had some of the best holidays of my life there; although I must admit I never stayed there during winter months, when I am sure it lived up to its name of Windwhistle.

After the war, when I was on holiday at Tisbury, I used to go with my Uncle George, who lived in the family cottage, on his cattle truck taking and collecting cows, mainly from Shaftesbury Market but sometimes Salisbury. I assisted with driving the animals on and off the lorry and I always remember him being very precise as to how this was done, and he always warned me to be very careful because two or three cows could crush you and cause a lot of damage or worse.

On one of my holiday visits, I had a driving accident, and I was only about eight or nine years old. The crash was in a cousin's toy pedal car which I had borrowed. I thought I would try and go faster than normal by taking it down a steep hill on a sideroad and down into the High Street in Tisbury, which was also downhill. It started all right, but soon the car was out of control and my feet had to come off the pedals, which was the only way to stop the car. I swept down the first hill, going faster and faster, and took the right-hand turn into the High Street all right, but the little car was totally out of control and I knew that if I did not stop, I would be going downhill for perhaps a half a mile before it would stop on its own. As I reached the Village Hall on the left-hand side, I took a decision that I had to turn into the road alongside, which was flat. I swung to the left and the car rolled over several times throwing me onto the road. A large bump on the head, and then I had to make a return journey up the hill to take the car back. It seems crazy today, not least because taking a toy car down onto any High Street, even in a village, would seem to be mad in today's world with heavy traffic, but in those days, there were very few cars around. It was good lesson in driving and taught me to be careful of taking corners too fast!

I sometimes stayed with another uncle, Eric, his wife Marion and family in a small sweet shop in the village. I always enjoyed that stay, and it was not just because it was a sweet shop. I sometimes cycled there from Windsor, and on one occasion, I did travel by train, and for the journey home I had to get the train from Tisbury; but for some reason we were late at the station and my uncle, who ran a car hire business as well as the shop, decided he would get me to Salisbury Station ahead of the train. He had one good leg and one artificial leg, but he could drive and he made it to Salisbury Station after racing around the bending country roads, by seconds, and I ran on the platform and just caught the train.

In 1944 my father and brother made the journey to Reading for their medical examination, to see if they were fit to be called-up for active service. They went together on the same day and they both came back A1. Dad was the most pleased I think, as he thought he might see active service in his third war. My brother wanted to be a pilot, but neither got the call as the war was coming to an end.

My youngest sister Judith was born on 5th May 1945, and within a couple of weeks my father received a War Office telegram to say that my elder stepbrother Leslie, a quartermaster sergeant, who was serving on detachment from the Royal Berkshire Regiment with the Africa Rifle Corps had died in Africa on 29th May; just one week after my other brother Bernard's nineteenth birthday. I had never seen my father so upset and although I got on well with Leslie, I think my main concern was the loss of my regular supply of chocolate when he was on leave. He had only been married a short while before his return to the oversea's posting and his new wife May had a son David after Leslie's death and he grew up to be a very successful international banker in the Middle East and Hong Kong.

I suppose ability in whatever field must come from parents and forebears and I think my running ability must have come from my father who had been an Army Boxing Champion in India and who at the V-E celebrations in Windsor, outsprinted all the opposition, even though he had a broken toe and was sixty years of age. I remember the victory celebrations in Windsor. All school children were entertained in the Holme Park by Uncle

Mac of 'Children's Hour' fame and I have never forgotten the singing of 'Jerusalem'. I remember our own V-E celebrations in Elm Road.

There were the above ground air-raid shelters spread down the road, one for every four or five houses and the one outside my home was used as the launch pad for a firework display as part of the street's celebrations, but disaster struck when a firework went off in the box containing the rest of the fireworks; it gave a very spectacular but short display. Although only a small terrace house, we had a flagpole in both the front and back gardens, and the Union Jack was hoisted on both as it was on all royal occasions during my father's life. We never actually lined up to salute the flag but it came pretty close!

When I was about eight to ten years old, I used to go to work with my father at the local laundry where he was a van driver. We often travelled over what seemed in those days to be quite long journeys, although in fact they were all within the Windsor/Ascot area. I quite liked loading the bundles and baskets of washing on and off the vans and there was a unique smell about laundries which had a strange attraction.

There was another attraction at the laundry. It was a 'what-the-butler-saw' machine that preceded television; I enjoyed winding the handle and seeing the moving pictures.

At the end of the war, both my maternal grandparents died, and as my grandmother died when the primroses were out, many of her children (she had fourteen) and grandchildren, including me, went and collected buckets full of the flowers from the local woods. There were masses of them; and then her sons wired the inside of the grave before putting bunches of primroses every few inches around the wire mesh.

I remember other details of early life in Windsor. On a Saturday the Co-op came round the road with a horse and cart selling bread, cakes and provisions. Most Saturdays I would be given a halfpenny to spend on a very nice little fruit cake that they sold.

The milkman delivered the milk by churn and my mother would take a jug out to him, and the milk would be scooped out from the churn into the jug.

On Sunday, a man would come on his cycle cart selling cockles and seafood.

From school we used to go swimming (not that I could swim), and the swimming 'pool' was a backwater of the Thames that was cut off by a wooden pole across the river; but it did have changing rooms, diving boards, and the water was graded by depth. Later we went to proper swimming baths at Maidenhead or Burnham Beeches, although I did not learn to swim until just before I joined up, and then it was thanks to girlfriend Marion who was a very good swimmer. Just as well, as it was pretty essential when I joined the police and I remember having to swim in the sea in early November as part of training.

About a year after the war ended, ice creams came back on sale and I remember when as a family we were walking along the river and my parents bought a couple of choc ices that were cut in half so that we could have a taste. They cost 4d, which was about the same as a loaf of bread.

When I was about nine or ten years old, I used to go on the River Thames in my brother's canvas boat; it was a sort of canoe/kayak but not that stable. On one occasion as we were pulling back into the millstream near Clewer Church in Windsor, we were passing a jetty where there was a small craft tied up. Suddenly we saw a naked boy on the jetty and he jumped off with the intention of landing on the tied-up boat. He missed his footing and pushed the boat away, to end up in the river which was around ten feet deep at this point. I remember seeing him sort of swimming around under the water, almost like a water baby, but he obviously could not swim. My brother knew he was drowning and we pulled over as close as we could to where he was submerged, and as he came up to the surface for the second time, my brother grabbed him while I tried to keep our boat upright. We both succeeded and got the lad, who was about my age, to the bank. I remember the reaction of that boy to this day. It was really quite strange; he thought he had enjoyed the experience floating under the water and did not realise how close he had come to disaster. Somebody collected him from the jetty, and a quick thanks and we were on our way.

If that was a near-death experience for that young boy, another incident happened much closer to home a little later. My family and I were at home one weekend when there was a knock on our front door. Dad opened the door and the lady next door staggered in covered in blood. I remember my parents getting a bucket of water and towels and tea towels to try and stop the bleeding. We did not have a telephone but someone, probably my older brother, must have gone to the phone box on the corner of the road, because an ambulance came, and later the police. The man next door had tried to kill his wife by hitting her over the head with a hammer, and a little later he was taken away. I remember he was only out of circulation for a short time and seemed to be back with his wife at their home next door very quickly. He was an old soldier from the First World War and had apparently had some temporary mental problem and was not detained for very long.

I mention elsewhere that I have never been a great fan of football, but as a young boy my father did take me to watch Windsor and Eton FC matches at Stag Meadow on the edge of Windsor Great Park. The club were know as the Royals in those days before the name was somehow highjacked by the county town and Reading Football Club. Windsor had a reasonable team and I will always remember one player, Billy Griffiths, and wonder what modern referees and players would make of him. He was a hard man and in almost every match he would end up knocking a player down with a punch, and I can only very rarely remember him being sent off. He was a good footballer and other players would be going for him, and it was not surprising that he took his revenge in this extreme way. He seemed to get away with it most of the time, and his skill probably helped to keep him on the pitch. He was a sporting character and I did meet him once very much later in life when we were both at an athletic event where one of his family was competing, and like so many sportsmen, he was very much a gentleman off the pitch. Footballers had a lot to put up with in those days; there were the very heavy dangerous football boots with those lethal studs made from leather and nails. Then there was that solid toecap; no soft leather like the modern boot. Tackling was hard but I do not recall seeing any more players injured, in fact probably less than today.

After the war, there were the 1947 floods in Windsor following a really bad winter. I lived about a mile from the River Thames and one Sunday afternoon we went for a family walk. Someone had told us that the river was high and there was some flooding, but we had only gone about a quarter of a mile towards the river when we found everywhere covered in water. Most of Windsor was underwater and in some areas nearer the river, the water was at first-floor level.

Quite naturally boys of my age turned the floods into a game, and we took a tin bath down to the flood water, a long way from the river, and paddled around in it, while my brother and others were involved in more serious activities; getting food and supplies to many of the homes underwater, in some cases up to the first floor.

A couple of years after the war, my family were hit by the plague; or rather it seemed like it. It was in fact scarlet fever. I was the first to go down with it around Christmas, but the doctor called it tonsillitis to avoid me going to hospital. I remember taking some rather large unpleasant pills (that was when someone was watching, otherwise they were hidden under the bed), but the ones I took did eventually improve the condition. But it did not help my mother, brother and sister who all picked it up from me, and all had to have a stay in the isolation hospital at Maidenhead.

By now I was better, and spent a lot of my time keeping my youngest sister amused. The funny thing I remember about this period, was the way we were partly treated like lepers. A very well-meaning friend and neighbour used to come along and put food she had cooked for us on the windowsill at the front of the house, tap on the window and run away. She had three children of her own, so this was an understandable precaution, although I found it strange at the time. After the scarlet fever had been diagnosed, and after my mother and brother had been removed to hospital, in came the local council to fumigate the house room by room. Each room was completely sealed and given the treatment; it really was like having the plague.

In September 1947, I had started at the Windsor County Boys' School, the local Grammar School. I had done reasonably well at the Royal Free School, where only two subjects were put onto the chart showing performance. Blue for Maths where I was always at or near the top, and red for English where I probably hovered below the halfway mark. There was then an interview in the library of the Grammar School and I thought I did OK. This was confirmed when I was awarded a place at the school. There were three classes at entry A, B, and C and I made it to the B class. I always thought, and still do, that I got there on merit, but my mother told me years later that I got there because we lived opposite the town mayor, Fred Fuzzens, and the headmaster thought I was related.

The cost of new school uniform and other clothes, were out of the reach of my parents, but fortunately we had friends who were quite well-off coal merchants in Windsor. They had two sons and their quality clothing was always passed on to me.

I started my new school in the September, and I well remember the watermarks in the classrooms where the school had been flooded. It had been rumoured that there were initiation ceremonies connected to the goats that were tethered on the school field, but I never suffered from this or other bullying. I remember just one occasion when someone did approach me on the field at break, but before I knew what was going on, one of the school rugby players gave him a flying tackle and sent him packing. I am not even sure he was going to pick a fight with me but I never had trouble again.

Rugby was the school game, and at the end of the very first term, I went with a school friend and his father to Twickenham for the Varsity Match. It was packed, standing room only and we were tucked in one corner behind a lot of other people. Fortunately my friend's dad was a big man and throughout the match he would lift us onto his shoulder in turn so that we could at least see something of the match, as well as soak up the atmosphere. It did something, because I have always enjoyed rugby far more than that other game of "football".

At my previous school, I had mostly gone home at lunch time, but at my new school I had dinner most days and it was very good, especially on Fridays; partly because we always had excellent fish and chips and probably jam tart and custard (I might have four or five helpings); but there was another attraction. The wife of my games master would be serving the lunches that day, and she was very attractive, wearing revealing low-cut dresses. In an all-boys' school this was a big attraction! As was the once-a-week session in the school gym for the girls of a neighbouring school, who came in for their PE lessons in their navy-blue knickers.

About the same time, my brother Bernard, who had completed his two years' National Service with the Tank Corps, was now a commissioned officer in the Royal Air Force Volunteer Reserve. He had always wanted to fly, and was very disappointed not to have had the chance while the war was still on. He became a glider pilot and was very good. I used to go with him to a small airfield at Bray near Maidenhead, and go out on the jeep to bring back the launch cable after it had been dropped from the gliders. He used to do displays and perform some very tricky manoeuvres when he was flying. He never crashed, although I remember one of my jobs was to stick patches on the glider after the outer skin had got torn on occasions. He always promised to take me up, but I was only around twelve years old, and whenever he was going to give me a flight in a two-seater, there was always some 'top brass' around, so the promised flight never happened.

I had been a Wolf Cub since I was eight years old, and had reached the dizzy heights of being a 'Sixer'. I moved up to the 2nd Windsor Scouts in 1947 and rapidly became a 'Patrol Leader' (mainly because I was taller than most).

Camping became an important part of my life for the next few years. There was very good camp site in Windsor Great Park, Bears Rail, and many weekends in the summer we would pull our heavily-laden cart, loaded with tents and equipment, from Windsor to Old Windsor and camp for the weekend; a distance of at least three miles. I was lucky to get the opportunity to go to camps further afield with the other scout troops in the town. One of these was to Porlock in Somerset, where we used to go into Minehead and where we could buy baked beans on toast for about a shilling (5p). After camp food it always tasted so good, and I suppose that is why I still enjoy beans on toast today. Another camp took me across the water for the first time to the Isle of Wight.

Between scout camps, there were occasional trips to the coast as choir outings, and as mentioned before, I had a great liking for ice cream, probably due to being deprived of it during the war, and the Lyons Corner House knickerbocker glories. Our trips were usually to Brighton or Southend, and I remember on one such trip eating something like thirty ices of various sorts during the one day. Maybe this contributed to my health problem later in life.

In about 1950, the magic of electricity came to our road and we had electric light for the first time, but the tin bath in the kitchen continued for the rest of my time at home.

I had a very happy childhood, even though we had very few comforts and six of my formative years were in the war. There was no bathroom, an outside loo, no electricity, no central heating and no washing machine or fridge; and a family income of just about £5. My parents must have done a great job of bringing up the family with so little money, because we always had enough to eat and had great Christmases. Our pillowcases that we used to hang up, were always full to overflowing with regular presents, like a toy post office, sweet shop, toys and a stocking filled with whatever small items were available; later fruit and chocolate, but not much of that during the war, unless my half-brother Leslie, who was in the Army, had brought some home. Even our holidays to Tisbury continued throughout the war.

Christmas was always magic, and when I had my own family, we managed to keep the magic alive for our own children. They would go to bed on Christmas Eve and nothing would be done; there would be no tree, no decorations nor any other sign of Christmas. When they were all asleep, the work would start to transform the house, so that when they woke up, very early next morning, everything was there and ready for them. Frequently we would only get to bed about an hour or two before they were rising. Normally the first thing we did on Christmas morning was to go to church, and then the presents would be distributed on our return.

By the time I was twelve years old, I was delivering groceries for a long-established family grocer in Windsor; Trudgeons. I remember my rate of pay, which was one shilling and three pence (6p) per hour, and I earned ten shillings (50p) a week for an hour after school on four days and four hours on Saturday morning.

My main task was riding one of several ancient delivery bikes, which either had two wheels the same size, or one that had the small wheel at the front so that it could have an even bigger load. Whichever bicycle I was on, I was always carrying the maximum load, delivering mainly to the large houses in the better areas of Windsor. Although I say it myself, I was good at the job and never fell off or lost my loads, and worked faster than other delivery boys who came and went, while I soldiered on for the whole time I was at school.

The only problem that my employer had with me, was that I did enjoy the biscuits, that in those days were weighed and put into open bags. Frequently the bag would be short of biscuits by the time I got them to their destination. The strange thing was, I never got told off about this, and I think the manager used to overweigh the biscuits in the first place to allow for those that he knew would disappear. I cannot have been too bad at the job as I collected many tips at Christmas, most of them around two shillings and sixpence, or the equivalent of two hours' work.

As well as the deliveries, I did carry out other work, including the weighing out of dried fruit (which I often sampled) and sugar. I also worked in the cellar of the shop, scraping the wax from the rind of the cheese and repairing the damage mice made to the cheese to make it presentable to the customers.

There was a row of glass-top biscuit tins in front of the counter, so that customers could select what biscuits they liked.

The owner of the shop was a dapper little man with a stiff winged collar, and he and his wife used to trust me with taking the money to the bank. I well remember those big white £5 notes, but I did deliver them all to the bank and did not do what I did with those biscuits. It was an interesting time and I think it probably helped to shape my future in retail trade.

In those early days in Windsor, I had my only short-lived interest in playing football and ran my own team. I got all the lads in the street together, and we went off to play against other similar teams in the area where I lived. Although we only had small back yards, we never played in the street and always went off to find a field or recreation ground for our games.

I enjoyed cycling and bought my first bike from the money I got for my grocery round. Sometimes alone, and sometimes with a friend from the scouts, I would cycle quite long distances. On one occasion with this friend, we cycled to Southampton and back; a total distance of over 100 miles in a day to see an aunt of mine. My lone trips took me to see other relatives in Wiltshire; about eighty-four miles away. Most of these trips were when I was twelve to thirteen years old; before I really got the running bug.

I was good at saving my money from my grocer's round, and when I wanted to buy my first running spikes, I went off to the Eton College sports shop. This was a shop that specialised in supplying the Eton boys with their sports clothing and equipment, so it was all top of the range kit. The sports at the college were always held before Easter, and as soon as they were over, boys would sell back to the shop those very expensive spikes bought for them by their wealthy fathers. They had probably only run one or two races in them, and so the shoes were virtually new but secondhand. I bought a pair of G. T. Laws handmade white snakeskin shoes for £3, and they remained my treasured possession for some years.

I also saved up and paid for a ski trip out of my earnings, and we were due to travel out on a Christmas Eve, but at the very last minute it was cancelled, due I believe to lack of numbers after some of my school mates pulled out. I was very disappointed but I did get my money back.

Chapter Two

The Start of Running

My athletic career started in 1948 when I was twelve years old. I saw part of the Olympic cycle race held in the area of Windsor Great Park, and then I remember going to the Playhouse Cinema in Windsor with my school to see the film of the 1948 Wembley Olympics.

I saw the marathon on the film, and at that ripe old age of twelve years I made up my mind that was what I wanted to do. Little did I know that someone in that film was to play a part in my future athletic career; Stan Jones, who finished seventeenth in that Olympic Marathon, helped me considerably in later years. It was the end of 1948 and I started running.

My first race was a Windsor Scouts Cross-Country in the early part of 1949, which I won. At school I was playing for the Colts Under 15 rugby team, but at every opportunity I was running. My games master 'Chick' Evans, was fairly quick to recognise that I was a better athlete than rugby player, and gradually I got more and more into athletics.

For a while I did follow my father and did some boxing at school. I only ever had one official fight, and that was very early on at school in an inter-house competition, which I did win quite easily. Official boxing contests were banned at school not long after this, but we had many unofficial fights in the school gym at lunch time with the supervision of a games master. I always matched up with the two biggest boys in my years because those of my size and weight were not much competition.

One of the big events at school was the annual cross-country race; an inter-house competition that scored points towards the overall competition between the houses, that were named after four boys who lost their lives in the First World War. My housemaster wanted me to run for the house, but no boy under fifteen had ever been allowed to run.

Appeals were made to the games master and eventually to the headmaster, and finally they decided that it would not hurt this thirteen-year-old boy to run three miles. I ran on Windsor racecourse alongside the river. I was running against boys from fifteen to eighteen years of age. I did not win but came third, only being beaten by two boys around four years older than myself, and it was well received by my housemaster and my house 'Burnett'.

The following year, although still 'under age', I ran away with the annual race and did so for the rest of my time at school.

My early track successes came in 1950, when I won eight athletic events in the District Scout Sports. In 1950, I progressed through to the District School Sports and won the 880 yards in a new record time of 2:26.2.

The following year 1951, I started to train with a purpose, and kept records of my training and races. I was only fourteen years old, but I ran against seniors in most club races and generally finished in the first three places. I was running 3.5 miles in about 19 minutes and up 4.75 miles in about 29 minutes. In March I won a schools cross-country race at Maidenhead, and recorded 13 minutes for the 2.5 miles, which was 51 seconds in front of the second boy.

Shortly after this it was the annual school race again, and this time there were no arguments about me running, even though I was 'still under age'. I won the 3.5 mile race in 19:18, which was 90 seconds faster than my nearest rival. I won the club road championship on 7th April with 12 minutes 40 seconds for the 2.3 miles. A win in the school sports 880 yards came next on 28th April; the winning time was 2:17, and then in May I won the District race in the same time, before moving on to the South East Berkshire 880 yards, which was won in the slower time of 2:22.8. It was slow, but was still a record for the under 15 age group.

The Berkshire race was next, and I reduced my record of the previous year to 2:13.1, and went to Southampton for the All England Schools, representing Berkshire. I won my heat quite easily in 2:8.4, and went into the final next day very confident. I will always remember the superb grass track at Southampton and that race for two reasons. The first being that I realised how good runners were when you competed nationally, and I remembered the race because of what happened as we all fought for positions around the last bend. A shot-putter dropped the shot on his foot and fell onto the track, blocking the two inside lanes, and some of us saw the obstruction and others did not, and I got knocked to the outside lane. I could only finish seventh out of a field of nine in the much slower time of 2:12 against the winner's 2:6.9. A time which I knew I could match. In my very next race, an 880 yards, running for Eton AC against Reading, I ran 2:8, in second place.

I carried on with playing rugby until 1951, and I think it was that year when I went over the handlebars of my bike outside Windsor Police Station on my way to the grocers for my Saturday morning work. They had just freshly gravelled the road and I think I picked up most of it in my lips. I went to work and did my Saturday morning, before going off to school in the afternoon to play rugby. I did not play, as my headmaster saw me and the state of my face, and refused to let me play; probably just as well.

In March 1952, I was invited to represent Berkshire in a special Olympic Fund Raising event; an indoor athletic meeting at Haringey Arena. This was my once only run indoors in my whole running career. The event I was running in was the 600 yards, and it was not easy. The track was flat with very small laps and no banking as they have today. I started on the outside virtually off the proper track, and could not get into the lead as I liked to in the first fifty yards. I had quite a good run though and enjoyed the experience. I remember the occasion, as on the same programme, were the big names of athletics in this country at the time, Arthur Wint and E. McDonald Bailey.

I won the Berkshire Schools 15 to 17 years age group 880 yards in 2:1.6, and went to Bradford for the All England Schools again. It was a very windy day for the heats, and running from the front, I paid the price not for the last time in my career, and just failed to qualify for the final.

Training in those early days consisted mainly of long steady runs; my favourite run was up the Long Walk in Windsor Great Park to the famous Copper Horse and then back again. Depending on where I started from, home or school, the return run was about six miles. I did a little training on the track, and when I was included in the Berkshire team for the All England, I had to travel to Reading by train and trolleybus to be coached at Palmer Park, Reading. The coaching here for the 880 yard runners was by Mike Dunhill, a runner from Oxford City AC. The school paid for my travel, which was just about four shillings (20p) for the train fare.

In 1949, I had joined the then Eton AC (now Windsor, Slough and Eton), where we trained and raced on a recreation ground grass track, and the cross-country races were run along the Thames on the north side of the river. I remember athletics was real fun in those days; I enjoyed racing and I enjoyed training.

The club was a very compact, small family, with the majority of members coming from two families; the Robsons and the Smiths. It also had a great secretary who became my mentor and guiding light, Len Runyard.

The changing accommodation for cross-country was the British Restaurant in Eton High Street. In those days there were no showers, just a tin bath of normally cold water, unless someone poured in a jug of hot water. There was also a big advantage in being back first, as the water would still be reasonably clean. After a few very muddy runners had been through, you were more likely to come out dirtier than when you went in. This primitive washing facility was commonplace at all cross-country venues, including major championships like the Southern Counties and National races at Parliament Hill in London and elsewhere.

Although the club track was marked out on the recreation ground at

Eton, there was a cinder track at nearby Eton College, that was very little used and was frequently covered in weeds. I did occasionally go there for some training on my own. The site of this track is where the new Thames Valley Athletics Centre, the home of Windsor, Slough, Eton and Hounslow AC is now situated. The new facilities are certainly one hundred per cent better than the old.

While at school, I took part in various sporting activities including athletics, hockey, boxing and rugby. We had a strong 'house' structure and there was tough competition between the houses on a whole range of activities, including music and drama, as well as sport.

I played my part and took part in the solo singing competition. I chose quite a tough piece for this solo effort; the largo from Handel's Xerces. It was a very difficult piece and had been selected by the organist and choirmistress, who must have thought I could do it justice. I practised quite hard, singing it from the organ loft at All Saints' Church, where I was still in the choir. I did not win but did get some points for my house, Burnett, by coming third.

We had some interesting teachers at the Windsor County Boys' School. There was just one lady teacher and she taught Latin, but it was reputed that she was well equipped to teach a few non-academic things as well; although I was not privileged to the special tuition and was only in her Latin class for one year. One of the masters had a reputation that went before him, and I remember stories from my brother about his behaviour in class. He was a great Maths master, but was a very strict disciplinarian, and had bouts of violent behaviour, supposedly breaking the arm of one boy, before my day. He did frequently throw the wooden-based blackboard wiper with extreme venom and accuracy at anyone who stepped out of line. Needless to say his reputation was enough to keep order, and every class of boys that ever came in contact with him behaved impeccably. I never had any trouble with him, but then Maths was my favourite and best subject.

There were some great teachers and characters at school. The Chemistry master was a very strong man and reputed to be an ex-wrestler. He could pick at least two boys, whatever their size, up at a time; one in each hand like weights, and if need be, literally bang heads together. I kept on the right side of him as I delivered his groceries, and his wife was always very generous with her tip at Christmas. The Physics master later became Mayor of Windsor, and in 1958 presented me with an Illuminated Address from the Royal Borough for my contribution to English Sport. My housemaster, who was also my History master and one time form master, wrote a special book on the history of Windsor later in his life, and I featured in his special book where I appeared in the index between the King Edwards and Queen Eleanor.

I wonder how some of these very dedicated and splendid teachers would have dealt with teaching today, in a world of over protection, lack of discipline, liberalization and legal redress for the slightest assault, real or otherwise, on a pupil?

Football with a round ball was banned at school, and no one was supposed to play soccer for a team in their own time. It came as a bit of a shock to Mr Fairhurst, the headmaster, when on one occasion boys from the Grammar School made up all but one of the schoolboy football team for the town of Windsor. To make matters worse for him, one senior prefect, who was also a very good rugby player, broke his arm playing in goal with this soccer team. The rule about playing this nasty game with a round ball outside of school, was then reinforced. Maybe some of this rubbed off on me, as I have never been able to get very passionate about the game either.

The highlight of 1951 was going on the school trip by train to Waterloo from Windsor, and a day at the Festival of Britain. Although we did not meet then, and unknown to me, my wife Marion was on the train with the girls from Windsor Girls' School, but of course boys and girls were segregated. Our only contact was by waving our trousers out of the carriage window!

The Festival itself was a great experience, and the timing of it was right; just six years after the end of the war. It is a pity the Millennium Dome did not take off in the same way, but sadly people's expectancy today is a lot more than fifty years ago, and only six years after war, that had deprived us of many of the pleasant things in life.

In 1952, I was in the fifth form at school, and I remember one PT lesson in particular. We had just come out of the gym to change and our games master came into the changing room very stern faced and announced that the king was dead. There was a deathly silence and we were then sent home. I remember the day of George VI's funeral in Windsor. Kings and queens are brought down from London on such occasions by train to the railway station in the centre of Windsor, which is kept open mainly for that purpose, and the processional route from there to the castle passes the Windsor Guildhall and Parish Church. As I mentioned earlier, I had an association with the Parish Church in Windsor, as I had been in the choir of its sister church All Saints' since I was seven years old.

On the day of the funeral, the Parish Church of St John the Baptist, had sold seats in the churchyard so that people could pay their respects as the cortege passed the church on its way from the railway station to the final resting place, and to enable the church to make "a bob or two" for the roof fund. I was on 'duty' at one of the gates, when a very colourful man approached me in his white robes and offered me a lot of money (wads of the old white £5 notes) to allow him in. The man was the well-known racing tipster Prince Monolulu. I called over to a church warden who was in charge and a deal was done; a few of those big fivers changed hands, and the 'Prince' took his place in the churchyard.

It was the same year that Eton AC added Windsor to its name, and became Windsor and Eton AC.

My final race at school was the one mile in the Annual School Sports. The record had stood for a little while at around 5 minutes 10 seconds, but I wanted to set a record that would stand for a while after I had disappeared from the scene. On the rough grass track that the goats used to trim, I ran the four laps in just 4 minutes 37 seconds. (For those who only understand metric distances and times, this would have been about 4:17 for 1,500 metres.) The record did stand for some years after that; in fact it may have carried through to the switch to metric distances. I did return to the School Sports a couple of times after this to run in the Old Boys v School relay.

Shortly after this, came the time to leave school. Sport had been my school life and academic achievement suffered. I took a total of nine subjects for my 'O' levels and achieved just one; in Maths; although I could claim some near misses!

We had some fun in that last year at school. I remember trousers of prefects, and on one occasion, a member of the staff's being flown from the white flagpole.

The headmaster had a 1934 green and black Austin 8 with running boards, and I remember we pushed it out into the middle of the school field and put a potato up the exhaust. Little did I know then that in 1960 I was to buy and own that treasured possession which I bought for just £5. I learnt to drive on it and then sold it to a scrap merchant for the same money. If only I had kept that splendid old car which was still in perfect working order.

We were not a well-behaved year and were always in trouble for something, but it was all good natured and very rarely did the head have to use his cane.

In August 1952, I was still cycling and went on holiday to my relatives in Tisbury, near Salisbury, and on a Saturday morning, I cycled the eighty-four miles back to Windsor and ran in the one mile at the Agars Plough Carnival in Slough in the afternoon. A meeting that I was to return to many times and enjoy. I won with a time of 4:29.6, one of the fastest times by a sixteen-year-old in those days.

Before setting out into my career, I joined the first party of young people from Windsor to go on an exchange trip with Goslar in the Hertz Mountains near Hanover in Germany. This was Windsor's new twin town, and we all had some brief lessons in the German language before we went on what, for many including myself, was a first-ever trip overseas.

We travelled by sea from Harwich and then across Germany by train, and as this was only seven years after the war; the devastation was still obvious.

While in Goslar, we went to a nearby running track where I ran what was to be my first 'international race'. The best senior athlete from the local club was given the privilege of running against this young sixteen-year-old from Windsor over 3,000 metres. I won this first international challenge in my running career.

One of our trips was to take us down a mine; my first but not last experience of this activity. I remember some of the tunnels were very low and they were extremely wet.

Not all went well on this trip though, as we were taken on a sightseeing tour near to the East German border. After returning to our hosts later that day, I realised I had lost my passport. This caused a few sparks, because passports were highly valued in the East of Germany. However after much panic, the passport was recovered and returned to me, although I cannot remember exactly where it was found.

The daughter of the family I stayed with, really did try to get her hands on me in more ways than one, but I resisted, as there were more attractive girls in our party. She did however get close to the family, when she eventually met my cousin while he was serving in the Educational Corps in Germany, and they eventually got married.

Chapter Three

The Start of Ten Years in Uniform

I made up my mind, long before leaving school, that I wanted to be a policeman. I think it was the adverts for Hong Kong Police and £1,000 a year that attracted me, but on my return from Germany, I joined the Berkshire Constabulary as a police cadet at Windsor. One of the first three in the county, and an interesting time.

There were no radio communications at the time, and I remember receiving instruction in 1953 when the first radio was placed in the Windsor Police Station. I received one of the first messages over the airwaves. Not that top brass trusted this new method of communication. Many messages were still transmitted via the teleprinter and the telephone, so that a stolen car or missing person details could be received in triplicate. It took sometime for the powers that be to accept one method of receiving urgent messages.

The first police dogs were recruited about the same time, and a little later the police frogmen team was formed in the Berkshire Police.

I was present in uniform for the second royal funeral in a year; that of Queen Mary; and by coincidence I was placed at the foot of the steps of the Parish Church where I had been as a civilian one year earlier.

I had an interesting two years as a police cadet. Duties were wide and various, and included going over the road to a working men's cafe to buy meals for prisoners being held in the station cells; also cleaning the cells, running errands for the superintendent and working in both the general office and admin office. My errands used to include getting on my bike and going into the park to collect a brace of pheasants for the 'Super'; a gift from the royal estate. I also collected occasional bottles of whisky from a local off-licence that had parking restrictions outside its premises, and where customers only ever received cautions if a police officer handed out tickets.

After the first few months, I was issued with the special uniform of a cadet, and one of my duties was to collect cash from the bank and put the money into the pay envelopes for everyone from the superintendent down to me. I remember being very envious of the superintendent, who received over £20 a week, whilst my weekly pay was just about £3.

One of the cells was an arsenal of all types of weapons; mainly I think surrendered in various amnesties after the war. On one occasion, close to Christmas, someone put a turkey in there for safekeeping. It was forgotten and we had mild weather, so the bird turned to maggots and flies. Guess who had to clean up all the weapons and other items in the cell!

When the police opened a small sub-police station on the outskirts of Windsor, I manned this on my own during office hours. I was well looked after by the wives of the policemen who lived in the adjoining police houses; they kept me supplied with tea, cake and company.

About the most exciting thing that happened to me there, was when a young lady came into the station one morning and said "I am going to have a baby." "Yes" I said. "When?" "In the next few minutes I think" was the reply. I got the ambulance there very quickly!

Part of my duties as a cadet, included sorting the wages out for all the policeman in Windsor, as mentioned earlier, which included the superintendent, Fred Salter, MVO. The pay details used to be given to me, and I would write up the pay packets with their appropriate deductions, and go to the bank to collect the cash. Then I would put the correct sums into each packet and make sure it balanced to the penny. A police constable in those days received about £7 per week and the 'Super' received something just over £20, but all had their little extras which could be three shillings (15p) for bicycle, two shillings (10p) for torch.

When I was working at the main police station, I also used to make the tea and sell chocolate biscuits to those who worked in the police station, and always made a small profit. Another duty included looking after the switchboard and teleprinter, as well as showing guests into the superintendent's office.

A fairly frequent visitor was a young Army major from the Household Cavalry, Major the Marques of Douro, who is now the current Duke of Wellington, and whom I have met more recently, when he allowed me to organize running events on his estate at Stratfield Saye between Reading and Basingstoke. The 'Super' was always very formal on these visits, and would make a very pronounced and distinct bow when greeting his guest; a real hand in front and hand behind deep bow.

My time as a police cadet was enjoyable and instructive, and I think it has helped me to have a responsible and fairly disciplined life. I certainly learned to type, make out reports, take phone messages and file complicated police files. Receiving phone calls was quite an art, and exact names and details of callers had to be taken; there could be no mistakes. Then there was the art of deflecting calls and callers that the superintendent would not want to be bothered with, or in many cases, no other senior person would want to be troubled with.

In 1953, I won the Berkshire Youth 880 yards title in 2:6.2, which was faster than the winning time in either of the older age groups; the senior or junior. The runner-up to me was someone who I have known throughout my running life as a competitor, training partner and athletic enthusiast; Brian Bacon (Reading AC). Later I ran and won my first road race. It was 3.5 miles and was part of the Langley Fete near Slough. There was also a seven mile 'marathon' for seniors; these were the forerunners of today's mass running events.

While in Windsor as a police cadet, I belonged to the Windsor Parish Players and acted in a number of productions with them, including 'Acacia Avenue'.

I was always busy and spent most of my Sundays in church attending three or four services in my capacity as a chorister, server, and even as a Sunday School teacher.

The social life revolved around a Christian club, the Anglican Young People's Association (AYPA). They were a great crowd and eventually nearly all the members were married off to each other. These included Marion and myself, who were both members, and we enjoyed a wide variety of activities, including that violent sport, mixed hockey. There were more gentle pursuits, and a group of us would meet at my house on a Sunday evening after service and have a singsong around the piano; luckily several were quite accomplished on the piano. We also provided entertainment at various social events throughout the year.

The dress for the young men at that time was a trilby hat, a walking stick and brothel creepers. At least that was what I used to pull the girls.

Along with about six of them, I queued all day at the Albert Hall on one occasion to get into the 'Last Night of the Proms'. We did not get a space on the floor, but managed to get standing room on about three or four balconies up. It was a great night, and although I have not been back, I always enjoy that special night on television and radio.

There was never a dull moment in our lives, and I cannot understand how today, when there are so many more activities and opportunities, we hear young people protesting there is nothing to do. It is very sad, and they certainly have something lacking in their education and family life.

Frequently on a Monday evening, it was off to the Theatre Royal to see the latest play; they changed every week, and a group of us had a seat in the 'gods', right at the back upstairs. There were some great characters at that theatre and I delivered the groceries to some of the top management. One actor who was there for many years, before making it onto television quite late in life, was Patrick Cargill.

I knew my future wife Marion while we were both still at school, and I started to go out with her just after I had left, and when she was in her fifth year. The Royal Show was held in Windsor at that time, and I was on duty at the show, which required me to cycle past the girls' school in my uniform. This got Marion into trouble for looking out of the window and eyeing up the young man in uniform. She also had the same problem a couple of years later, when I was going home to Windsor on leave from the Army. We had to wear uniform on weekend leave, and because she was seen with me, it was assumed by some that she was going out with soldiers from one of the local barracks. Some well-meaning but misinformed person tried to stir it up with Marion's parents, but were promptly put in their place.

I had a very good cross-country season at the start of 1954 and won ten races in a row, which prompted a small mention in the *London Evening News* after my ninth win:– *Windsor and Eton Athletic Club in their first cross-country season, appear to have a real find in S. Eldon. His ninth successive victory was in a race between Windsor, Vale of Aylesbury and RAF Halton clubs.*

In March, I ran in the Southern Counties at Parliament Hill. I was in the Youth (under 18) age group, and there were 222 runners taking part. With three-quarters of a mile to go, I had won myself a good lead but disaster struck and running fast downhill, I had a heavy fall and was overtaken by four runners. I got up and fought on and with 600 yards to go had caught all but Nat Fisher (Eton Manor AC). We battled on over the last 400 yards, but the fall had taken its toll and Fisher broke the tape first. One report on the day blamed my failure to win on my race number which was 13! I then went on to Liverpool for the National Championship and came ninth out of an entry of 603.

My running continued to go well, and on the Whit Holiday I ran my first of many races at the White City. I was only just eighteen, but ran for Berkshire in the Inter Counties meeting as I had won the county three mile in a new record time of 14:43.6. I finished ninth out of the twenty-nine taking part, behind a man who I was to clash with many times in the future, Gordon Pirie. In the Reading Trophies Meeting, held at Palmer Park, Reading, in June, I won the Junior mile against a field of thirty-six runners, including John Herring, who was ranked second in the country at the distance in the previous season, and many county champions. It was a very wet weekend, and according to reports of the day, the track was largely underwater. In those days of cinder tracks, if it was wet it normally meant finishing a race with half the track sprayed up your back, and running on this type of track almost turned into cross-country running.

I continued to run for the club and breaking records right up to my call-up in the second week of July. My club records at that time were 880 yards, 2:0.6; mile, 4:23.2; two miles, 9:28.5, and three miles, 14:43.6.

I finished third in the Southern Counties mile at Battersea Park with 4:23.2, behind Roger Dunkley 4:19 (the fastest ever junior miler at that stage with 4:12), and Laurie Reed 4:22. My very last match before entering the Army, was against Finchley Harriers and Watford Harriers. I won the mile again in 4:23.2, and the 880 yards in 2:0.6. This latter record was my thirteenth for the club.

Chapter Four

National Service in the Redcaps

The next step in my life was National Service, and I remember being asked to list my choices in order of preference. I did select the Army and listed my top choice as the Horse Guards, who were stationed at the bottom of my garden; although that was not the reason for that choice. They had a very good athletic team at that time, and I had got to know their sergeant major PE instructor, as he coached at the athletic club. My second choice was logical, it was the Military Police, because I intended picking up my police career when I finished my two years' service.

My call-up came in early July 1954, just two months after my eighteenth birthday. Where was I going, and what unit was I going to? It was none of my preferred choices; not even number six on the list. I was off to Catterick Camp and the 3rd Signals Regiment. It was pretty tough there, being kept on the go all day with square-bashing, and being woken as early as 5 a.m. on the whim of some little corporal. The food was terrible. I don't think I have ever had anything anywhere to come even close to the shocking standard of food at Catterick Camp.

Fortunately this did not last long as after two weeks of square-bashing and guard duty (we were not let loose with rifles but carried pickaxe handles as our weapons), and where on one occasion I was in trouble for allowing the Yorkshire sheep to enter the barracks and attack the colonel's roses, I was summoned by the unit commander and told I was on the move. He was not happy because I had kept my athletic prowess quiet, and at the same time he received the orders to ship me out, he had received a letter from the secretary of my athletic club at Windsor, Len Runyard, who was possibly the nearest I ever had to a coach. It explained how good I was and could expect to be, and asking that I be allowed to continue my progress in the Army. The Signals Regiment had a very good reputation for looking after sportsmen, and they had rugby league players, footballers and Ken Norris, whom I subsequently took the British record for six miles from, had also been at Catterick a couple of years earlier, as were several league footballers, rugby league players and boxers.

I was off to Inkerman Barracks, Woking, in Surrey; the training centre and headquarters of the Royal Military Police; returning south, where I would be only a short journey from my then girlfriend Marion at Windsor. The course lasted thirteen weeks, and although there was strict discipline, I enjoyed it much better than Catterick; even the food was ten times better, but that was not difficult.

The training was of a good standard and I think I actually enjoyed those three months, though not perhaps one small part of it. This was learning to ride a motorcycle which we had to do towards the end of the course. Some of our training was done close to barracks, and some on trips out further afield. On one such trip to the Guildford area, I was riding my motorcycle at the back of the column of about twenty-five. There was just an instructor behind me, and when driving in any sort of convoy, you always seem to have to drive faster at the back than the front just to keep up. I came round a bend at about 60 mph, under a railway bridge and lost it, crashing into the bridge and ending up sprawled on the road. The instructor pulled up alongside and was actually quite nice, thinking that I must have been injured, but my ill-fitting helmet and rough motorcycling gear had saved me more than the bike. I think I damaged or destroyed three Army motorcycles during my short involvement with them. Even on the day of our driving test I got things wrong. I did not crash on this occasion but got lost and missed all the spying instructors/testers; arriving at Aldershot well after everyone else. I have not attempted to ride a two-wheeled machine since then.

If motorcycling was not my scene, one thing I did enjoy was shooting, and the trips to the range for whatever weapon we were going to use, was always something to be looked forward to. We had to be able to use any sort of shooting implement, from revolver to Bren gun, but the rifle was my favourite, even if I normally finished a session with a swollen chin from the powerful recoil of the weapon. I did get very good scores and did qualify as a marksman.

Being on the range was not without its incidents though, and there was always someone who did not realise the dangers. We had one member of our squad who was not that bright; in fact I don't know how he ever qualified for the Military Police. Yes, we were in the main bright young men, contrary to popular belief. On the range one day, this chap's rifle jammed. Some of us had finished shooting and were standing up, when he stood up and turned round pointing the weapon at us and the officer in charge, still pulling the trigger and saying "My gun won't fire." Knowing he still had live ammunition in the chamber, we all dived to the ground in case his rifle did go off. He was suitably chastised by the NCOs and officer present, as well as the rest of us, and we were always very careful when he was around with any weapon in the future. I do not think he survived his full two years in the 'redcaps'; he was busted back to private later in his service, and I think sent back to another unit.

At the end of the course, there was the usual passing out parade and relatives attended. My mother and Marion were there for the big day, and afterwards there was some leave before we all got sent off to our various postings. I have always liked military music and ceremonial, and it was great to be part of this special event where the Military Police Band played the 'Watchtower', its signature tune, and we marched up and down in our best battledress; white belts, holsters, rifles and bayonets; with those sparkling boots, that had hard hours of little rings polished into them. Not that I was like one lad, who early in his training, got sent by the rest of us to the NAAFI to buy some packets of black, shiny 'rings'. Of course he was sent back by the staff who were obviously used to having at least one recruit from each squad sent to them for the same purpose.

Our squad's specialty was slow marching, and the powers that be congratulated us and said that it was some of the best they had seen anywhere. It was good that we could do something well together, as we were a mixed bag like any squad of mainly National Servicemen.

Then we were off on leave before being sent to our many and varied postings. These varied from Korea, Singapore, Hong Kong, Berlin, SHAPE in Paris or Brussels. My posting was not so exotic, probably because they wanted to keep me handy for the unit running team. I was going to Bulford Camp on Salisbury Plain; Provost Company 147, a small unit of about twenty-five to thirty men. The CO was a Major Goebbels (yes, I believe he was a relation) and there were two other officers, a company sergeant major, a staff sergeant, a couple of sergeants, and all the rest were lance corporals like myself.

This turned out to be a very pleasant posting for me. Much of the time we were left to our devices, and I was able to go off over the plains and get some serious training in. I put in a lot of hard work and I have always been convinced that it was my period there that built my fitness up for the later success. I even managed to get a team together to run for the unit in the Salisbury Plain District Cross-Country Championships while I was at Bulford.

The major had other ideas for me. He was a keen horseman and wanted to see one of his men go to the top in the Modern Pentathlon, which was dominated at the time by a Corporal Hudson in the Horse Guards. I was a marksman and a good runner, and I could just about swim, but horse riding and fencing, I had no experience of at all. The CO said he would teach me to ride and I could use his horses, and he would send me on a course to Aldershot to learn the art of fencing. I declined and he accepted my decision that I would prefer to make it in athletics, although I have often had doubts as to whether I missed a great opportunity.

My introduction to the Inter Counties Cross-Country Race was on 15th February 1955. It was held at Childwall Park near Liverpool, and it was cold; very cold. There had been snow and the ground was frozen solid, and as a lot of it was ploughed fields, this made the surface very uneven, as well as frozen. There was even talk of the race being cancelled after we all arrived on the Saturday morning, but it did go ahead, although some of the track stars at that time, including Gordon Pirie, were not happy. The real cross-country runners triumphed, and the winner was Ken Norris in 37:34. Pirie did run in spite of his protests that it was too dangerous and finished 6th in 38:43. I had a good run considering I was only eighteen years old at the time and finished 67th in 40:26.0, which was fourteen places better than Frank Sando, who on any other day would have been challenging for the title. In those days all distance runners took part in a full cross-country season and the entry in that race was a catalogue of all the runners who were around at that time, and for some years to come.

In these early days as a junior, I ran in the Kodak Sports at Harrow, and against Chris Chataway in a 3,000 metre race, where I finished second in 8:44. This was a good meeting that I went to a number of times, as the prizes were always some of the top products of that company, and we could always request and get what we wanted by way of a prize. I had always admired Chataway up to that point, but when I saw this scruffy runner in tatty Oxford sweater and old trousers, and even dirtier running kit when he stripped off, I vowed I would never look like that. I had heard someone say that even if you are not a champion, always try and look like one. From that race on I was fanatical about turnout. I would always wear clean kit, and I would even wash the laces in my running spikes. Frequently, and whenever possible, I would have a haircut before a big race and would only ever wear clean kit but never new kit.

My oldest proper training diary starts with races from September 1955 while in the Army, and the actual training is logged from 1st November of that year. I had kept a brief training diary while I was at school. I was running six to twelve miles every day, and running twice on some days. I had various circuits for training worked out. There were laps of three miles where I could run one or more to make up the distance. Good times for the three mile circuits were around 15:15 and for the double lap 31:20. There was an eight mile run from Bulford to Tidworth and back and another to Amesbury. Other runs I described as uphill, covered various distances up to seven miles; these were all on Salisbury Plain.

In September, I had run in the Maidenhead Road Relay and recorded 21:48 for the 4.25 miles. I was still stationed at Woking then, before moving to Bulford in October.

After running for Guildford and Godalming AC, my second claim club near Woking, I joined Salisbury AC and started to run for them over the country. If I could get back to Windsor, I would run for my first claim club, and I did this twice in November, winning one race and getting second in another. In the December, I ran three times for Salisbury in home fixtures, winning two and getting second in the other.

While at Bulford, I had a very convenient job as batman (unofficial) to the sergeant major. This gave me plenty of time to train as well as cleaning his kit and my own, so that I could never get into trouble on parade. I had my own room in the Sergeants' Mess, and I was now training quite seriously and running more or less every day. Some of my runs were quite long; probably ten to twelve miles, either along the top of Salisbury Plain or on the roads to Amesbury or Tidworth.

My training now was up to a good level, and a look at my training diary for the start of 1956 shows this. The first week in January, I totalled seventy-three miles from twelve training runs. The following week this went up to eighty-five miles in fifteen sessions, and on several days this included running three times a day. The following week it was up to ninety-one miles and sixteen training sessions, including one day when I actually ran four times. The last week in January, I seemed to have a great number of rest days, but perhaps this was to work in my favour.

There were some good runners in the forces in those days. Derek Ibbotson, who in 1957 set world record figures for the mile, was in the RAF along with many good runners; in the Army we had Basil Heatley (silver medal winner in the Olympic Marathon 1964), Gerry North (who won the National Cross-Country title), Mick Firth and Laurie Reed (South London Harriers) and other runners who were in the top twenty distant runners in the country. Some were little known then, but became very well known later, like Mel Batty (Thurrock Harriers). Even the Navy had a couple of star runners, and one of them was a particularly good marathon runner, E. R. Pape.

I floated between Bulford and Woking, depending on who required my running services. Generally it was summers at Inkerman and winters on Salisbury Plain. There was a small shop near the station in Salisbury, where they produced handmade shoes, and it was there that I bought my second pair of running spikes.

Training on the plain was always fun, especially where the Royal Air Force were practising dropping bales of straw from low-flying transporter aircraft. They used me as their target but they never got too close for comfort.

One winter there was a lot of snow and vehicles could not get out, so I was dispatched with various military papers and ran through the snow to deliver them to HQ several miles away. That was when I first found the use of woollen socks over running shoes to be very effective in giving more grip in snow and ice conditions.

While at Bulford, I even managed to get some senior and very mature NCOs running, and we were able to enter teams in races in the Salisbury Plain district.

I was sent back to Woking on one occasion for a signals course, which was all about radio communication and Morse code. I passed the course, which entitled me to have crossed semaphore flags on my sleeve and an extra couple of bob added to my twenty-five shillings (£1.25) per week pay. Later in my service this 'qualification' was to get me a couple of interesting days at the Military Staff College at Camberley, where I was one of two or three selected to act as the communication's control, on a major military exercise.

After the course, it was back to Bulford and life on Salisbury Plain. I think I enjoyed Bulford better than Woking, as it was a small unit and life was pretty laid-back. There was a very good corporal cook there, and the food was always good; especially on a Sunday, when we would have tinned salmon for tea, followed by tinned fruit. This was not part of the normal catering budget but he used to find a way of fiddling the system.

Wherever I was stationed, I did manage to get home pretty frequently, although the trip to Bulford was always a bit of a bind. I used to leave the Windsor Riverside Station as late as I could on a Sunday night, normally about 10.30 p.m., after a quick kiss and cuddle on the platform, and travel to Waterloo, where I would get a train to Salisbury which used to arrive at about 1 a.m.; fortunately a truck used to meet the train to take us back to Bulford, but it did not give much time for sleep that night. The journey to and from Woking was a lot easier, and I used to be back in my room in time to listen to Radio Luxembourg and the popular hit of the day, Eddie Calvert and "Cherry Pink and Apple Blossom White".

On another occasion, when I was going home on leave from Bulford, I went to Tisbury, my mother's village in Wiltshire, to collect a new bicycle from her brother's shop in the village; a present for my sister which I had to get back to Windsor. I cycled the eighty-four miles on a girl's cycle and it was not the most comfortable ride, but I did get it home to the Royal Borough in a still new condition.

Although I used to escape a lot of duties, I did get pulled in on a Saturday night to patrol Salisbury and keep order. A truck full of 'Redcaps' would descend on the city at about 7 p.m., and we would patrol in twos around the city, especially the NAAFI and bus station areas. Sometimes it was quiet but not very often.

One of the largest units in the area was the 3rd Battalion of the Highland Light Infantry, a great bunch until drink took over and then no one or anything was safe. This also applied to their NCOs, particularly one of them, a corporal. He was a man who was as broad as he was tall, about five feet five inches, and a fearsome sight in his kilt. When he had a couple of drinks he was all for discipline and order, and if any of his 'mob' got out of hand, he was the first to pick them up and throw them into the back of the truck; something he could do without help. BUT if he had more than a few drinks he became very protective of his lads, and would fight with them against us 'Redcaps'. Then it would take almost our entire squad on duty to restrain and deal with him. Fortunately more times than not he was on the side of law and order.

One Saturday night there was a lot of fighting in the bus station, and I saw one of the Jocks kick someone in the face while he was on the ground. It made a great indentation and I rather unwisely saw red in more ways than one, and although alone I waded in to try and stop the violence. I tackled one of the offenders and threw a punch at him; I did not hit him that hard but I was wearing leather gloves and I slightly cut his face. Once his mates saw blood they were after me, about a dozen or more of them, and they surrounded me and got me up against a wall in the bus station. I thought that was it until a local civilian policeman with his Alsatian dog came to my rescue, and with some other help they got me into the police station opposite, and I stayed there for my own protection until all the HLI had left town.

I enjoyed my time at Bulford, even these sometimes violent duties which were a contrast and break from running long distances over Salisbury Plain every afternoon, which was helping my fitness level improve rapidly.

On one Saturday night we had no trouble in Salisbury, mainly because there was some of the thickest fog I have ever seen. We had to take our usual trip into the city in case of trouble, but it really was a real "peasouper". It was so thick, the only way our driver could guide the truck was by me and others walking in front with torches, from the camp to the city centre. It really was impossible to go faster than walking pace, and even then vehicles were all over the place, going off the road and going in the opposite direction to what they intended. Even the HLI could not find their way into Salisbury that night, so we had a quiet night and don't really know why we bothered to struggle into Salisbury.

Apart from the signals course at Woking, I spent my other time there as a waiter in the Officers' Mess. Plenty of time to train, and good food, and just like Bulford I had my own room, but it was not as pleasant for running, except that it gave me the chance to travel to some track meetings for my own club and for Guildford and Godalming AC that I joined second claim while at Woking.

While at Woking, I went off to run one evening in a club match at Ealing on a very hard five laps to the mile track. After the race I had to get back to barracks, and I remember getting back to Woking and hardly able to walk. Getting from the bus to barracks was a real struggle, as I had a terrific pain in my left foot. I reported on sick parade next morning and got sent off to the Cambridge Military Hospital at Aldershot for an X-ray. They discovered a march fracture; a splintering of the bones behind the toes. The MO wanted to put it in plaster for six weeks, but I had the unit championships in only a few days plus other races, so I persuaded him just to put a pad under the damaged area and some heavy strapping. He virtually told me that it was up to me, but if I was mad enough to run he would not be responsible for what it might do. I did run two days later and won the three miles almost on one leg. The time was very slow, around seventeen minutes, but I was streets ahead of the field anyway, and won by over a lap. Because I had insisted on not being plastered, I did suffer for much longer than I should, and in fact felt pain for some years.

Like many of the runners of my generation, I think the two years in the forces did help to shape our athletic careers. I am sure the training I was able to do in my two years in uniform, helped me prepare for my successes in the following few years. I suppose it was easy to see why the Soviet Union and other Warsaw Pact countries used the military for most of their top athletes in this pre-professional era.

In January 1956, I finished second in the Berkshire Senior and went to the Inter Counties where I came 126th. Then came a series of good results. I won the Salisbury Plain and District Championship, which I followed up with a win for Salisbury AC, and then the Berkshire Junior Championship. I had seven races in February; it was good job it was leap year with that extra day. I won the Southern Command, and then took second place in the Army Championships behind Basil Heatley. In between, I finished third in the Southern Counties Junior and won another Army race on 29th February.

March was a quieter month, and there were two major races; the National Junior where I was ninth, and the Inter Services where I was eleventh.

In April 1956, I had run the Maidenhead ten mile for the first time. The race winner was Jack Heywood (Herne Hill Harriers) and an almost permanent student at Reading University. His time was 53:05, and Mike Barrett (Ealing) was second in 53:44, just in front of me in the third spot with 53:51. I won the Army three mile title and other races during that summer.

At the end of April, after I had won a six mile invitation race at the White City in 29:48, I started training on the track, which meant running to Tidworth or running on a local grass track at Bulford. My first track session of the year was about nine miles in total, and started with running two 880 yards in 2:7.5 and 2:8, with 440 yards recovery, followed by two 440 yards in 59 and 56.8 seconds, and then 6 x 220 yards, run in between 26 and 28 seconds, and finishing off with 2 x 100 yards in about 10.5 seconds. I took a 220 yard jog between every fast run after the 880 yards. A word of explanation about my sprint times; they were always taken from a flying start. This pattern of training, progressively getting faster in a training session, was to be my main training for the rest of my running career, and helped me to develop a fast finish.

In May I had quite a few club races; some for Salisbury and others for Windsor. These included a 2:05 880 yards, several miles in around 4:30, and a 440 yards in 54.5. I ran for Berkshire in the Inter County Championships at the White City, and finished sixth in 14:0.8. Wins in the Berkshire Championships followed; the one mile in 4:18.4 and the three miles in 14:27.2. My next run was not so good, I ran in the Southern six miles and could only finish sixth in 29:59, but within four days I was back to my best. Winning a three mile race for the Army against Hampshire in 14:14.8.

Most of my training was on the track at this time, and typical sessions could include up to 28 x 220 yards, with the same recovery and all run in under 30 seconds. Other sessions would include up to 14 x 440 yards, but these were normally as part of a longer session where I would run other distances as well. Another typical day at this time would be 6 x ¾ mile, with a two lap jog between each ¾, and finishing with 6 x 220 yards.

Other races in June included finishing sixth in the Southern Counties three mile in 13:59 (first time under 14 minutes), the Army three mile title in 14:10.2, run on a very heavy track at Aldershot, and a 3,000 metre invitation, on the same track one day later, in 8:33.

July was a very busy month, both before and after finishing my National Service in the second week. I ran for the AAAs against Kent in a two mile race; 4th in 9:17.6. I was ninth in my first AAA senior championship three miles at the White City, where I ran 14:02. All together I had over twelve races in that month, plus an unusual event. Just before I left the Army I was sent to Aldershot for the Army Modern Pentathlon Championship; the event I had declined to enter. Not to take part, but to run the 4,000 metre course and set the standard that the competitors had to match to score maximum points. I was not open to bribery, so I ran as fast as I could and set 13:01 as the standard over the cross-country circuit.

I had a busy July and I was back at Inkerman Barracks, Woking, for my demob from the Royal Military Police. I had a total of around fifteen races during that month, both before and after leaving the Army. Apart from the Inter Services Championships, where I finished third in the three miles in 14:19.4, most of these runs were in club matches.

While in the Army my running had progressed rapidly. I set a world best for the three miles for a junior under nineteen years of 14:19 in 1955, and in April 1956, I set a world best by six seconds for an under nineteen-year-old of 29:48.3. I was only eighth and it was my first six mile race, but I did have some good names behind me, including Chris Brasher who later that year won the Olympic steeplechase. The Kenyans have probably got fifty or maybe hundreds of young runners running faster than these times today. I had been the Army Three Mile Champion, but had not managed to win the cross-country because that was held by Basil Heatley, the man who was to win an Olympic silver medal at the marathon in 1964.

Chapter Five

On the Beat

I left the Army in July 1956 and applied to rejoin the Berkshire Constabulary. I had to report to my old police station at Windsor to see if I measured up to their requirements. I had no problem education wise, but the inspector who was checking me out, started to take my measurements. Everything was all right until it came to my chest measurement. He put the tape around my skinny frame and it was barely thirty-four inches; quite a bit below the required thirty-eight inches. Luckily the superintendent came in to see how things were going; the inspector conveyed the disaster of my chest measurement to him. The 'Super' then asked the inspector to measure me again, and he put his hand behind my back and twisted the tape to take up a few inches, and I was in the police. The only problem was that every year when I got my new uniform, it was like a sack and always had to be tailored to fit. In these early days we had two different uniforms; one was the now familiar open-neck collared tunic with lapels, and the other was a relic from the previous century, the buttoned-up to the neck tunic.

Shortly after my interview at Windsor, I was at the Police Training College at Sandgate, in Kent. There was a slight panic when some of the ex-servicemen on my course were called back to the forces for the Suez crisis. I was under threat of being called back for a few days, but they did not require my running, signalling or shooting skills, so I was able to settle into the course. Surprisingly for someone who had never been very good at exams, I had top marks all the way through the course; all over ninety per cent; much to the annoyance of my class mates who studied every evening, while I ran along the seafront between Sandgate and Hythe. I enjoyed the time at Sandgate and got plenty of training.

Other memories of Sandgate were not so good. The chief constable who took the salute at our passing out parade, went to prison shortly afterwards for corruption, and not long after that there was a scandal around the commandant of the training centre. It was a time when the practises of the past had got out of hand and were being jumped on.

I managed to keep up with regular racing and was getting more invitations. Somehow I managed to get away from Sandgate to take part in quite a few of these events. I won a two mile race at one of my favourite events, the Agars Plough meeting at Slough, in 9:10.8, and then two days later I was at the White City in an invitation 3,000 metres, where I managed fifth in 8:28.6. I went back to the White City again for the Fire Brigade Sports, where I ran the 3,000 metres in 8:32. I had plenty of club races to take me up to November, when I finished fifth in the five mile race at Rochester in 25:53.

Once that was over, it was into work as a police constable on the beat at Wokingham. I lived in digs and got home to Windsor as often as I could. It was a very uneventful year of policing, apart from racing home on my cycle one lunch time, and not watching the traffic in front of me in the main shopping street of the town. I hit a car that had stopped and went clean over the top, with my helmet flying off in another direction. The populous of Wokingham were amused and I was suitably embarrassed but not damaged.

On another occasion, I set off the Broadmoor alarm early one Sunday morning and had everyone in a panic for miles around.

There was, for a few weeks, some trouble on Saturday nights at the Drill Hall in Wokingham, where gangs of teddy boys from Slough and Maidenhead used to congregate, but it did not last long as our 'governor' believed in treating force with force, and after a few Saturday nights of "pressure" from us in blue, they decided Wokingham was not the place to be. Today it would be called "zero tolerance" — nothing much has changed over forty-plus years!

It was on the beat at Wokingham that I first came across real poverty. It was in an unexpected place, in cottages between the very good Rose Inn on the Market Place in the centre of the town and the local bowls club, a short distance behind it. I had to make enquiries at one of these cottages, and I never forgot the scene that greeted me. A place with hardly any furniture and very young children on the bare floors eating crusts of dried bread, taken from the floor, which they had also used as their toilet over a period of time. I did report it and something was done to help those poor children. I just hope they eventually grew up into a better life.

Night duty in Wokingham was very interesting, as the town had some strange acoustics. If I was in the town centre sitting on my dustbin behind the town hall, a favourite resting place for me when on night duty, I could hear men speaking to each other quite clearly at the Explorator Fish Depot, over half a mile away.

I had a very good police superintendent at Wokingham, and he and all the staff there were very helpful to me as I progressed my running. After I won my first Police Athletic Association Cross-Country Championship, they presented me with a special certificate, that had been designed and painted by a patient at Broadmoor, and a pair of red Adidas running spikes. I never did know who the special painted certificate was by, but I was told he was a mass murderer. I still have and treasure that special presentation.

The CND marches from Aldermaston were taking place during my time in the police. They were at Easter weekends and normally passed through our territory on Good Friday. I was on escort duty with the march on a few occasions, and enjoyed my walk with them, even though I was in uniform and on the 'other' side. It was always good natured and trouble free.

My police duties were mixed and various. In February 1958, I was working for a short while with CID at Wokingham, and used to run the seven miles from my home in Reading to work and back again. The fourteen miles a day was a good way to keep up my training while working for six days a week. It was while on CID duty at Wokingham, when I heard the devastating news about the Munich air crash of the Manchester United Busby Babes.

During my time both at Woodley and Wokingham, I did have to deal with quite a few sudden deaths of one sort or another, and was 'Coroner's Officer' on a number of cases. This required my attendance at postmortems, which I never had any difficulty with. In fact I was fascinated by the work of pathologists and often used to act as assistant to them. The difficult part of this work was dealing with relatives, especially when one was the first bearer of the bad news about the death of a relative or loved one.

Other more mundane duties could be the Christmas turkey patrols. Keeping an eye on anywhere that turkeys were being raised for the Christmas trade. This also included a watch on growing Christmas trees, and on the sports clubs who had a bar, to make sure no one broke in for some easy booze. We also did a lot of farm inspections and supervision.

Throughout the year there could be other observation duties, which included spending all night under hedges in front gardens trying to catch a persistent burglar, whose wife later worked for me as a secretary, and laying in wait close to a pigsty trying to catch 'criminals' stealing pig food. I wonder if even a country bobby today would get caught up in this small type of crime.

Police work was never without unusual and funny instances. When people went on holiday, they asked for their house to go on the unattended house list, so that the patrolling officers could look in during the night and make sure the property was secure with no unwanted visitors. Customers used to tell us when they were going and when they were due to return, but they were not very good at informing us if they returned from holiday a day or two early. On more than one occasion I checked a house and found a door unlocked. Quietly and gently I would creep into the house, truncheon at the ready, through the ground floor, and then finding no one, I would climb the stairs to the bedrooms. Then I would hear a noise and burst into a room with torch blazing, only to find a couple in bed. A shock for them and for me, but after a quick explanation about their early return, I would leave them to it.

There was another activity I could come across at night when patrolling down country lanes or off the main roads. A car or van with steamed up windows and may be with a little rocking motion. It was naturally my duty to shine my torch and make sure there was no illegal activity taking place. Frequently one of the two people in any car was the same young lady who had a rather appropriate but unfortunate name (she had the same surname as Sir Vivian, the British explorer and geologist).

Another annual duty took me to Oxford for November 5th celebrations. There were always celebrations at the famous Randolph Hotel, and huge numbers of students used to gather for some rather riotous fun there, so extra police were drafted in to protect the property and keep the peace. The university proctors were always in attendance, and they dealt with most problems.

At this time, Oxfordshire, Berkshire and Reading Borough were three completely separate police forces, and this led to some interesting activities on the county and borough boundaries. Between Woodley and Reading, we used to persuade vagrants and other undesirables to seek refuge in the county town, and between the two county police forces, that met at Sonning-on-Thames, it was not unknown for a body in the river to be persuaded to float across to the other side.

In my early days in the police at Wokingham, and later at Woodley, the local constabulary were inundated with gifts at Christmas time. These ranged from turkeys to cases of beer, wines, spirits and other goodies. Various methods were used to share these out, and towards the end it was normally by holding a draw and everyone received something. Towards the end of my service, the clampdown started on these 'gifts'. There had been a couple of high-profile cases of senior officers, including that chief constable, being found guilty of bribery and corruption, and everything was tightened up and gifts of any kind were not encouraged. At the modest local level I never thought it did any harm, and it helped to keep a good relationship between local business and the police. It was like another perk of the job, that I benefited from on a number of occasions with the full approval of my bosses. If there was an accident, especially at night, and we called out a certain garage to collect a wrecked car, there was always a fiver in it for the reporting officer. At that time this represented about two days' income from the 'job'.

Father William Frank Eldon before the First World War

A very young Eldon at Tisbury in 1937

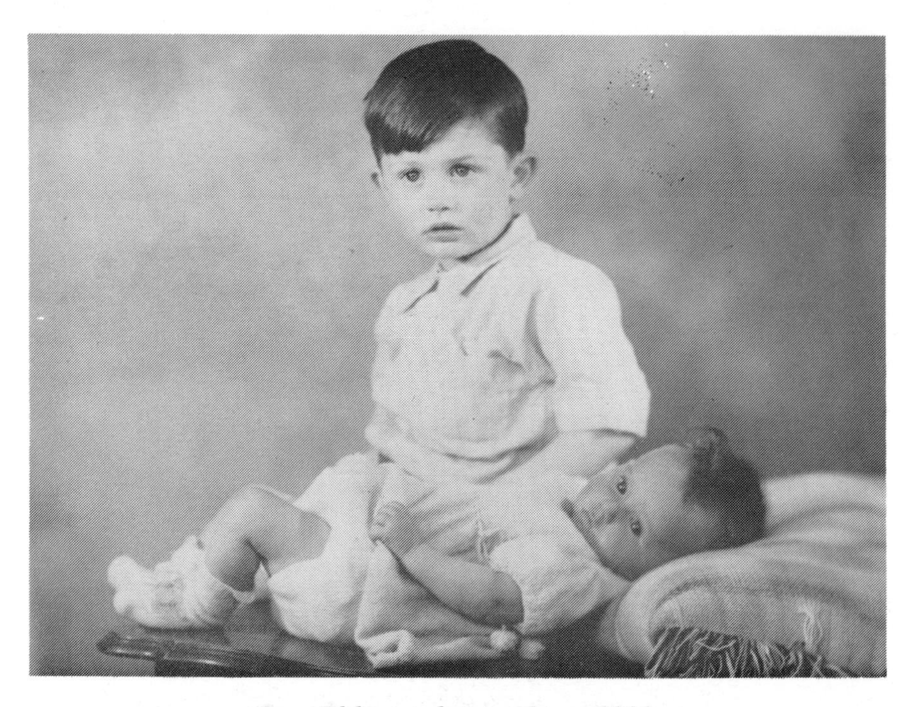

Stan Eldon and sister Janet 1939

Centre front choirboy Eldon with choir of All Saints', Windsor

"EXPRESS" Picture 504/A/1

Scouts 1950 Cross-country winners

The two winners of the 1950 Scouts' cross-country race are pictured here with their District Scout Master, Mr. E. C. Ilsley.

Runners set off from the Scout headquarters in Charles Street on a three-mile course which lay partly through Windsor Great Park.

First was patrol-leader Stanley don of the 2nd Windsor Troop, (left), with patrol-leader Peter Pomfret of the 3rd Windsor (Clewer St. Stephen) Group a close second.

Stanley Eldon, aged 13, spent two-and-a-half years in the Cub pack and has been in his Scout Troop for another two-and-a-half.

Peter Pomfret, aged 14, came up from the Cubs in 1947, after two years' service. He also is a second-class Scout.

☆ ☆

The first win

The young glamour girl I married

A display of trophies won by age 16 years

Leaving All Saints' Church, Windsor, Wedding Day 1957

Passing Out Royal Military Police 1954, Eldon 4th from right front row

Passing Out two years later as a police constable, nearest the camera

Superintendent Alf East sees the young Eldon off on his beat with TV crew in attendance

On duty alongside the Thames at Sonning, mixing training with duty

Phew! Thank goodness that's over

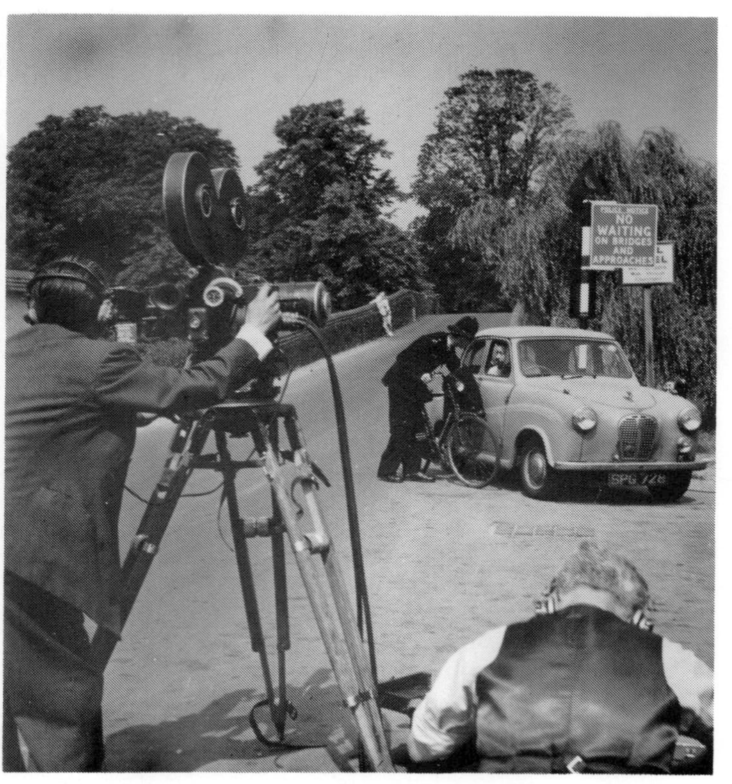

"You can't park here madam"
with news cameras recording as usual

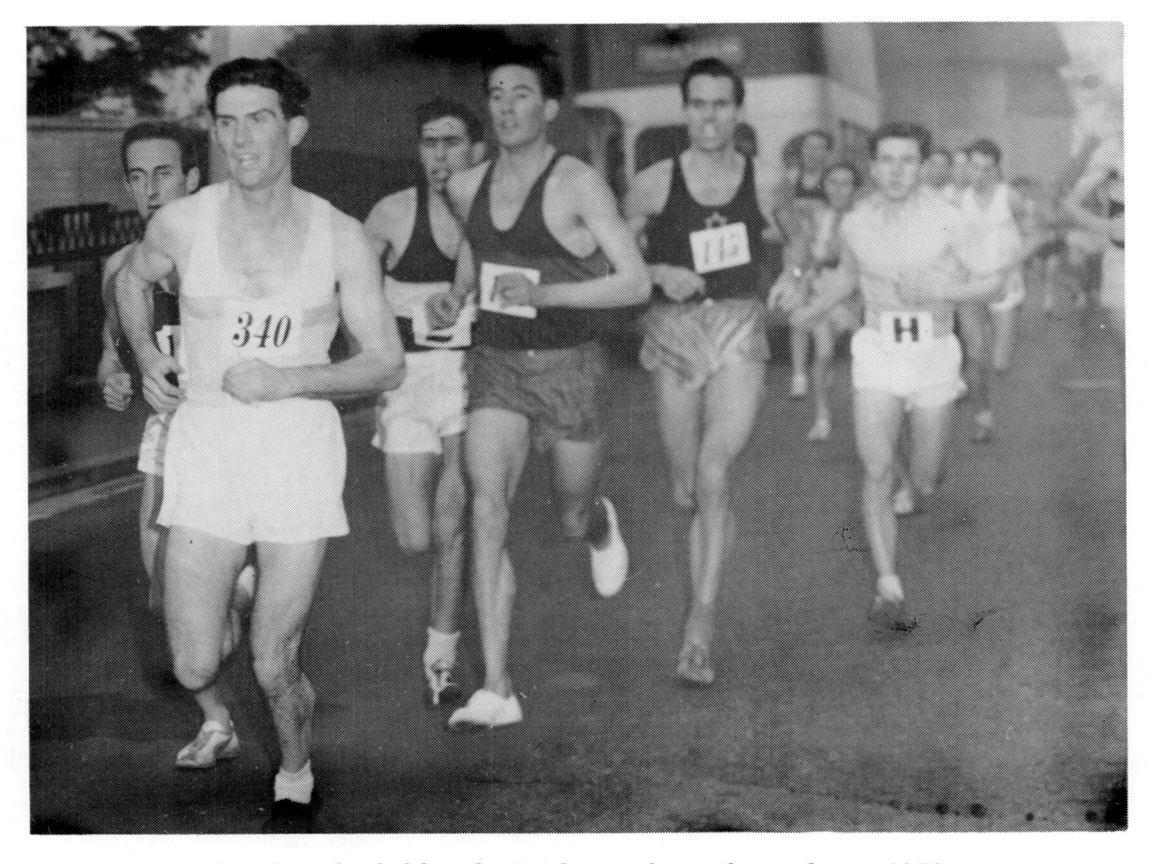

Leading the field in the Rochester five mile road race 1959

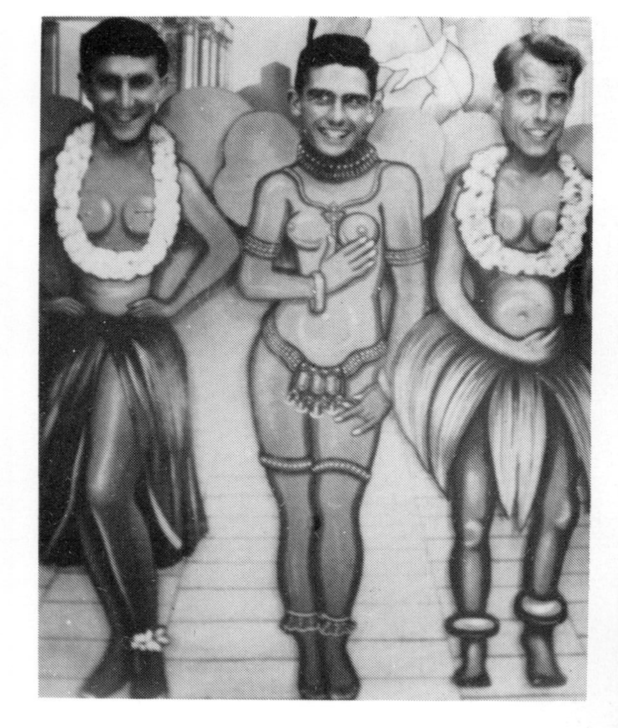

Tivoli Gardens, Copenhagen in 1957 with Dave Shaw and Derek Ibbotson

Primitive weight training, a flat iron on each foot

A quick rub down from wife Marion at 5 Eldon Road

Running home to Eldon Road, Reading

An abundance of police trophies and others

THE TWO ELDONS

Stan Eldon, the athlete, beats the best in Europe in the international cross-country race at Cardiff. Inset: Stan Eldon, the policeman, going on duty last night

Duty follows major win

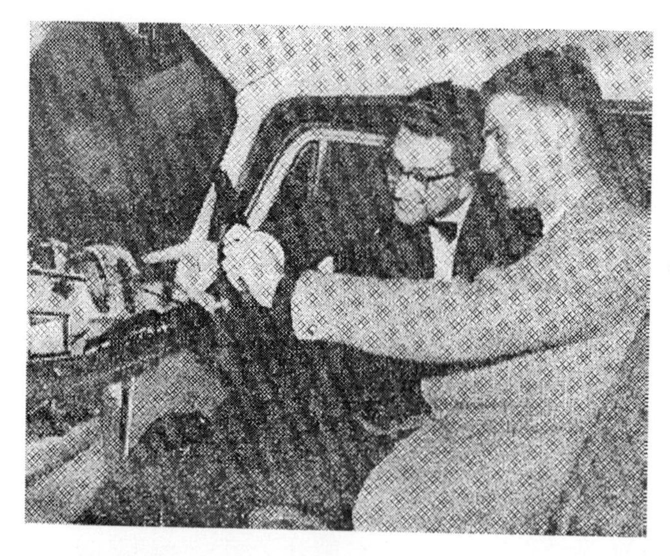

One of my driving lessons with BSM

PRESENTED TO

P.C.385

·STANLEY·EDWARD·ELDON·

BY THE

Berkshire Constabulary

("B" DIVISION)

Recreation Club

HIS ACHIEVEMENT

WINNING

THE POLICE ATHLETIC ASSOCIATION

CROSS-COUNTRY CHAMPIONSHIP

21ST MARCH, 1957.

The special certificate presented by police colleagues at Wokingham

Chapter Six

The Running Really Takes Off

The year of 1957 started with an abandoned County Championship at Reading on 5th January; but the year did start off with my winning the Berkshire Cross-Country, with a time of 47:34 for the nine miles in the rearranged race the following week. This was followed by the Inter Counties at Rugby, where I got away to a very fast start but faded badly between three and six miles, before coming again at the finish to come in twenty-ninth in 39:17.

I then started my usual increase in mileage, and in the week ending 26th January I ran seventy-five miles, with a win on the Saturday in a club cross-country match. I won, but I actually finished and dead-heated with a club colleague, and treated the race as a training run.

The following week my training was down to one of eight miles on the Saturday as I had flu, and it must have been pretty bad because I actually had two days in bed. My diary note on the day I got back to training says "Marion did about two miles"; this must have been a historic moment, I do not recall her running very often.

The following week I missed running on the Sunday, probably due to a quick turn round of my shift. If I had worked on Saturday night and finished at 6 a.m., I was probably back on duty at 2 p.m., so there was not much time to train. On the Monday I got cracking again with a fifteen mile run, and followed this up on Tuesday with another fifteen miles, but with some fast running over one mile to four miles. The next day it was up to sixteen miles, made up of five fast stages of about two miles with slight rest in between. On Thursday I had two training runs, with fourteen miles in the morning, which included 4 x 1.5—3 miles, and in the afternoon six miles with lots of short fast sprints up to 300 yards at a time. On Friday I did just twelve miles, made up of 3 x 2 miles fast, with slow running in between, and on the Saturday I had a 5.5 mile race which I won, but training as well on road and country. The total in the six days, ninety-two miles.

The following week I had to prepare for the Southern Counties Junior champs at the end of the week. Sunday was a rest day (changing shifts again), followed by twelve miles on Monday with 6 x 1 mile fast. On Tuesday I did sixteen miles with two training sessions. The first one in the morning was progressive training, four miles, two miles, one mile and 880 yards, all fast and flat out and obviously getting faster as the distance got shorter. This was followed by four miles of short fast bursts in the evening. The following day, Wednesday, I had two sessions again with a total of fifteen miles. This was made up of eleven miles in the afternoon, that consisted of a fast three miles, and 2 x 2 miles fast and then a short four miles in the evening. On Thursday I did ten miles with a two mile, followed by 2 x 1 mile and then 20 x 100 yards fast running. Friday was a rest day, and then it was the Southern on Saturday, where I finished second in 32:18 for the six mile course. The total for the week was only sixty-three miles which was normal on a big race week.

The following week it was back up to eighty-three miles, running every day with a mixture of fast and steady running and culminating in my winning the Berkshire Junior Cross-Country Championship. Another week followed of about eighty miles of running, which included another club win where I ran with a club colleague and treated the run as training. It was then the week of the National Junior Championships. My mixed week of training of sixty miles helped me to achieve a fourth place for the 6 miles 700 yards course with a time of 35:58. The following week I did seventy-five miles of mixed training as I prepared for my final race of the 1957 Cross-Country Season, the Police National Cross-Country Race at Harrogate. The police were always good to me, and sent a sergeant to Harrogate with me as a 'minder'. I had a very light week of training before this of only forty miles, and won the 6.5 mile race in 37:37. My win robbed a policeman, DC Pemble from Kent Constabulary, from winning his fifth title.

The final week of March saw me preparing for the start of the track season and the road races that would fill the gap between the seasons. I only did fifty-three miles, but it was quality fast running over shorter distances, and at the end of the week I ran for Windsor and Eton AC in the Thames Valley Harriers Road Relay at Cranford. I set a new record for the 4 miles 1,500 yards single lap of 22:31.

The next week it was really down to track training and a total of sixty miles, made up as follows. A steady run on Sunday of five miles, then on Monday eleven miles, which included eight miles on the road and three miles on grass, with fast stretches of one to three miles. On the Tuesday I did ten miles on grass, which included one mile in 4:37, half a mile in 2:17, 440 yards in 67 seconds and then 12 x 220 yards in between 29 and 33 seconds, all with about one mile of jogging in between each fast element.

Then came another of my favourite races, the Uxbridge Road Relay. The race started outside the Uxbridge Swimming Pool, and each of the four runners ran two laps totalling 5 miles 1,000 yards, and I set the fastest time with 27 minutes. The laps included running up the A40 twice. Imagine trying to do that today.

My next race was on Easter Monday at Maidenhead, where I finished second in 52.11, worth about 50 minutes for ten miles on the two-lap course, that ran out from Maidenhead to Cookham and back. Every Easter Monday, for a number of years, Marion and myself would have tea at Cookham with my friend and advisor Stan Jones. It was always a pleasure, as also there every year was Sam Ferris, the Olympic Marathon Silver Medallist from 1932. Sam was always at the 'Ten' to write up on it for *Athletics Weekly,* and it was sad over the years to see this once great marathon runner struck down with Parkinson's disease.

At the end of the week, I ran in the Southern Counties six mile at the White City and finished third in 28:53. I will always remember this race as my girlfriend Marion was in the stands, and on the last lap, just as I was about to strike for home on the back straight, I tripped over someone's legs and fell sprawling onto the track. I felt inclined to give up at that stage, but a voice screamed at me from the stands, "Get up you fool, you can still win." I didn't, but it nearly worked.

My training continued at the fifty to sixty miles a week mark, and I was now getting used to running twice a day on two or three days a week. The training was mixed with plenty of 220, 440 and 880 yard fast running with up to a lap of recovery. I also started on my 'progressive training' as I called it. Running a fairly fast ¾ mile in 3:24, and then 2 x 880 yards in 2:14 and finishing with 440 yards in 63 seconds. I kept up this training but adding much more to it over the next three years.

Compared with the next three years, my number of races in this season was pretty small and well spread.

In the middle of May, I ran in a Invitation 3,000 metres at Thurrock. The result third in 8:38.2. The following week I had a double win in the Berkshire Championships at Reading, winning the one mile in 4:22.2 and the three miles in 14:12.6.

My running continued on the up, and on one evening in May, in an inter club match at Maidenhead, I had three races in about ninety minutes. I won the mile in 4:19.2, then the 880 yards in 1:56.6 (my best ever for the distance), and finally I won the two miles in 9:13. All this was done on a five laps to the mile grass track that was like a switchback. About ten days later I took second place in the Inter County three miles at the White City in 13:47.8. I followed this at the same meeting, with fifth place in the six miles in 28:46.

A few days later, I was in Glasgow for the Glasgow Police Sports. This was a very major meeting in those far-off days. It had a big budget, good prizes, and it attracted some of the best athletes in the world. I took second place in the three miles in 13:49.2.

I then won the Southern Counties three miles at Hurlingham in 13:49. It was then onto the White City again for the AAA Championships. As always the six miles was on the Friday evening, and I took second place in 28:50.8. I followed this up with third place in the three miles in 13:52.2 on the Saturday.

The Police Athletic Championships were held at Iffley Road, Oxford in July, and I won both the three miles in 14:16, and the one mile in 4:9.3. My memory of that meeting was that when I walked into the changing rooms at Iffley Road, I met a new recruit to the police service. It was such a shock as it was a pretty good 400 metre runner who had been a lieutenant in the Royal Military Police at Bulford with me. In his Army days he had been a bit more than just an ordinary bastard, and I thought he was destined for a long Army career. I think it was my running there that got me onto police posters in Oxfordshire, no not as a 'Wanted Man' but as a recruitment campaign.

Later the same month, I won an invitation three miles in Dublin in 14:4 around the famous rugby ground of Lansdowne Road. It was only a marked out grass track, but there was a huge crowd and the stadium was packed. It was here that I met the Olympic three mile gold medal winner of 1908, Joe Deacon. The meeting was promoted by Billy Morton, the well-known Irish character who loved his athletics, as a way of raising funds for the new stadium that he had planned for Dublin. He was a great showman, and the meeting was promoted with the message that an Olympic gold medallist would be taking part. That was sort of true as Joe Deacon ran around the track nearly fifty years after his Olympic glory.

My AAA's results earned me my first full international vest against France at the White City. This was a great thrill, but ended in disaster with photographs of me laying prostrate on the grass after the race, and headlines *"The flop by the galloping cop"* and similar. I was not last but third out of four in 30:40.6. I had suffered in the heat, a problem that stayed with me throughout my athletic career; more of that later.

Only four days after my failure, I bounced back with a win in the three miles for the Combined Services against the AAA and Combined Universities. The winning time was 13:55.

In September I was selected for my first full overseas vest, and I was off with the British team to run in Hanover, Germany, and Warsaw in Poland, and in between I had a trip to Finland to run in a 3,000 metres race, where I finished sixth in 8:27.4. It was a very memorable and enjoyable trip, even if my performances were not quite what I had hoped for. I well remember some of the characters who were on that trip. Of course there was the famous Gordon Pirie who I suppose I had a love/hate relationship with, and there was big George Knight from Essex Beagles, who was a very fine 10,000 metre runner, and a vegetarian. In Poland I ran the 10,000 metres, and in Germany the 5,000 metres, both were not good runs and I was last of four in both races.

Lads always lark about, and while at the school in Germany where we were staying, I went down to have a shower which was on the ground floor. After the shower I was running back upstairs with just a towel around me, and was confronted by the women's team manager, and as I was just in front of her on the stairs, me going up and her coming down, someone pulled my towel away leaving me starkers in front of someone who was the doyen of women's athletics for many years.

In between the two full internationals, a small team of about fifteen went to Copenhagen for an invitation meeting. We flew from Hanover to the Danish capital in one of the two Elizabethan aircraft. One of the athletic team officials, Bob Adams, was also Deputy Chairman of British European Airways at the time, and he accompanied us on this trip. This enabled me to do something that was a once in a lifetime experience. At the time BEA were looking for pilots; the stock they had carried over from the war were slowly retiring, and the airline was getting desperate for some new blood. As we were getting closer to Denmark, Adams suggested I might like to fly the plane! He took me up to meet the captain and I was put in the seat and told what to do. I remember how difficult it was to control the level flight and keep the wings level and watch all the instrumentation, even though it was a lot less than in a modern aircraft. A message came up to the cockpit from Derek Ibbotson, who complained of feeling sick because of the movement of the aircraft, I think he was only kidding. I did fly for some way until we were in sight of the runway, then the professionals took over. I did not get offered a job, but it was a very exciting experience, and I still have the letter that I sent home to Marion telling her all about it.

The visit to Warsaw was a great experience for a number of reasons. It was my first visit to an 'Iron Curtain' country, and we arrived within days of some student riots in the city, and the bullet damage was still clearly visible on the damaged buildings. There was also a great black market in the Polish currency, the zloty. The official rate of exchange was sixty to the pound, but because there was such a demand for sterling, up to five times that could be fetched in an exchange on the street. I did not take advantage of this, but I worked out that for about £50 you could buy an excellent grand piano, but how could I get it on the plane home! The visit also showed how well off we were compared to the population of Poland. The food was terrible and it was fortunate that one of the two aircraft we had flown out on had carried a hold full of Lucozade. The water was so bad we were advised not to use it for anything, and we even cleaned our teeth with the amber drink.

Soon after I arrived at the hotel, I had just settled into my room when I received a phone call, very unusual in any circumstances at that time, but this was even more unusual. It was a young lady and she did not say much, but that she would like to come up to my room. I wondered what temptation was going to be put in the way of this young man just weeks away from his wedding. The visit was of a much more serious nature. The first thing she did on entering the room, before she said anything, was to look under the bed, along the skirting and into the air vent. After she had satisfied herself that everything was OK, she explained that she thought the room might be 'bugged'. She wanted an interview with me for a student underground newspaper, and had picked me out because I was young and a policeman in England. We had a long conversation about life in England, my life, and in particular about young people.

I was a bit of a daredevil, and one night in Warsaw I went out onto the roof of the hotel and climbed someway up a radio mast — and I was not even drunk.

It was on this trip that I first got to know some of the top sports journalists of the day, in particular Peter Wilson of the *Daily Mirror*, Desmond Hackett of the *Express*, and Roy Moor of the *News Chronicle*. I learned something about journalists. I remember getting into a discussion with Peter Wilson, when I asked him "Why do you make such glaring errors in what you report and say?" His response was "If you do not make a few mistakes, no one will be interested and no one will write to the paper or remember what you have written." I was very surprised at his knowledge of athletics, and it was not the perception that I and many others had of this top professional.

On this first international trip I had the 'reward' of the special fifteen shillings a day (75p), that was paid to all athletes when they were abroad competing in international races. It was always a source of amusement to Marion that I used to keep an accurate account of all moneys received, whether the fifteen bob a day or expenses on trips. These always included every small detail, including the purchase of a newspaper or stamps. I learned over my few years in international athletics to make a profit out of almost every race I ran in. If I had a way of making a few bob, some of my team mates were more inventive. I remember the rows over expenses that shot-putter Arthur Rowe used to have, and some of the items he tried to claim for. Because he used to carry the heavy 16-pound implements around with him in a holdall, he claimed that the bag rubbed on his trousers and wore them out quickly, so on at least one occasion he claimed for new trousers. He also had trouble with claiming expenses for his food when travelling, but I always thought this was not unreasonable as he did have an enormous appetite, and would consume huge quantities of milk and other food. I suppose today the big men just add supplements or 'other' things to their diet.

The last race of the season was at Birmingham on 5th October in an invitation three mile. I came third in 13:50.6, which was not a bad end to the season, especially as I had other things on my mind; my wedding to Marion and the start of married life.

Before that could happen, I had to apply to my superintendent in a written report to see if I could marry Marion. This was not just a formality in those days but a serious matter. The enquiry was passed to Windsor where she lived with her parents (I was at Wokingham now), and an inspector checked out her family. Her dad ran a small motor repair shop under the arches in Windsor, and was a very honest hard-working man, and he easily passed the police enquiry, so we were given permission to marry.

Back home I was preparing for the big event, my wedding which was to be on the 12th October. The big day came and it was a beautiful October day; the sun shone and family members and friends attended the marriage service in All Saints' Church, Windsor, where I had sung in the choir as a boy and man, as well as being a Sunday School teacher and server. It was a long wedding, as we had decided to take Holy Communion as part of our celebration. Our many friends and family were there, and as we left the church many of our athletic friends formed a guard of honour with running shoes mounted on poles. The wedding was conducted by a number of clergy, including the Reverend Creed Meredith, a Chaplain to the Queen, and the Reverend Harry Stanbrook whose mother Annie had made me promise when I was only in my teens that I would write a book one day. The wedding cake was provided by the White family, who had a daughter, Shirley, who was a very good sprinter in the Windsor and Eton Club. They had a local business and were very good to me in my early career, helping me with some of my athletic costs as they knew my own parents could not afford to help. I suppose they were the nearest I ever had to a commercial sponsor.

The honeymoon was in Guernsey, and I had just embarked on a training programme that was to make sure I ran every day for a year. So every night before dinner in the Les Rocketts Hotel, St Peter Port, I sat Marion in the bar and off I went training. People there who knew we were on our honeymoon could not understand this strange man.

We had to return from honeymoon a couple of days early, as I had to go on a refresher course at Sandgate, and the police had found me a police house.

So it was back to Sandgate for the first of two refresher courses, but my marriage and running did not stop me from continuing with successful exam results, and I again hit the ninety per cent plus in the examinations. My new bride went home to mother for the week, although she did go and take a look at our new home at 5 Eldon Road, Reading; yes it was Eldon Road, not named after me, but I think the then Chief Constable of Berkshire had a sense of humour. It was a rambling three-storey house with a large cellar and many rooms, including attic rooms that had been used as servants' quarters in days gone by, when a chief constable had it as his residence. I returned home and we moved into this mausoleum. We only had a few sticks of furniture, so many of the rooms remained empty. I did have an unusual use for the large basement; I bought some day-old chicks and reared them down there until they were able to go outside and eventually moved with us to a new home.

I patrolled a beat that covered a huge area from the village of Sonning-on-Thames and across Earley and Woodley. An area that was largely a mixture of urban and rural. I remained here for the rest of my time in the Berkshire

Constabulary. I believe my cycling contributed to my all-round fitness, especially as I was known to cycle much faster on my police bike than the norm. In fact my supervising officer very seldom came out to meet and cycle with me as he could not keep up with me.

I had great support from my colleagues while I was in the police. They generously swopped duties with me, to enable me to get to as many races as possible, but I did work my six days a week like the rest. Yes it was six days a week; our official working week was five days, but it was compulsory to work the sixth day as what was called ED.P (Extra Duties Performed). This extra day did put more money in the pay packet, but did not give much time for outside activities. Many of my races were run between shifts, an early turn from 6 a.m. to 2 p.m. one day, and then a night shift the next day from 10 p.m. to 6 a.m. I had to catch up on sleep somehow, and I found various ways of grabbing a short nap when I was on nights. I developed a way of propping myself up in a telephone box and going to sleep leaning on the telephone shelf and sort of wedged in the box with knees bent.

While I was living in my first police house, I had my first of many postmortems. I had always joked with Marion that the day I had one she would give me hearts, kidneys or liver for lunch; and that is exactly what happened. I was only told on the morning and the PM was going to be in the afternoon at the Royal Berkshire Hospital, only a short distance from home. I went home for lunch and Marion had prepared something I was very fond of, liver. I ate it and enjoyed it before making the short journey to the mortuary, where I found myself, not just watching, but weighing out human liver and organs. It did not put me off and I attended many more, especially as I had a sergeant who could not face up to this part of police work.

There were some characters around in my early days in the police and I think I learned a lot from them. I remember one detective constable in particular who was an expert at interrogation, and I could never understand why he was still at the bottom of the ladder, after well over twenty years of service before gaining a promotion, although in his last five years or so he did rise very rapidly to superintendent. I suppose it was partly looking at him that made me leave the constabulary after a few years. I would not have wanted to wait that long for promotion. He, like many of my other colleagues, did a very good job, and they knew that their job was catching the villains. They more or less did it by the book, but they could not have survived in the modern service with all the politics of the job.

While I was at Woodley, I had a sergeant who drank too much and was frequently inebriated on duty in the evening and especially at night. One night we had an emergency call; someone was breaking into a factory, and he wanted to drive the police vehicle to the incident. I flatly refused to let him drive and took over the driving. I suppose it was insubordination but he never mentioned the incident again.

During my service, I did act as a court usher on quite a few occasions, and one of the interesting aspects of this job was shutting the jury away and having to stay outside the door where they were deliberating and hearing their discussions. Later as a civilian I did act as chairman on a jury and so saw the job from both sides. I must admit that in neither case did it inspire me with great confidence about the legal system. I remember one comment from a juror in particular. While others tried to be fair, this chap said "I know he is guilty. I know the family and they are all a bad lot." Maybe it was true and it certainly persuaded the jury on that occasion, as a swift guilty verdict was brought in.

Because of my athletics, I frequently had the press knocking at the door, and they loved to take pictures of me next to the road sign 'Eldon Road'. After a year living in Eldon Road, I was given a new police house that had just been built at Earley. There were many photographs and articles written about me and Eldon Road. One of them that did cause a stir, was a photo of me running along the road with my black Labrador Simon, who was only about eighteen months old and full of energy. When I came back from a training run, he would be waiting at the door making sure that I took him for a run around the block. The photograph shows me doing just that, and it appeared in the *Sunday Express*. The next day the RSPCA came to see me because some idiot had seen this picture and thought it was cruel to the dog. Fortunately the RSPCA senior inspector that came, saw how stupid the complaint was and that was the end of it. I wonder what that crank would have thought about dogs running all the way with their owners in half marathons today? It was another incident that showed me just how careful you have to be if you are a celebrity that is always in the news.

We moved from Eldon Road to Falstaff Avenue in Earley, and it was while I was living there that I learnt to drive. I had a couple of drives with a police colleague in my old ex-headmaster's Austin, and also five lessons with the British School of Motoring. A photograph appeared in some papers of me in the BSM car. Today I would probably have been paid for such a promotion, but I actually had to pay them for the lessons. Within a couple of weeks, I had passed my test and shocked one of my neighbours. A lady opposite knew I was learning to drive, she had had several attempts herself, and when I returned home the day I passed the test, I went out in the car to take part in an 'Any Questions' at a community club at Cholsey in South Oxfordshire, about eighteen mile away. I remember that night as there was heavy snow and I had never driven in conditions like that before, and had never driven on my own. My neighbour thought I had just taken a chance, as she could not believe I had passed my test so quickly.

Within a couple of weeks I took another test, the police driving test, a little tougher but I passed so that I could then drive general police vehicles.

One unusual happening around this time, was that Marion had to go to

Reading Borough Police Station to be interviewed regarding the A6 murder. I don't think she was a suspect but she had worked with all the parties involved.

Whilst living at Earley, I used to have some company on night shifts. Depending on where I was supposed to be patrolling on my bicycle, I would go home in the early hours of the morning and collect my dog Simon so that he could 'assist' me while checking properties on my patch. He was great company but would not have made a very brave police dog. On several occasions I sent him round the back of garages and the like, while I would go around the opposite way. He would dash round the back of the property and as we met up he would come and sit by me still shaking from the fright of seeing my torch and thinking I was a villain. With no radio and no communication with anybody during the night, it was comforting to have him around and he enjoyed the exercise trotting along by the side of my bike.

Several times during this period, I would be the escort for prisoners being taken to Oxford Prison. They were normally only taken one at a time in the police station's small van. There would be just a driver and myself, but I never handcuffed my charges and we would stop off at a transport cafe on the way to the prison so that the prisoner could have his last free meal for a while, and we could have some refreshment as well. I never lost a prisoner or had any trouble with them. Before we set out from Woodley, I would introduce myself and most of them knew very well about my running ability, so I would warn them that if they took off I would always catch them. There was another reason we did not have trouble, whatever the criminal had done to get sent down. In those days there was a relationship between police and the public and that included the criminal element. There was a certain respect for the uniform, and I suppose the attitude of most of the criminal fraternity was "fair cop guv", and they got on with their sentence.

I remember a couple of occasions that proved this point, and which also shows the difference between then and now. One of these was when I was alone late at night and I had to confront three or four yobs. During my 'debate' with them, one pulled out a knife and threatened me. I told him not to be so stupid and to put the thing away. He stared at me and then decided that it was good advice. It all settled down and that was that. Another incident was when I was called to a caravan after someone reported hearing a shotgun being fired. I went to the caravan and picked up one or two discharged cartridges as I approached. I knocked on the door and this chap opened the door holding the still smoking gun. He started off being aggressive with something like "Do you want some too?" I told him to put the bl...... thing down and don't be silly. He did and we went and had a chat and I discovered that he had fired the gun outside at his stepdaughter who lived with him, his wife and children. There was a cosy family arrangement where the two women slept in turn with the man, and on this particular night the stepdaughter, who was about sixteen, did not want to know. After reporting the incident to my inspector the next day, I was told to go and see his employer and see what sort of man he was. I did and he was very good at his job of delivering coal, and his boss did not want to lose him. The end result; he was warned about his future conduct and that was that.

My father in the First World War had also been an escort for prisoners, but this was much more serious. He told the story about one particular prisoner he had to take, I think it was from London to Edinburgh, but it may have been in the opposite direction. This man had been arrested as a German spy and was being taken to his execution. He was apparently a German baron and very wealthy, and my father was offered many inducements to let him escape, but he did not succumb and the sentence was carried out. I was never put in that very difficult position while carrying out my duties.

The year of 1958 started quite well; my training had gone well and I was clocking up the miles. In 1956 my total miles run were 2,437; in 1957 that had increased to 2,655 and in 1958, I passed the 3,000 mark with 3,061 miles. The first week in January, I started to up my training levels after a quiet time before Christmas. I always eased off the training between the end of the track season, in about October, until early January. The first full week of the new year, I clocked up eighty-five miles, running twice a day on four of the seven days, and finishing the week with a good win in a six mile cross-country race. The following week I dropped back to seventy-one miles, although this did include some hard days in the early part of the week, running up to sixteen miles a day. This was the week of the Inter Counties where I finished tenth, the only race I did not win that winter. After that 'failure' it was back to hard training, and the next week I was back up to eighty-six miles and all my training was in the morning, so I must have been working the 2 p.m. to 10 p.m. shift. This was followed by weeks of 102 miles and 100 miles.

The 102 mile week was made up as follows:—

Sunday — 5 miles on road in afternoon.
Monday — 12 miles on road in evening, fairly fast pace with some sprints.
Tuesday — total 20 miles, 7 miles on road in morning, 7 miles fast running in 34 minutes in evening, followed by 6 miles fast and slow.
Wednesday — total 20 miles, 7 miles in morning in 38 minutes, 7 miles in evening in 37 minutes, followed by 6 miles interval running. Weight Training.
Thursday — total 20 miles, 7 miles in morning in 39 minutes, 7 miles in evening in 40 minutes, followed by 6 miles interval running. Weight Training.

Friday — total 12 miles, 8 miles in morning, 5 laps around Palmer Park, with 4 miles on road in evening.
Saturday — total 13 miles, 6 mile race which I won in 29:50, but I ran three laps in 46.05 and did other training.

The training the following week was identical, with another race win at the end of the week.

I then dropped back to seventy miles in the week of the Southern Counties Championships at Parliament Hill, although the mileage was down, I still trained very hard, and had a good session of eleven miles as close as on the Thursday. I ran away from the field early in the race, and went on to record a great win; there were some great runners in that field, including Gordon Pirie and Frank Sando. My time was 49:50 for the 9 miles 100 yards, heavy and as usual very muddy, course. On the Parliament Hill course with the mud and hills, once you broke away from the field, it was comparatively easy to keep the other runners behind you. While you were running fast downhill, they would be running much slower up the other side.

I was then confident that I could win the National, and training went back up to 100 miles a week, before easing back the week before the big race. As always the National Championships were in March, and these were held at Birkenhead. So as to be there in plenty of time, and so that I could be prepared properly for the nine mile race, Marion and I went up to Manchester a couple of days earlier and stayed with her aunt. What should have been another triumph for me turned into a disaster.

Chapter Seven

From Disaster to Triumph

We had to make our way from Manchester to the venue at Stoke Park, Birkenhead, and after staying in bed longer than we should, we left Manchester for the race and thought we had plenty of time, but problem followed problem; partly because I had misunderstood the start time, and not least of all because when we took a taxi for the last part of the journey the driver did not know his area, and we arrived at the start when the runners had run their first few hundred yards. Bitterly disappointed I did not know what to do, so I watched the race and saw Alan Perkins (Ilford AC) win the 1958 National Cross-Country title. I had beaten him very easily in the Southern a few weeks earlier. I explained my predicament to the officials after the race, before they did the traditional thing of selecting the first nine athletes for the International Championships to be held that year in Cardiff. When the team was announced at the prize giving I waited, not really expecting to be selected, as the rules had always been very strict about selection. The team was announced and they put me in the list. There were mixed reactions from other runners; congratulations from some and not very happy comments from those who had been pushed further down the list by my inclusion. I knew there was only one thing I could do to make up for their disappointment, and that was to make sure that I went to Cardiff and run my legs off for a top place.

There were only a couple of weeks, but I trained hard for another ten days, including another week of the magic 100 miles. During this time I won two more races, including the Police National on the Thursday before the big day. The Police Championship on this occasion was close to home. As a result of my winning in 1957, the Berkshire Constabulary had the task of organising the event, and it was staged at the Royal Military Academy at Sandhurst. My winning time was a new Championship best of 30:37.4, although to this day I do not know how they could talk about records when every course was different and certainly not measured with any accuracy. I treated the race as a serious training run and I had a very comfortable win, which was just as well, as just twenty-four hours later, on the Friday, I was at Cardiff for the biggest race of my life.

After we had all met up, we went for a light run around the course with the rest of the team. It was a flat, fast course but to my horror there were around thirty hurdle-type fences to be jumped in the three laps. I was not alone, and some of my team mates were talking about running a little further and going around the obstacles rather than trying to jump them.

The Saturday came and it was very cold, but the cold never worried me, it was the heat that caused me problems, although I did wear gloves on this occasion. The favourite for the race was Alain Mimoun from France, a great athlete, even if a little eccentric, who had beaten me in that first international race at the White City. He was so fussy about his food that he had insisted on going into the kitchens at the hotel and helping to prepare his own food. He was now thirty-five years of age, but had won silver medals in the 1952 Olympics, and was the Gold Medal winner in the Olympic Marathon of 1956. He also had a great incentive to win the race, as no one had ever won four titles in a row, and this was his fourth title chance. I did what I always did, I went out at the front, not worrying about the opposition, but at every obstacle Mimoun got ahead of me; he was so fast over the fences, but as soon as he knew I was over a fence he would slow and wave me to the front again. This was repeated many times and I thought 'He thinks he can outsprint me at the finish.' As we neared the end, I kept up the pressure and we turned towards the finish, running stride by stride. I seem to remember he passed me and made his strike for home, but I was ready and I started my finishing dash for the line. I always could muster a strong finish however tired I was, and I was not going to lose now. My final kick took me ahead and I crossed the line around thirty yards ahead of the great runner. My winning time was 46:29 for the nine miles, and with all the obstacles this was a pretty good time.

I had done it and rewarded those who had kept faith with me by putting me in the team. The England team ran away with the team prize, packing all six in the first ten places. Our captain Frank Sando was third and he was the opposite to me, he did suffer from the cold and was the first athlete I knew to wear tights or track trousers in races to keep his legs warm.

The excited commentator that day, was the well-known Welshman Bernard Baldwin. As soon as he could after the race, he rushed up to me and invited me to run in his special New Year's Eve run; the Nos Galan in Mountain Ash. I agreed and over the next forty years I was to return about thirty times to be part of that very special event on New Year's Eve, where I always received great hospitality from the families that put me up and looked after me each year.

Fresh from my first major win, I ran at Cranford in the Thames Valley Harriers Road Relay the following Saturday, and recorded 22:19 for the fastest lap of the 4 miles 1,500 yards circuit, which took twelve seconds off my record time the previous year.

In those days it was traditional to run on the road between cross-country and track seasons, and I had a number of road races over the next few weeks. The first week in April, I started my speed training to get ready for the track season, and these included sessions with groups of 220 yards in 28 to 32 seconds and 440 yards in 63 seconds upwards.

The one race I should have won, but didn't, was the Maidenhead ten miles on Easter Monday, 7th April. It was a race over two laps and the actual distance was 10 miles 700 yards. A very good road runner, Tony Redrup of Wycombe Phoenix Harriers, was the surprise winner and I was second in 50:52, after a race where we had never been separated by more than a few yards. It brought me down to earth with a bump and it was back to the drawing board. Club track races followed in April, where I won an assortment of distances from 880 yards to three miles.

On 6th May, I ran for the AAA v Oxford University; the annual meeting where just four years earlier Roger Bannister had clocked the first sub four minute mile. I won the two miles in 8:53.8, a good start to the season. A week later I was at Hornchurch in Essex for two races; a 2,000 metres where I finished second in 5:19, and a 3,000 metres which I won in 8:16.4.

On a Tuesday evening, about one week later, I was in Dublin at the opening of the Santry Stadium to run a one mile race against some of the best milers of the day. The money for the stadium had been raised mainly by the work of one man; the bubbling outgoing Dublin jeweller Billy Morton, who had been promoting athletics in Ireland for a number of years. It was a very windy night, but I decided to run my usual way and run from the front, even though I knew I was over ten seconds slower than most of the field. The opposition included Ronnie Delaney (Olympic 1,500 metre champion), Derek Ibbotson (World record miler), Brian Hewson (European 1,500 metre champion), Gordon Pirie, Mike Berisford and several other sub or near four minute milers. I was leading until the last 100 metres or so, and at the finish Delaney won in 4:7.3 — I was fourth in 4:9, my best mile time to date.

Back in London four days later, I won the Inter County Three Miles at the White City in 13:40. This was followed two days later on the Monday, with fourth place in an Invitation two mile race where I ran 8:47.6 behind Pirie, 8:46.4, Szabo (Hungary) in the same time, and Derek Ibbotson, 8:47.4. Five days later I was back at the familiar Palmer Park in Reading, where I ran two invitation races at ¾ and 1.5 miles,winning them both in 3:8.3 and 6:39. These were good training runs and were much the same as the training distances I used a lot.

At this time of the year, May to June, I would put in a lot of track and speed work. Mileage could be anything from fifty to seventy miles, and a typical week would follow this pattern. My training between 11th and 17th May was:—

Sunday — 6 miles in the evening, with steeplechasing and sprints, plus weight training.
Monday — 12 miles in evening , 9 miles on the track and rest on

road to and from training. 12 x 220 yds in about 30 seconds each, followed by ¾ mile in 3:19 and 4 x 440 yds in 62 to 64 seconds, plus my unconventional weight training.
Tuesday — 10 miles in evening, 7 miles on grass and 3 on road. Fast and slow running, followed by weights.
Wednesday — 10 miles in afternoon, 7 miles track and 3 miles on road. 8 x 440 yds in 64 to 67 seconds with sprints and weights to finish.
Thursday — 9 miles in evening including the two races at Hornchurch.
Friday — 8 miles in evening, 5 laps around the perimeter of Palmer Park with some road and sprints. Weight training.
Saturday — 10 miles which included two races and some sprint training. I won a mile in 4:36 and a 2 mile in 9:16.4.
Total miles for the week 65.

The following week was a busy one, with my runs in Dublin and the White City, so mileage dropped back a bit to only fifty-five but I was still running every day.

The last week in May started with the two miles at the White City, and finished with the two invitation races at Palmer Park, and I clocked up a total of seventy miles. My training this week was all in the morning, as I must have been on a late shift. This included a session where I did 16 x 440 yards in 62 to 67 seconds (all as usual with just a 220 yard jog in between). Another faster session of 8 x 440 yards in 59 to 60 seconds and another of 6 x 880 yards in 2:11 to 2:15 (as always the fastest run was the last). Away from the track I ran around the perimeter of Palmer Park, a distance of 1 mile 150 yards. I ran the alternate laps fast and slow, and my fast laps were 5:12, 5:15 and 5:15. The fastest time I ever recorded for running around the park through the trees was 4:34.

The following week, the first week in June, it was similar, clocking seventy-one miles, and I ended the week by running in the Berkshire County Championships. I did my usual double and won the three miles in 13:37.8, and the mile in 4:19.3. The Southern Counties followed shortly afterwards and I won the three miles again in 13:37.6. Near enough the same time as the county race but with much tougher opposition. It was after this race that Gordon Pirie was quoted as saying "Stan Eldon cheats, he runs too fast at the start." He was of course referring to my front running, which I used so effectively again in that race when I led all the way from the first lap. Pirie was second in 13:43.6, with John Merriman third in 13:43.8, Dave Chapman (Woodford Green) fourth in 13:50.8, George Knight (Essex Beagles) fifth 13:50.8 and Hugh Ford (Brighton) sixth in 13:54.4. My training in the following week was as follows:—

Sunday — 7 miles in the evening, 3 miles on road and 4 miles on

The first lap of record-breaking six miles — Chiswick June 1958

Leading the field, British Games, White City, May 1958, Ibbotson, Pirie, Szabo and Shirley in pursuit

The British All-Comers' record run at five and six miles

Young Eldon leads Chataway at Kodak Sports

Some you win and some you lose, outsprinting Bruce Tulloh at London Fire Brigade Meeting, White City, August 1959 — both recording 8:50 for two miles

A narrow defeat by Steve James in Inter County three mile 1959 — both recording 13:36

HOME AGAIN

Home after her triple success in an international athletics meeting in Rome is 19-year-old Mary Bignal, who has announced her intention to concentrate on the long jump for next year's Olympic Games. With her at London Airport is Stan Eldon, who took second place in the 5,000 metres at the meeting.

Return home from Rome with Mary Rand (Bignal). One of several photographs that got me into trouble at home!

Winning the Southern Cross-Country at Parliament Hill a month before winning the International Title

Finishing in third place at National Cross-Country at West Bromwich 1960

track, sprints up to 220 yards and some weight training.
Monday — 12 miles in the evening, 8 miles on track. 660 yards in 86.8 followed by 8 x 440 yards in 62, 63, 63, 61, 64, 56, 61, 60 seconds with 220 yards rest. Weight training.
Tuesday — 10 miles in evening, 8 miles on track and two miles on road. A 220 yard race (in about 24 seconds) and 7 x 220 yards in 29/30 seconds, finishing with an 880 yard race and some fast and slow running.
Wednesday — 11 miles in the afternoon, 3 miles on road, 2 miles on grass (sprints) and 5 laps around the outside of Palmer Park with three fast laps in 5:20, 5:15 and 5:14. The distance of the lap was 1 mile 150 yards. Then weight training.
Thursday — 10 miles in the evening, 3 miles on road and 7 miles on track. 330 yards in 42.4 and 8 x 220 yards in 25/28 seconds. Weight training.
Friday — 5 miles in morning, 3 miles on road, 2 miles on track, jogging with sprints. Weight training.

Perhaps a word of explanation about weight training; it was nothing sophisticated. I did not have money for weights, but using an old metal pudding basin as a mould, which I filled with concrete and using a cut-off a broom handle, I made myself some dumbbells, and my training was mainly resting them on each leg in turn and lifting the leg to help strengthen my leg muscles. I also used them for my arms. With these modest implements, my cycling on the beat and my twice-a-day training, I continued to develop my fitness, stamina and speed.

The week after the County Championships ended, with what was for me a poor performance, when I finished only sixth with a time of 14:18, running in a South v Midlands v North athletics match. My training race diary only says 'Poor' so I do not know why I ran so badly, except looking at the time of day I trained that week, I could have been on night duty right up until the race. I kept up my training every day that I had started the previous October, and it was in the main producing the results I hoped for.

On June 28th 1958, I ran in the AAA six miles championship at the Kinnaird Meeting at Chiswick. I knew I was going well, and in that race I proved it, as I broke Ken Norris's British record for the distance and on the way broke the five mile record as well. My new record for the six miles was 28:05, and the five mile record was 23:20. After the race Harold Abrahams, the former Olympic champion sprinter, later famed by the film Chariots of Fire, wrote to me and explained that if only I could run more even lap times, the world record could be mine. Harold continued taking an interest in me for the rest of my running career. I had a good win and a British record but it was a wasted opportunity, as I know I could have got much closer to Kuts' world figures, which were only twenty seconds faster.

Perhaps the most flattering comments of my running career came after this race. The man who coached Roger Bannister to that first four minute mile, Franz Stampfl, could not believe I had to get back to Reading to work a 10 p.m. to 6 a.m. night shift. He was quoted as saying "A policeman? I can't think of a worse job for a world-class athlete. This Eldon must be fantastic to combine the two. He really ought to get another job. Slow striding on the policeman's beat is bad for him." He then suggested that six months' training like Zatopek or Kuts and the world record could be mine.

This success brought me instant fame, and I was awarded the Ronson Sports Achievement Award of the Week. It was not a cheque for £5,000 which runners would probably get today, but a specially inscribed cigarette lighter. I still have this lighter, although it has never been used, and I can image what a modern athlete would say to such a presentation.

This race gave me a very unusual television experience. Peter Waterman, the British Featherweight Boxing Champion (brother of Dennis), was hosting a children's TV programme at the time, and he invited me on to talk about my record run. He picked me up from my home and we went to the studios for the live programme. After the usual make-up treatment and test for sound levels, I was sat on a sofa for the interview with Peter. The programme started OK and it then came to the point where he had to introduce and interview me. He completely dried up and left me sitting there. The producer then started frantically waving his arms, and from his gestures I could tell he wanted me to carry on by myself. They rolled the film of the race and I talked through it and it went all right apparently. It was an interesting programme, with the singer Lita Rosa and Nigel Lythgow the dancer.

Articles and cartoons appeared in newspapers, comics and magazines about the 'galloping policeman' and some were written by myself, including a section in a book that was produced by the then *News Chronicle*. Six sportsmen of the day contributed. They were Billy Wright, Matt Busby, Jimmy Armfield, Colin Cowdrey, Eamonn Andrews and myself. The local newsagent was very good and would deliver to me any newspaper that had a mention of me. Sometimes this was quite a lot of newspapers, and just as well they were not as bulky as some of today's editions.

My new celebrity status brought with it some extra activities, including opening a casino in Windsor, crowning beauty queens at local carnivals and opening church and village fetes. I also had to make my first after-dinner speech at a dinner for the newsagents from the Windsor, Slough area. Proposing the toast to the association was Air Vice Marshal 'Pathfinder' Bennett, and I had to reply on behalf of the guests.

I did not play football after about the age of twelve years, but in the 1960s I turned out for a Celebrity team in a charity match at Windsor, replacing Peter Osgood the Chelsea player who had a broken leg at the time. I think the team would have done better with him.

Television was still the coming media in the 1950s, but athletics was always on BBC radio with commentators like Max Robertson and Harold Abrahams. I had my share of interviews on the radio, and I also got to appear on television quite a few times. There was a little money beginning to creep in and I received about £10 an interview.

Between the Commonwealth and European Championships, I went to Portsmouth with Martin Hyman and Percy Cerutty (Herb Elliott's coach), to do a television programme comparing us with greyhounds.

On the 1st July, I was running in an invitation 1.5 mile (6 lap) race at Paddington. This had been well publicised as a race between this new star, me, and the established favorite Gordon Pirie, who held the unofficial world's and British best time for the distance. In the changing room before the race he told me how he would beat me at this event and I did not stand a chance. The race started and I ran in my usual way at the front; first lap in 63.6, 880 yards in 2:8, ¾ mile in 3:13.6, mile in 4:20.6 and 5:28 at the bell. Pirie followed until the last lap, and on the back straight he made his move and went past me. He gained a few yards but I responded and held him round the bend, and as we came off the bend into the final straight I pounced, remembering that he said I could not outsprint him, and I went for the line winning by a few yards in 6:27.6. A second outside his best for the distance but that was of no consequence. I had won in grand style and won a suitcase as a reward. The third placed runner was Eric Shirley with Tony Redrup (Wycombe Phoenix Harriers), my frequent rival over ten miles, fourth.

The next day I was in Devon running at the cricket ground in Torquay. This was the annual Devon Police Sports which always attracted large crowds; something around 5,000/6,000 was the normal attendance. It was a handicap meeting and I ran two races. The first was the mile, where I ran off 25 yards, but I was the back marker and finished fourth in 4:11.2. Then it was the three mile, and here I was off scratch, and ahead of me at the start with a lap handicap advantage was the local hero and a very good runner, Dennis Crook. I chased him hard around the grass track, but I was running twelve laps to his eleven, and it just proved too much, so I took second place in 13.55.

During the busy years of 1958 to 1960, I was always on the move with races every few days in all sorts of places, and much of the travelling was done between my police shifts, working nights, travelling next morning, running in the evening and then travelling back and starting work again on the next evening or even earlier. I could be running up to six races a week in far-flung places and over many different distances. Wherever I was, I could nearly always get some assistance from the local police by way of a lift in a police car to catch a train or flight; even abroad; and I remember having a great deal of help when I was in Helsinki. The local police chief took me to their police museum and put a car at my disposal for my stay.

Although life was very hectic and I spent a great deal of time on night duty, this did have its compensations. Any sportsman will tell you that they dream of success and often see their moment of glory in their dreams. Well, I was not in bed very much, but on night duty, cycling or walking around the country lanes, I would go over races time and time again, lap by lap, in my mind and hopefully reach the finish line in number one position. Sometimes the dreams did become reality.

Trains were my main mode of transport in this country, and it often meant arriving at Paddington at about 1 a.m., after all normal trains had stopped running, but there were what they called in those days milk trains and newspaper trains, and I was always able to get a lift back to Reading on one of these. Life was very hectic, but I did have that facility of being able to sleep anywhere and I found luggage racks could be quite comfortable.

At the end of that busy week, I was back at the White City running National Police Championships. These were comparatively easy runs, but I did set two best performance times when I won the mile in 4:9.8 and the three miles in 13:43.6. I received my plaques on that occasion from HRH Princess Alexandra.

A week later I was at the White City running in the AAA three mile championship, which I won in 13:22.4; just outside Derek Ibbotson's British record. The winning of a second AAA's title won me the Harvey Memorial Gold Cup for the best champion of the year, and I was only just passed my twenty-second birthday.

I was selected for the six miles in the Commonwealth Games to be held at Cardiff in July. My final warm up race for this was a club match at Windsor, where I ran a comfortable 4:11.5 mile on grass. The press were pressing for me to be either switched to the three miles or to run both events in Cardiff. The selectors would not be moved on this occasion, and I lined up for the six miles at Cardiff Arms Park knowing that I was something like thirty seconds faster, or nearly half a lap, better than my nearest rivals. It was a very hot day, ninety plus degrees in the stadium, and after a few laps the heat started to take its toll. I could not break the field as usual and I soon started falling away, and getting slower and slower. It was left to an Australian, Dave Power, and my old rival Welshman John Merriman, to race it out for the gold medal, which Power won with 28:47.8, just one second ahead of Merriman, who won the silver. I finished, I think it was ninth, with a time over two minutes slower than my best of a month a earlier. I could see these two fighting it out on the last lap as I was nearly two laps behind them. I was not the only athlete to suffer in that race. The man who followed me home in the AAA six miles, Hugh Ford from Brighton, faded, as did Alistair Wood from Scotland, another very good distance runner. We all suffered from the extreme heat.

I have mentioned elsewhere about my strange relationship with Gordon Pirie, and it was on this occasion that he showed the very best side of his nature, and he did something that I have never forgotten. I had only been married about nine months, and my young bride Marion had travelled down to Cardiff to see me run. She was bitterly disappointed at my performance and when we met up after the race, Gordon took us to a pub and after a drink he climbed onto the bar and addressed all those there. He introduced Marion and myself, and made a request that someone should offer this newly-married couple a bed for the night, so that they could be together. It worked and the volunteers came forward and we had our night together. Prior to that arrangement, Marion had been offered a space in a tent with four of the New Zealand male athletes, which she declined.

It would be easy to make excuses for my poor performance. I had probably run the wrong event, the three miles would have been better, and I had been selected for that event in the first place but was switched to the longer distance after breaking the British record. I was a new sensation and I was plagued by the press and not just the UK people, but from all over, including East Germany. They followed my every move and every bit of training I did at St Athan where we stayed. But the real problem had been the heat, and this was to be an ongoing problem, even though I did enter a research programme to try and find the cause and solution.

After the Games, I was taken to hospital in Cardiff for a couple of days, and Dr Roger Bannister carried out research on me and some other athletes, including one of the first successful Kenyan athletes. I still have the note Bannister sent to me asking me to take part. We ran on treadmills in cold conditions and in rooms heated up with electric fires. The thermometer was placed in an unusual position within my body! He found that I did have a problem in temperatures above about seventy degrees. When running in warm conditions my temperature would keep rising, where another runner would steady off at just over 100 degrees, mine would not cut out but keep rising. That information was never put to good use, as many years later Dave Bedford had the same problem, and they researched it all over again. Medical research for similar problems and injuries has been a backwater in this country for a very long time.

After that it was back to hard training, and fighting for a place in the British team for the European Championships in Stockholm. I did not race again for ten days, and then it's a 1,500 metre at Paddington, again on a Tuesday evening, but I was not so successful there this time and only finished ninth in 3:53. I was still racing or training every day of the week, and on the Saturday I ran for Great Britain against the Commonwealth in the three miles. I was narrowly beaten by Albert Thomas the top Australian runner, who ran 13:20.6 to beat Derek Ibbotson's British All-Comers' record of 13:20.8; although the time ratification was awaited on the winning time in the three miles at Cardiff, when Murray Halberg (New Zealand) ran 13:15. My time behind Thomas was 13:23. Again I had Gordon Pirie behind me in third place with 13:34, fourth was Peter Clark (Thames Valley) in 13:38, Mike Bullivant (Derby and County) was fifth in 13:57.

This was an occasion when I had another interesting experience. I had agreed to run in the Annual Carnival meeting at Agars Plough, near my home in Windsor, and as soon as I had run the three miles at the White City, I had to find Marion and make our way to a taxi that had been sent for to take us to my next race. We left the White City and were swamped by crowds, more adults than children, and we literally had to fight our way through with police help to the taxi. I know what it feels like to have this sort of adulation and understand what it must be like for the pop and sports stars today. I am afraid I was not very complimentary to some of those surrounding us on that occasion, and would probably have been arrested today for my language! There was the usual large crowd at Slough for the carnival running, and I won the mile in 4:14.3, less than two hours after running at the White City.

On the Monday, I was back at the White City for an Invitation two miles, where I finished fourth in 8:49.

It was also about this time that I discovered another problem of being 'famous'. I used taxis quite a bit, getting about from Heathrow and in London. The London taxi drivers are always very generous and inquisitive; they always talk and find out who you are. I have been given free rides on a number of occasions as a result of these conversations. But their generosity can be misplaced. On one such occasion when I was taking a taxi from Heathrow, the driver realising it was me, suddenly realised his mistake a few weeks earlier when he had apparently picked up someone claiming to be me and given him a free ride.

I made the team and went off to Stockholm with much of my confidence restored. My training had gone well and the atmosphere in the Swedish city was ideal for running; fresh clean air and not too warm. The race started and I set out to run as I always did from the front. It went almost too well and quickly built up a lead of over forty metres by the end of 3,200 metres (8 laps). The only runners chasing me at that stage were Zhukov, Krsyszkowiak, Ozog, Pudov and my old rival Mimoun. I went through 5,000 metres in just under fourteen minutes, which was well inside the world record schedule. The trouble was I had never run in such ideal conditions as Stockholm, and I did not realise how fast I was running or how far I was ahead of the opposition. There were no big screens in those days, and no track-side coaches to tell you how fast you were going. At 6,000 metres I still had a huge lead, and the only change in the chasing group was that my team colleague John Merriman had taken over from Mimoun. I kept my lead until the last couple of laps, when half a dozen runners caught me and there was a real dash for the line on the last lap.

The winner was a Pole, Z. Krsyzkowiak in 28:56, with Y. Zhukov (USSR) second in 28:58.6 and N. Pudov (USSR) third in 29:2.2. I was the first Britain to finish in fourth place in 29:2.8, a new British record. I didn't win but I certainly felt I had done a lot better than in the Commonwealth Games in Cardiff, and had gained my revenge over John Merriman, who had trounced me in those championships. I had mixed it with some of the best distance runners in the world, in fact the best, as most of the top distance runners were in Europe in those days. The runners behind me were Ozog (Poland) 29:3.2, Merriman 29:3.8, Mimoun 29:30.6. Further back in nineteenth place was another great cross-country runner, Marcel Van de Wattyne (Belgium) with 30:45.4. I got more sports coverage for that defeat than many athletes got for winning gold medals. I appeared on sports placards for newspapers all over Sweden and even featured in a cartoon alongside Dana the wife of my great running hero Emil Zatopek.

Only nine days before I ran in Stockholm, I was in Weisbaden in Germany for the European Police Championships. Although this was a closed meet for the police forces of Europe, there were a lot of good athletes; even world class athletes, taking part. As the British Police Champion at both the mile and three miles, I was selected for both the 1,500 metres and 5,000 metres. In the 1,500 I had to face Roger Moens from Belgium, who held the world 800 metre record at the time of 1:45.7. We had a very close race, and with his extra speed he just got up to win in 3:49, with a very good Finnish athlete second and me in third spot with 3:50.6, my best time for the distance. In the 5,000 metres, I had to face another very good Finnish runner and it was a very hot day. Before the start while I was warming up, I ran through the water coming from the hose that was filling up the water jump for the steeplechase, and I soaked a handkerchief and put it on my head. It worked and I had a good win in a respectable time of 14:13.2 for the conditions. A best champion was always selected at this meeting and Roger Moens had won the 800 and 1,500 metres, but when they announced the winner it was Stan Eldon. I was as surprised as anyone and poor Moens was very disappointed.

Chapter Eight

'Fastest PC Seldom Puts His Feet Up'

It was about now that I had my first contact with an American athlete, Fred Wilt, himself an FBI agent; so we had something in common as well as our running. Fred was now thirty-seven years old but had run in the UK a few times and was very interested in the training patterns that were emerging, hence his corresponding with me, not just to know about my training, but also about anything I might know about other European athletes and their training methods.

After my European exploits, it was back to England for domestic races in September, and I ran 8:45.4 in a two mile invitation at the White City. Only three days after this race, I won the Southern Counties six mile championship again, this time in 29:6.8. Then it was off to France and a match between GB and France. I was selected for the 5,000 metres with Peter Clark who had come on the international scene at the distance. I did not run that well in this race, that was run on the Saturday in very hot conditions (not good for me!), and took second place behind him. He won in 13:53.8, a good time in the conditions, and I finished in fourteen minutes exactly which was good enough to give us the maximum points. The French pair of Michel Bernard 14:8.6, and R. Bogey 14:21.8, were well beaten, even though Bernard's time was the fastest by a native in France.

That was not the end of my running that weekend. The British squad were staying at a school/college on the outskirts of Paris, which had its own running track, and on the Sunday morning I thought I would do some training. I ran about seven miles in very hot weather, and for a bit of fun I put out the steeplechase hurdles and ran over them on quite a few laps. When I was nearly through, I heard Gordon Pirie call out from a dormitory window that the team management wanted to see me. I finished my training, showered and went to see the team management of Les Truelove and Jack Crump. They had a request, would I run the steeplechase that afternoon? In fact it was only about two hours away. They explained that Pirie, who was due to run his first international steeplechase, had withdrawn because of 'injury' and they needed someone to run and pick up a point. I agreed and rushed off to get something to eat in the canteen, as I could never run on an empty stomach. Then it was on the team bus and off to the Colombe Stadium.

I lined up for the 3,000 metres steeplechase, and was an instant sensation as I knocked over the first hurdle that I encountered. I don't think anyone has done this in an international, either before or since that day. I still grabbed some headlines, even if one of them did say *"The French Laugh at Eldon"*. I steadily improved, and although I was closing rapidly at the end on the two Frenchmen, I took fourth spot in 9:37.8 for the one point I was asked to get. I was in fact only two seconds away from moving up a place. The spectators in France and the British Press enjoyed my one appearance as a steeplechaser in international competition. Two British athletes did have a good weekend by winning two events; Brian Hewson took the 800 and 1,500 metres, and Peter Radford the 100 and 200 metres. In the 1,500 metres, Michel Jazy set a new French record of 3:42.5 in third place behind the other Englishman Mike Blagrove. Jazy later became the world record holder at one mile, when he set figures of 3:53.6, and was the first runner not from the British Commonwealth to hold the record following Bannister's four minute mile.

The reason why Pirie withdrew was always surrounded in mystery. He was the first really professional runner in those days of shamateurism, and travelled to where he could get his money. He had been running that summer in Scandinavia, where he could pick up £150 a race, and had asked to be included in the team to compete in France. There had been a dispute between him and the management over the expenses he had asked for to cover his travel from Sweden with his wife. They were prepared to pay for him but not his wife Shirley, so he used what many athletes have used since then, the excuse not to run if the payment was not right. He had a friendly doctor on the team who was able to say he was unfit to run.

Back home it was off to a floodlit meeting at Brighton, where I won the three mile in 13:40, on the Saturday evening. I note that in that week my training diary had something very unusual. On Tuesday 15th August, I had a rest from running and no distance was recorded. This was the first day off in 1958, except for the 8th March when I missed the National at Birkenhead.

I learned to live with the media and so did my bosses in the police. On several occasions, either Pathe News or BBC TV, spent days with me 'on my beat'. I remember Paul Fox as a young producer spending a day at Woodley with his crew filming me at 'work' and training at Palmer Park. It was a long day and they even had to send a motorcycle back to London for more film. The film was meant to be a documentary about me, and was to have a prime spot on SportsNight in the middle of the week, but a big sports story broke on the Wednesday it was due to be shown, and the day of filming turned out to be about two minutes. Paul Fox (now Sir Paul) kept in touch with me for quite some years with

Christmas cards, as did many of the journalists I knew from the National newspapers.

On another occasion I had a day with Pathe News, who also filmed me on the beat in Sonning and at Palmer Park track in Reading. Here I was filmed chasing small boys along the river bank, and stopping a lady motorist on the bridge over the Thames, and this was a speaking part as I had to tell her "You can't park here." Marion and I went to the cinema to see this when it was being shown, and the audience found the scene funny and were all laughing. I kept a low profile and no one knew I was sitting in the middle of them.

During my international years the newspapers always had a story about me; win or lose. I think it was fairly novel for them to have a running policeman to write about, because it was not many years before when most of our international squad were from the universities, and in particular OxBridge. The headlines were always big; the sort that would dominate the back sports pages today. Here are just a few of the headlines from 1958 to 1960.

"THE FLOP BY THE GALLOPING COP"
"ELDON COPS TITLE"
"ELDON LEADS ENGLAND TO VICTORY"
"SPEED COP GETS A SHOCK — EXCEEDING THE LIMIT"
"ELDON PLEADS 'LET ME OFF NIGHT WORK'"
"ELDON — FAIR COP"
"SCORCER BY ELDON"
"RECORD BREAKING ELDON CAN BE NEW ZATOPEK"
"ELDON SMASHES 3 RECORDS in AAA 6 MILES"
"FASTEST PC SELDOM PUTS HIS FEET UP"
"DAZZLING ELDON'S RECORD 6 MILE".

These were main sports page headlines, above all other sports news, and ELDON was often in letters over an inch in height. The sports writers like Peter Wilson, Desmond Hackett, Alan Hobey, Terry O'Connor and Ken Hawkes, loved to write something about the "Flying Cop".

It was round about this time that I met Henry Cooper for the first time. As a local celebrity I had been invited to a Sportsman's Ball at Slough as the special guest. I was taken around the room to meet the other up-and-coming sportsmen and sportswomen who were there. One of these was Henry, along with his twin brother and his manager Jim Wicks. He was not a big name at this time and was not well known, as he was only just emerging.

At the end of the 1958 track season I had a few races, including a 5,000 metres at the White City for GB v Finland, where I came third in 14:10, and in the same week I ran the same distance in Wuppertal, Germany, and finished second in 14:13. My final race was at the Birchfield Harriers floodlight meeting on 4th October, where I finished second in the three miles in 13:49.8. This meeting was always good fun and ended with a great party at the home of one of the members of the club. I went to this event for several years, and on one occasion when the party was in full swing, the police called to tell us to cut the noise. The other runners made sure I went to the door to deal with them.

The week after that last race my training dropped off, and I took my usual semi-rest, only running on three days and only for a total of fifteen miles. Over the next couple of weeks I won two cross-country races, and my total weekly mileage stayed below thirty-five miles. The first week in November, I got back to the routine of running every day, and back to training up to seventy miles a week. In the middle of the month I won the Rochester five mile race in Kent, in a new record time of 24:57.4. It was a pretty tough five miles, and most of the current good distance runners were there. On Sunday 23rd November I was in Brussels for the 'Le Soir' cross-country race, and in the senior event finished second in 29:16 for the 5.5 miles.

The following Saturday I won a 7.5 mile cross-country race, running for Windsor against Thames Valley Harriers, Aylesford Paper Mills, Herne Hill Harriers and the Parachute Regiment. My time for the race was 41:26. I was then back into serious training, running every day.

I have an interesting note in my training diary about a club race on 6th December. It was against Wycombe and Southall clubs. In the place where I would normally have my position and time I had "Race Abandoned", but I did clock up ten miles of running, so I guess it must have been very foggy and we all got lost.

Towards the end of 1958, I was invited to the Guildhall at Windsor by the Mayor and Councillors of the Royal Borough, and presented with an Illuminated Address in appreciation of my athletic achievements. The presentation was made by the Mayor, Councillor Joe Proctor, who had formally been my Physics master at Windsor Grammar School, although I do not think there was any favouritism, as Physics was one of my worst subjects, where in exams I think I averaged about eight per cent. My wife Marion, parents and family, as well as my old headmaster, the police superintendent who 'fiddled' my entry into the police in 1956, Fred Salter, and my own 'Super' Alf East from Wokingham, were there. There were speeches of course, and Alf East said his few words which pleased me — "He is a good champion, he is a good sportsman, and incidentally, he is a good copper too." I said a few words to the gathered group, and I have never been allowed to forget what I said, or rather what I didn't say. I thanked my parents, my school, the police, the athletic club, but I forgot my wife, and with the scroll still hanging on our wall, she gently reminds me from time to time.

I kept up with training every day in December, including five miles on Christmas Day.

At the very end of 1958 I kept my promise to Bernard Baldwin, and went to Mountain Ash in South Wales to run in the unique Nos Galan race, that was being run for the first time. The atmosphere for that race was terrific. It was a bitterly cold night but the whole town had turned out onto the streets to watch the race. The runners changed in the pithead baths where the miners came up and showered. As we prepared for the race, some of them were coming up to end their shift. The race was to start from very close to these facilities, and before the start the 'Mystery Runner' came down from the grave of Guto Nythbran to light the torch and set the runners on their way. There was great speculation as to who would carry the torch, and the crowd were not disappointed as it was a local hero, forty-eight years old Tom Richards, who had won the silver medal in the marathon at the 1948 Olympics. He had set out from the graveside from the misty heights outside Mountain Ash, and ran the nearly four miles in twenty minutes. At ten minutes to midnight, we lined up and the race took us over three laps, up through the terraced houses on the hillside overlooking the valley. There were no streetlights, but the children of the miners were out in their dozens holding flaming torches to show us the way. At midnight all the sirens at the pits were sounding to welcome in the new year. It was a tough course, and as hard running down the steep inclines, as having to run up them. It was very cold and there was a lot of frost on the roads which made running a little treacherous, and I did not lead all the way as usual, but was always in the front two or three places. I took the lead with a mile to go, and when we came back down into the main street it was packed with people; local estimates put the crowd at over 10,000; and the race finished over the bridge and in front of the Town Hall. I had won in 18:46, beating Frank Salvat (Finchley) 18:52 and Mike Price (Bristol) 18:55. Just under 100 runners had taken part, and other leading runners were Eddie Strong (Bristol) fourth, John Merriman fifth, and Ken Norris (TVH), who had won the big Sao Paulo Round the Houses race in 1955, was tenth. This event has always remained in my memory. I do not think any other event I have ever taken part in had the same terrific public support and excitement.

I was to attend Nos Galan many times in the future, including my turn as Mystery Runner in 1964, running down from Llanwonno Churchyard and the grave of Guto Nythbran (Griffith Morgan), a celebrated Welshman who died in 1737, and who was reputed to have run twelve miles in "seven minutes within the hour". The ritual of a secret well-known runner acting as the Mystery Runner, and running the three miles or so down the mountain prior to the start of what was then the midnight race, was part of the fun and magic of the special Nos Galan race. The first runner to have the privilege was Tom Richards, the 1948 Olympic silver medallist; and others in the early days included Ken Norris, Martin Hyman, John Merriman, Ron Jones and following me in 1965 and 1966, were two of our great women Olympic gold medallists, Ann Packer and Mary Rand. I escorted the mystery runners on more than one occasion, and in particular 1986, when the race was reintroduced after a break of thirteen years. I ran down with Kirsty Wade, double Commonwealth gold medal winner. There was always a short dedication at the graveside, and then it was into the pub for drinks all round, before lighting the torches and running down what could sometimes be snow-covered and treacherous roads. On one run, the land rover escort could not make it through the snow. Each year those that lived on the route would turn out to cheer, and out would come trays of drinks and we would be kissed by all the females, whatever their age, and even by a few of the fellows. The last time I ran I think I was kissed by grandmothers who had been young girls when I first ran in 1958. With the drink it was a wonder any of us arrived at the start still sober. There are bigger events, but there is still nothing to compare to the Nos Galan races, which were the brainchild of Bernard Baldwin who ran them for many years. His enthusiasm was infectious, and whenever I was attending the event, he would take me and others to the nightclubs in Mountain Ash and elsewhere, and introduce us to the packed clubs. He was always overpoweringly generous in the way he introduced any of us, and could turn a non-sports star, like my wife Marion, into a star by his introduction. We supplied the Nos Galan running vests for many years, and Marion used to cut out the letters and sew Nos Galan onto the vests, and Bernard always made a great thing about this.

The following year 1959, I had quite an exciting time over the country, on the road and on the track. I had tied myself to Puma Shoes, although no money changed hands, but they did send me regular consignments of their latest shoes for my use and comments. The letters were always signed by Armin Dassler, the boss at Puma himself, and we corresponded regularly. Both Adidas and Puma were started by the Dassler family.

The year did not start off well though. I ran in the Berkshire Championships at Newbury and although I won easily, as usual it was at a price. During the race one of my feet went into what looked like a puddle, but was in fact quite a deep hole in some concrete surfacing and I damaged my lower leg quite badly. I took three days off at this critical time and then managed to get back to reasonable training, but only around fifty miles a week for a couple of weeks, leading up to the Inter Counties Championship at Parliament Hill in London. On the usual tough, heavy going on this course, I finished fifth in 38:43 for the seven mile course, behind the winner Basil Heatley 38:01, John Merriman 38:21, John Anderson 38:28 and Alan Perkins 38:39. Not bad, but I had been looking forward to having my best ever run in that particular race.

It was then back to serious training, and the mileage again climbed back to 100 a week. The last week in January started off with a run in the San Sebastian Cross-Country race in Spain. I did not have the best of runs for the seven mile race and finished seventeenth in 40:24. It was never the easiest of journeys to this race, which I ran a couple of times. The team would leave Victoria Station in London on the 11 p.m. wagons-lits train to Paris, and although we had comfortable sleeping accommodation, we did not get much sleep. When the train arrived at Dover, it would be driven onto the ferry and the chains would make a lot of noise as the train was secured in the hold. Then it was the crossing which sometimes could be rough, and we would arrive at the Gare du Nord in Paris at about 6 a.m. It was then another train journey down to San Sebastian.

This was my first visit to Spain, and I well remember one incident which gave our team a big laugh at the time. In those days when teams went abroad, it was quite common, in fact almost recommended, that we took some familiar food with us. On this occasion I had taken Weetabix for my breakfast. I tried to explain to the Spanish waiter that I wanted some milk and sugar to go with them, but he insisted that he took them away for the chef to prepare! After a considerable time, a dish was put back in front of me; it contained a brownie-white milky liquid but no real evidence of my Weetabix. Inquiries were made and it turned out that they had never seen this breakfast cereal before, and did not understand what to do with it. They had boiled the Weetabix in milk and then strained off the solids, and presented me apparently with what was left. Nowadays when breakfast cereals are universal, it is easy to forget that forty years ago this was not the case.

After my return from Spain it was back to that 100 miles a week, only easing off in the week before the Southern Counties Championships at Aylesford in Kent. I had another easy win in 48:25 for the nine mile course against good opposition again. Frank Sando, on his home course, chased me home in forty-nine minutes and George Knight was third in 49:06. Ken Norris was ninth, Bruce Tulloh seventeenth and Derek Ibbotson twenty-sixth. My training continued at the 100 mile level, and I was running every day with quite a few double training days. Most weeks I was running between nine and twelve times, with the hardest days totalling over twenty miles.

I eased off in the first week of March, ready for the National at Peterborough, where I failed to make up for my disappointment of the previous year, and only finished fifth in 48:14 for the nine miles.

I was again selected for the English Cross-Country team because of this fifth position in the National Championships. The team were flying out to Lisbon, Portugal, on the Thursday, twelve days later, ready for the race on the Saturday, but I could not go with them as I had the National Police Cross-Country on the Thursday, and I felt it was my duty to run for the Berkshire Constabulary and win my third title, which I did with a time of 35:59 for the 6.5 mile course. I then made my own way out to Lisbon on Friday to meet up with my team mates.

There was a good race on the Saturday, but I could not repeat my win of the previous year; the race on the Thursday had taken the edge off my run, but I did not mind too much as Fred Norris, one of our team won, and Frank Sando was third, with Basil Heatley (the silver medallist in the 1964 Olympic Marathon) coming in fourth and me fifth.

I always felt a little cheated by the official result as Basil and I ran in together, but they decided to split us. As always, England won the team race quite comfortably.

There was quite a do after the race; a dinner with plenty of drink, cheap brandy and wine. Up to this stage in my life, I do not think I had hardly ever touched alcohol, so I indulged a little, drinking the brandy of some of my fellows. Afterwards we all went to a cellar nightclub but my evening there did not last long. I remember sitting at a table with a couple of girls (topless I think) leaning over me, but I quickly passed out and slid off my chair. Luckily Frank Orton, an athletic official who I knew from Reading, was there and he got me into a taxi and back to the hotel, where I slept it off. Next morning I was up earlier and a lot fresher than my team mates who had stayed much later at the club.

Another cracking run followed the next week in the Thames Valley Cranford Relay, where I set another record fastest lap of 22:01 for the 4 mile 1,500 yard circuit. Only two days later I did win the event I had failed to win the previous year; the Maidenhead ten mile race which I took with 51:18. It was sweet revenge as I beat Tony Redrup (Wycombe), who had beaten me in 1958, by just under two minutes. These were good days for Reading AC who had three teams in the top ten team places. Thirty-three runners ran faster than the hour, but allowing for the fact that the distance was about 10.4 miles, the first fifty-four would have beaten that time. These included no less than ten from Reading AC.

It was then onto another favourite event of mine, the Uxbridge Road Relay, which was run around two laps, mainly on the A40. It would be a nightmare trying to run the same circuit today. The record for the fastest lap was held by Frank Sando with 26:43. I had a good run and took the record down to 26:30 for the 5 miles 1,000 yards distance.

It was then on to track training to sharpen myself up for the season ahead. My first track race was at the White City in the Southern six miles, where I only came fourth in 28:48. That did not worry me as I knew I had a long season ahead of me, and the Olympics were the following year. A typical week at this stage of the season was:—

Day 1 — 4.5 miles on road and grass with 2.5 miles running on the track doing sprints from 50 to 150 yards.
Day 2 — 4 miles on road, one lap around park and 7 miles on track, including 10 x 440 yards in 64 to 66 seconds with half a lap jog

between, and finished with more sprinting and some light weight training.
Day 3 — 4.5 miles on road, lap of park and 6.5 miles on track, including 5 x 880 yards with 1 lap jog in between. The times for the 880 yards were 2:15, 2:18, 2:14, 2:15 and 2:12.
Day 4 — 12 miles made up of 4.5 on road, 1 lap around park, and 6.5 miles on track running 6 x ¾ miles.
Day 5 — 10 miles — a mixture of road and track running with sprints.
Day 6 — 13 miles — including road and track running. 1.5 miles in 6:52 (lap times 66, 68, 68, 68, 74 and 68), followed by 4 x 440 yards in 61.8, 65, 63.5 and 62 seconds, with short fast sprints to finish.
Day 7 — 8 miles — mixture of road, grass and track running, steady running with some sprinting.

On the last day in April I was back at Iffley Road, Oxford, for the annual AAA v University match, where I again ran the two miles and came second in 8:52.2. Two days later I was completing the double for Windsor in a club match, winning the one mile in 4:23.1, and the two miles in 9:10.8.

The following week I won a 1,500 metre race in the middle of the week, and on the Saturday a two mile race at Southampton in 9:5.4.

On the 10th May my first daughter was born, Caroline Louise. She was born at our new police house and I was present at the birth. She weighed in at just five pounds twelve ounces, and was so small I held her up in one hand.

I was straight back in to racing and travelling, and again ran in the Hornchurch Harriers Invitation meeting on 14th May, where I ran 2,000 metres in 5:20 to finish third.

Two days later it was back at the White City, to run for Berkshire in the Inter Counties at three miles. On this occasion I was narrowly beaten by Steve James, and we were both given the same time of 13:36. It took the judges fifteen minutes to decide he had won and it was not a dead heat.

On the Bank Holiday Monday, two days later, I ran the six miles at the same meeting, but only finished fifth in 29:4.6.

After this it was back to the training with some good sessions, including my usual 4 x 880 yards and 4 x ¾ mile. I also packed in the 220 and 440 yard distances to sharpen up on my speed. It paid off and I had two good runs in the Berkshire Championships at Palmer Park, Reading. I had very comfortable wins in the three miles, where I ran the season's fastest time in the world of 13:35.6, and an event I was not very good at, the 3,000 metre steeplechase, where I won in 9:35. I think I ran this because the tight programme did not allow me to run my usual double of the three and one mile races.

During the next week I had two races; the first at Brighton, where I finished second in a two mile invitation race in 8:48.4, and a one mile invitation at Chatham, where I came only fifth in 4:16.6.

On the middle Saturday in June, I ran in the Coronation Trophy at Guildford, and had a busy afternoon finishing second in the 880 yards in 2:2.8, winning the two miles in 9:10.5, and even running third in the 440 yards in 57.2, not a very good time considering I won my first race at school in that time in 1949, ten years earlier.

My programme of racing now got very busy, and my next race was in a handicap at Middlesbrough in the middle of the week, where I finished third, running from scratch in 8:40.6. A time that was to be my best ever for the distance. On the Saturday after I returned, it was the Southern Counties three miles at Motspur Park. Not a good run, only fifth in 13:50.6.

A few days later I was in Paris for a 3,000 metre international, and won in 8:16.2. Three days later, I ran against the man who had held the British six mile record before me, Ken Norris of Thames Valley Harriers, in a one mile race at Camberley. He got his own back and won, leaving me in second place, 4:17.2.

On the Wednesday of the following week, I ran for England as opposed to GB, against East Germany and won the 5,000 metres in 14:6.4. It was described as a shock win by the press, and not least because I stayed back for the first mile and then took off. An East German, Hans Grodotski, was second in 14:12.2, and my team colleague Kevin Gilligan, was third in 14:13. The *Times* described my run as *"front running at its best"*. This may have been the first occasion that flowers were presented at an athletic meeting. There was an exchange of flowers between the two teams instead of playing the national anthems!

A few more club and invitation races followed before the AAA Championships in the middle of July. I entered and ran both the six miles on the Friday evening, and the three miles on the Saturday, which as usual meant two tough races in less than twenty-four hours. I repeated my win of 1958 in the six miles, although the time was seven seconds slower than my British record of 28:5. My old rival John Merriman was second in 28:15.8. I was still a little tired on the Saturday when I lined up for the shorter distance, but still managed third in 13:38.

There were some good races in 1959, and not all of them were serious internationals. My daughter Caroline had been born in May, and one of the invitations I had was to run in the Devon Police Sports at Torquay as I had done in the previous year. Myself, Marion and baby Caroline went off to Torquay in the holiday season. We had a very good few days; I won a one mile handicap race off twenty-five yards in 4:11, and took second place in a three mile race, where I ran off scratch in 13:57, which won me some prizes and about £20 in a brown envelope, as well as my travelling expenses. In those days £20 was more than twice my weekly pay as a beat policeman, so with the few days' holiday and the prizes worth around another £20, it was a lucrative week.

Of course, between my training and many races, I was carrying out normal police duties for the whole period between 1956 and 1962. Some of these were the usual, dealing with accidents and minor crime (there was not much serious crime on my beat), but it did include some special duties, like attending Ascot Races for the Royal Meeting. I used to get an early shift, and was normally on the entrance to the racecourse from the Great Park at 7 a.m. as security for the royal family, who used to go onto the course at that time for a canter. I would be there in my white gloves and give a quick salute to the party, which was always quite large, with the Queen, Duke of Edinburgh, the old Duke of Gloucester and others. After their canter around the course, they would be back at the gate to return to the castle.

On another occasion, I was on special duty in Bracknell when the Shah of Persia made a visit to the town. I remember moving from one part of the town to another as he moved around to take up different positions, so I suppose there was a shortage of manpower even in those days.

At the end of that week I was in Brighton, and won my usual double in the National Police Championships for the third time. My winning times were 4:17.8 for the mile and 14:9.8 for the three miles.

The invitation races and club races kept me busy, and some of my weekly training totals were quite low as a result, varying from only thirty-five miles to about sixty miles in a week. I ran in the invitation meeting at Paddington again, and finished fourth in a 1,500 metres in 3:54.1. I also ran in a special mile race at Motspur Park, finishing only seventh, but in 4:11.8.

These low-key races warmed me up nicely for another international race. This time for GB against West Germany at the White City, and the distance was six miles which I won in 28:18.6; so in the space of a month, I had won races against the best in the two German states.

I liked running at the White City; it was such an intimate place to run. There was always a huge crowd and warming up had to be done under the stands, running through the spectators arriving and buying refreshments during the meeting. I would do a little warm up an hour before my race and then go back to the changing rooms, lay on a bench and go to sleep for thirty minutes, before completing the warm up. Then it was under the tunnel and up onto the centre of the track by the water jump and you were in the arena. I imagine it was a bit like a gladiator would have felt, but if I failed I knew my life was safe. We did not worry very much about supplements in those days, but there was always Horlicks available at the White City, both in drink form and tablets. I don't think any of us would have failed a drugs test with this our only stimulant.

More club races and a trip to Paignton in Devon for their Regatta Sports, where I ran 4:6 for the mile, but off thirty yards, so it was probably worth about 4:10 for the full mile. I was only there as a showpiece to draw in the crowds, and the weather was not good; it poured with rain. The crowd was less than normal, and the promoter was full of apologies that he could not give me the sort of money they had given the main attractions in previous years; I believe about £100. I think it was about then that I started to realise what went on in those happy shamateur days, if you were lucky. As my earnings were only about £7 a week, the £25 I received was still very acceptable. That was on the Wednesday, and on the Friday I was back in London running for Great Britain, again at three miles, against Poland. I had to be content with second place behind the top Polish runner Zimny. My time was 13:27.8.

A trip to Cheltenham followed for another one of those special handicap races over the one mile. This time I was off twenty-five yards, and finished seventh in 4:7.5. In these handicap races, although I was running around twenty-five yards less than the full distance, the other runners could be running off anything up to 300 yards less than the full distance, and most of them were just on grass tracks and not proper running tracks.

My last race in August was the usual London Fire Brigade meeting at White City, and this time I won the two mile race in 8:50, just getting the verdict over Bruce Tulloh, and we both did the same time.

Chapter Nine

Two Trips to Moscow

One of my main memories of that year was a trip to Moscow, with the first British athletics team to ever compete against the then Soviet Union. My event was to be the 5,000 metres, and my running partner for the first time was to be a new discovery who would be running his first international event, Bruce Tulloh from Portsmouth AC. I remember warming up in the underground track beneath the Lenin Stadium. I introduced Bruce to the two Russians we would be competing against, as I had met them previously in the European Championships the previous year. With very little verbal conversation but with body language, I think we gave them the message that we were very confident, although I am not sure whether they considered Bruce to be a threat as he looked like a young boy straight out of school, and I think they were even more surprised when he dared to line up without spikes. We had a plan and it was based on my liking for leading from the front. We would lead for alternative laps and run as fast as we could, the other one of us would follow and keep in close contact.

This worked well, and by halfway one of the Russians had dropped off the pace, but the other one was persistent and even tried to take the lead at the bell with one lap to go. I always had a fast finish and took off and built a lead all around that final lap, and Bruce did his bit by chasing me. My lap times were thirty seconds for the first 200 metres, then 66, 66.5, 66.5, 66, 69, 67, 70, 66, 68, 68, 69 and 60 seconds. We crossed the line in first and second place, with the noise of tens of thousands of Muscovites ringing in our ears. My winning time was a respectable 13:52.8. An official then grabbed me and said "Come with me" and I wondered what they wanted me for. I was taken into a small room at the back of the stands and I did not know what was going to happen next. I need not have worried, as all they wanted was for me to write my name so that they could engrave it in Russian on the very large medal I was to receive.

The food in Moscow was not good, and my diet before and after the race was soup and ice cream, both of which were excellent. I remember being asked if there was anything I would like by the hotel staff, and not realising the task I was setting them I said "oranges". They sent someone off and it took him hours to find a few oranges from somewhere in Moscow, and I expect they were on the black market!

There was a big dispute between the British team management and the Russians about our flight from Moscow to our next destination, Helsinki in Finland. The Russians wanted to fly us home instead of on to Helsinki, but all the athletes went 'on strike' and we sat on our cases and sports bags in the foyer of the Moscow hotel, and refused to move while the management negotiated with the Russians. Eventually they relented and we flew off to Helsinki.

I had kept my training up, both in Moscow and when we arrived in the Finnish capital. The race against the Finns was on the Saturday, exactly one week after the Moscow race, and I knew I was still in good form. My partner was again Bruce Tulloh, who lined up in his bare feet yet again. I tried to persuade him to wear shoes as the red shale track of the 1952 Olympic Stadium was very coarse, and I knew it would play havoc with his feet. It did and I had a much larger winning margin than in the previous race. I led from the start to the finish, and Tulloh was in second place all the way from the third lap. My lap times were 66, 66, 67, 67, 67, 66.5, 69.5, 70, 68, 70, 69 and 62.4, and I won in 13:59.4. The last lap was slow for me, and Bruce ran a much faster lap of 58 seconds to finish in 14:19. He must have had quite a race to keep that second spot, because the better of the Finns, Soloranto, ran 58.6 for his last lap and finished just that .6 behind my team mate.

Because of my double win in good times, I was given the bonus of being selected to go with just a few athletes to the famous Turku track in southern Finland. Many top athletes had run on the famous Turku track and the Finns were great athletic supporters; they wanted me to break the world record of 13:35 held by Vladamir Kuts of the USSR. This was the track where Zatopek and many other top runners had set world best performances.

My race was to be the 5,000 metres again, and it was billed as world record attempt at the three miles and 5,000 metres, but when the opposition appeared I was dismayed. There were only two runners to race me and, not like these days, there was no pacemaker. The race started and it was soon clear that neither was going to give me any trouble. I rolled off the laps, but it was hard with no one pushing me, in fact it was more like a training run or time trial. One runner dropped out and the other was lapped, but I went through the three mile mark in 13:23.6 and finished the 5,000 metres in 13:47.8. The second runner T. Virtanen was over a lap behind in 14:59.4. My lap times had been 64.5, 64.5, 66.5, 65, 68.5, 65.5, 67, 67.5, 67, 69, 69, and for the last 600 metres 93.8 (last lap my usual sixty seconds). This was about twelve seconds or one second a lap outside V. Kuts' world best for the distance. It was not a bad run, but I know I could have run very much faster with some real opposition. I did have the satisfaction of running the fastest ever 5,000 metres in Finland. Our select little team did quite well, with Dave Segal winning the 200 metres in 21.4, and John

Wrighton second in 21.7. In the 400 metres the positions were reversed with Wrighton winning in 47.0, and Segal running a rare 400 metres, third in 47.6. The other member of the team was the late Mike Rawson, who had to be content with second place in the 800 metres.

After the race I had a sauna and sat out on the balcony of the sauna house to cool down. There were a couple of us and we were completely nude, but this did not stop girls climbing up onto the balcony with their autograph books for us to sign. So we sat there and let them all come, keeping our modesty covered with one hand and signing with the other.

It was then back home and a three mile race at Welwyn Garden City, where I was well beaten by Martin Hyman, better known for his 10,000 metre running; his time was 13:31.4, and my time for second place was only 13:46.6.

The season was not over, so it was back to the training ready for the three races I was to have in the space of four days at the beginning of October.

My next race was for London against Stockholm at the White City, and here I teamed up with old rival Gordon Pirie, and this was one occasion when he got the better of me. He outsprinted me at the finish, and my time was 13:25.6.

Two days later I was at the White City in Manchester, to run a two mile race for the newly-formed International Athletes Club against The Rest of Europe, organised by the Mancastrian Club and sponsored by the *Evening Chronicle*. According to newspaper reports I was the sensation of the evening, although not quite good enough to be awarded the Munich Trophy. This trophy was presented by the National Union of Journalists in Manchester, in memory of the eight of their profession who died in the Munich air crash eighteen months earlier. The trophy went to shot-putter Arthur Rowe, for a distance of over sixty feet and repeatedly beating the Olympic qualifying standard. Most of the British athletes competing were beaten by overseas competition. The runners in the mile were especially criticized, including my conqueror from a few days earlier Pirie, who could only manage fourth in 4:9.5. The leading opposition in my two mile race was a strong East German, Herhard Hoenicke. According to one newspaper report after the race, I was tired and hungry. After my run at the White City, I had been on duty all next day from 9 a.m. to 6 p.m., and on the Friday I was working my beat again from 6 a.m. to 11 a.m., before dashing to Euston to catch the train to Manchester. I only just reached the stadium in time, and my only food all day was, I quote "two bobs' worth of railway bread rolls". I reached halfway in the race in 4:21.6 and was apparently looking very tired, the German then took over for three laps before the bell and took a ten yard lead into the final lap, before I challenged with the crowd shouting their heads off. I won the race in 8:47.2 and tired Hoenicke had to be content with only third place in 8:49.6. I like a quote about that final lap *"His legs lost that rubbery look. His head, instead of rolling, stayed firmly forward. His eyes were glued to the tape. His reward was victory."* I learned another lesson about how athletics was changing. After my win I was invited by a well-known journalist to accompany him down to the 'Gents'. I did wonder what was going on, especially when he sidled up to me and thrust something in my hand, it was a brown envelope which contained some cash. It was my pay for a good night's work. I think it was £25 or so; not much by today's standards but still the equivalent of three weeks' pay for a policeman on the beat.

The very next day I was in Birmingham for the usual Birchfield end of season meeting, and I won the three miles in 14:7.6; pretty slow but I had a busy week.

In the October of that year, I had become the first Brit to notch up the Olympic qualifying times at both 5,000 and 10,000 metres. My best position on the international ranking lists was in the 5,000 metres with the 13:47.6.

In October I went with a small British squad to compete in a pre-Olympic meeting in Rome. I wanted to keep training, and the only way I could do this was to run around the streets of Rome. This was quite a hazardous experience that grabbed me even more headlines. All the top ranked 5,000 metre runners in the world were there, and I managed to get second place behind Zimny (Poland), with the man who topped the rankings well behind me. Not a very fast race, but a tactical one, and my time was 13:54.2. He led the first two kilometres, and then I took over before he regained control at four km. He took a small lead and I could not catch him, but I won the battle for second place with the famous Hungarian world record holder Sandor Iharos.

We stayed in a new hotel in Rome and had quite a weekend. The team included some of the star (and attractive) girls of British athletics at the time, including Mary Rand (the former Mary Bignal). I was sharing with another male athlete, and a couple of others joined us as well as Les Girls. We had a bit of a party, and romping about on the bed, someone pulled an electrical wire and threw the hotel into darkness. Next thing we had knocking on the door; the girls disappeared into the bathroom and I opened the door. The team management were not amused and told the spare fellows to return to their own rooms, not realising the girls were also in the room. I recall they locked us in and what happened after that I cannot remember.

It was round about this time, when I was living in my new police house at Earley, that I received a visit from a young man who lived in Caversham. He knocked on the door, introduced himself and asked me if I would attend his school and give a coaching course and training session. I instantly agreed and only realised my 'mistake' when a letter arrived from Downside Abbey at Bath — that was the school! I had not bothered to ask and had assumed it was in Reading. I took a train to Bath and went to the famous abbey and school to carry out my promise. I had a very enjoyable and unusual day. I gave the boys a talk and took them for a cross-country run. All the teaching staff were monks and the games master had a very good cellar of wine in the wall of the changing room. I had lunch with the abbot and staff; the Abbott of Downside was a well-known figure who appeared regularly on radio's 'Any Questions'. It was a very good lunch, but it was a little strange as they ate in complete silence, but told me before we entered the dining room that I could talk as much as I liked; my friends and family would say that this would not be difficult for me, but it is difficult to do if no one can respond; but I think I did chat a bit and they nodded and acknowledged. I got to know the lad who invited me quite well in future years as his mother lived near to my shop, and when he was about he used to call in and see me. Unfortunately he was an epileptic and would nearly always have an attack in the shop. The first time it happened we did not know what it was, and when he went down on the floor hitting his head on some weightlifting weights, and appearing totally unconscious, our first reaction was that he was dead. Fortunately he recovered on that occasion but it became a very regular occurrence after this, and even my customers got used to it. Sadly his illness got worse, and he eventually had an attack while on his bike and was killed by the accident that followed.

I paid a similar visit to Bradfield College (much nearer to home), during the track season as part of my training as a coach. International athletes were expected to do this, and I worked alongside a famous national coach of his day, John Le Masurier.

The following winter was not to be a good one for me. I had run the qualifying times for both my events, and selection for the Olympics in Rome should have been automatic, but I had problems with my stomach. Every time I trained I would have to rush to the loo. It was worse as I got into the spring and summer of 1960, and I had numerous trips to my doctor and samples went to the Royal Berkshire Hospital for analysis. There was a suspicion that it was related to diet, and at one stage tomatoes were blamed. Nothing conclusive was found and my running continued to suffer. Looking back, and now understanding my problem of diabetes, I do wonder if that was the problem I had then which very rapidly reduced my capability of running as I had in 1956 to 1959.

My first race after the Rome trip was a month later in the Farnham Cross-Country Relays in Surrey. It was a 6 x 1.5 mile relay, and I set the fastest time of the day 7:29.

Then it was back to the Rochester five mile in Kent, where I had set the record the previous year of 24:57.4. I was looking forward to this race, as I always like running on the road and I had trained well leading up to it, clocking seventy miles in the previous seven days. I was on the 2 p.m.—10 p.m. shift, which was quite convenient, and meant I would get proper sleep in the week leading up to the race.

Things went wrong on the Friday, just as I was about to knock off duty, I got sent to a house on my beat where a man had been found dead in strange circumstances. It was difficult to tell whether it was suicide, accident or murder, and I had to seek higher authority before I could arrange to have the body removed. It started with the sergeant and ended up with calling out the detective superintendent after midnight. After much discussion, it was decided that it was an accident, even if a bizarre one, and so I had to arrange for the removal of the body and tidy up. I remember waiting in this cold house with the body for everyone to come, and I had to collect a lot of material found in the house which later ended up in Scotland Yard's Black Museum. Needless to say it was a very late night and I did not get very long in bed, so it was not the best preparation for my race.

I went off to Rochester next day, or rather later the same day, and had a good run but was beaten into fourth place, but my time was 24:57, the same as my record of the previous year.

In December I was at the Sportsman of the Year Lunch at the Savoy in London. I had hopes of following in the footsteps of many athletes who had won the coveted award since it was first presented in 1946, but it was not to be. The list of those at that function was like a sporting Who's Who.

Just five days later I was at the other big sporting occasion, the BBC Sportsview Personality of the Year Award at the BBC Television Theatre, Shepherds Bush. I had been warned I was in the running, and on the night I was one of half a dozen who had major film presentations of their achievements, but I missed out again. I left the theatre with another disappointed sportsman Billy Wright, the England football captain; we travelled on the tube together and it was my only meeting with this gentleman of football.

Wins in a couple of club cross-country matches followed, before New Year's Eve and my annual pilgrimage to Nos Galan at Mountain Ash in South Wales. This year a mile race had been introduced, and in the afternoon I lined up in Penrhiwceiber to run the mile. It was quite tough with climbs and twists and turns through the rows of terraced houses. The winner of this first race was Bruce Tulloh in 4:37, and I managed second place in 4:44, and it was a good warm-up for the real event at a few minutes to midnight. As always there was a huge crowd in Mountain Ash. Before the race I had the usual visit to the cottage hospital to meet the patients there; mostly pregnant women and a few miners. Then it was changing in the pithead baths, before lining up and waiting for the beacon to be lit by the 'Mystery Runner' to set us on our way. The Mystery Runner this year was Ken Norris. It was another great race, but this time I had to accept second best and Frank Salvat won the race, but my second place time was 18:49, just three seconds slower than my record time in 1958.

Two days later, I was winning the Berkshire Cross-Country in 43:38 for the eight mile course.

We were then in 1960, Olympic Year, the aspiration of any athlete was to take part, and my performances the previous year set me up to be there, or so I thought.

The next race was the Inter Counties at Brighton, and this was the race I always liked to use to test how my training was going, as it was always just when I was getting into full winter training. I had a very satisfactory run in fifth place with 36:31 for the seven mile course, which was pretty tough with some steep hills.

After one more club race win, I was off on that trip to San Sebastian again where I fared no better than the previous year, finishing twentieth on this occasion, but two minutes slower. The San Sebastian races were great events, and there was always a crowd of around 25,000 watching the races, mainly from the hills around the course. Gerry North was the winner this year, and the England team won the team race.

Just one week later I was in Hannut, Belgium, for another major cross-country where I did a little better, coming third in 36:15 for 11,000 metres, behind the winner Hedwig Leenaert (Belgium) in 35:51, and Allonsius, also Belgium, in 36:09. There were some good men behind me, including Vandwattyne (Belgium) fifth, Michel Bernard (France) who was eighth, and the great Gaston Roelants (Belgium) fifteenth. The England team, which included Brian Hill-Cottingham running his first international in sixth place, were well beaten in the team race by the home team. Looking back to the press cuttings of the race, I see that the English squad were far from happy about the race. I was quoted as saying *"We didn't even know the race had begun until we saw the Belgians move off. It was a farce of a start"*. Another member of the team Mike Maynard, who finished seventeenth said *"And when we did get going, we had to push spectators out of the way. It was awful"*.

The Southern Counties race followed within a few days and the travelling had taken its toll, and I could only finish third on the tough Parliament Hill course, behind the winner John Merriman and second placed Bruce Tulloh.

Over the following four weeks, I won four club and police races quite easily and I was beginning to get back to form. On 12th March it was the National Cross-Country at West Bromwich, and I had eased back on my 100 mile a week training, and it paid off with third place in 45:45 for the usual nine miles. The event winner was Basil Heatley in 45:15, from John Merriman, 45:42. Gerry North was just behind me with John Anderson fifth, Fred Norris sixth, Gordon Pirie seventh and Bruce Tulloh eighth.

I was selected for the England team again, and the international was to be held at Glasgow just two weeks later. In between I had the usual ritual of running and winning the Police AA race again, and fortunately it was nine days before the Glasgow race and not two days as in previous years. The race was won by A. Rhadi (Morocco) in 43:33, Gaston Roelants was second, John Merriman (Wales) third, Basil Heatley fourth, Fred Norris sixth, the very consistent Frank Sando eighth and Harry Minshall ninth. I finished tenth in Glasgow and scored for England for the third successive year, and we won the team race again. It wasn't bad but I had slid from first to fifth to tenth over the three years.

One more cross-country race between the police and REME, which I won, and then it was back on the road and one of my regular favourite events the Uxbridge Road Relay, with another fastest time of 26:38, but just outside the record set the previous year.

I again won the Maidenhead 10 on Easter Monday, in 51:33, just seventeen seconds slower than my 1959 winning time, and forty-one seconds slower than my best time set when I came second in 1958. They were all good times, and bearing in mind the course at Maidenhead was 770 yards over distance, and that extra bit would have taken over two minutes, it was still the equivalent of around 49:30 for ten miles.

My first track race was ten days later, when I again ran in the annual AAA v Oxford University match. I only finished fourth in 8:52.8, but two days later I did win the Southern Counties six mile in 28:44.4.

A friendly invitation two mile race followed at Alton, where my opponents were Martin Hyman and Bruce Tulloh amongst others, and I took second place behind Tulloh in 8:56.

Races at Hornchurch and Portsmouth followed, before I had a very special invitation to run a 5,000 metres crowd warmer at Hampden Park, Glasgow, before the European Cup Final between Real Madrid and Eintracht. Things did not start well, as I had to fit it in with my police duties and was due to fly up from Heathrow on the morning of the race. I arrived at Heathrow too late for my flight, and although they were used to me arriving late and were always very helpful at getting me on the plane at the last moment, they could not help on this occasion as the plane was in the air. I explained my plight and I was lucky. The big wigs of the FA had a charter flight going to the match and Sir Stanley Rous, who was one of them, was approached and I got my seat.

There were only six of us invited to run in this crowd warmer, and these were Derek Ibbotson, Basil Heatley, Graham Everett (British mile champion in 1958), Alistair Wood the holder of the Scottish records at four, five and six miles, Andrew Brown the holder of the other Scottish distance record the three mile, and myself. The crowd was already very large when we were sent on our way, and the atmosphere was electric. I finished third in 14:26.6, and then the big match started. We had very good seats to watch the game, and although not a great football fan, it was a great match with many goals and the game flowed one end to the other. Afterwards we joined the dinner for the teams, and next morning it was back to reality and the beat. I did get my flight home; they made sure by depositing me at the airport in plenty of time.

I was well known at Heathrow and always got VIP treatment. I seldom went through the conventional customs routine, as I was nearly always met by a member of Special Branch who was a friend of the family, and he used to meet me from the plane and take me straight to wherever I needed to go. I remember on one occasion when I was taken through the VIP lounge as usual, I was amazed to see so many photographers and press men. I didn't think my recent exploits justified such attention, but my attention was then drawn to a man in white; it was Pundit Nehru, Prime Minister of India.

A home match at Windsor followed, and then a rare treat, a whole week without a race but some good solid training with eleven sessions which included some very good ones. On the Tuesday I ran a three-quarter mile in 3:18, followed by two laps slow, and then 880 yards in 2:01, one lap slow and then 440 yards in sixty-four seconds; finishing with 4 x 220 yards in 30, 28, 30 and 25 seconds. That was the first of two sessions that day.

The first Saturday in June was the usual bank holiday meeting at the White City, and running for Berkshire on the Saturday I only managed fourth in the three miles with 13:54.2. Within two hours I was at Harrow, taking part in a two mile race at the Kodak Sports (there were good prizes at this meet) and I was second in 9:15 on the grass track. This was followed by a light run on the Sunday, and back to the White City on Monday for an invitation 3,000 metres, where I was badly left behind and came ninth in 8:15.8. A few days later I was running a 1,500 metres at Hayes where I came fifth in 4:5.

My health problem was playing me up, and my running was very erratic at this time. Some good training sessions but not very successful races. Apart from minor races I had not won a race since the Southern 6, in April.

My luck was to change; at least for one race. I was selected to run 10,000 metres for England against Italy at the White City, and I did win in a reasonable if unspectacular time of 29:30.

A 5,000 metres running for the South against the North and Midlands followed, and I could only manage second in a very poor time of 14:33. At the end of June I ran the Southern Counties three miles, but no win as I had in previous years, and I ran my fourth place in 13:36.8.

On the 1st July 1960 I flew to Moscow for a meeting I will never forget. It was only a very small group that flew from Heathrow with me. There was an elderly team manager, Arthur Rowe the shot-put king, and two others. The first sign of trouble was when we arrived at Moscow Airport. We were kept waiting for a long time and the officials there picked on the biggest of us, Arthur, and having examined his passport, they claimed it was not genuine, or forged, or something. It was of course complete nonsense, but it was a way of mucking us about. What was the problem and why were they doing this?

During the last week in June, the 'big three', Eisenhower, Khrushchev and Macmillan, had been having talks in Paris, and at the end of the week the U-2 pilot Gary Powers was shot down spying over the Soviet Union.

The talks were broken off, the cold war was on with a vengeance and there was great anti-American and British feeling in Moscow.

Eventually we did get released and taken to our hotel off Red Square. The atmosphere was very tense and we were told to stay in the hotel. It was not like our triumphant trip to the city twelve months earlier. On Saturday evening we were conveyed to the Lenin Stadium, and I did not think any of us were in the right frame of mind to perform at our best. I ran in the 5,000 metres, came sixth in 14:22.8, and on the Sunday evening the meeting continued, and I ran 10,000 metres and came tenth in 29:42.8.

That was not the end of the story; after the Sunday evening meet we went back to our hotel and were told that we would probably not be allowed home; in effect, I suppose we were under house arrest. Back in the hotel I was elected to try and sort the problem as our old retired schoolmaster manager found the whole situation beyond his understanding. The first thing I did was to telephone the British Embassy. They told me they were also confined and could not get to us, and their advice was that there would be a BEA plane taking off from the airport very early, I think about 7 a.m. on Monday morning. They advised me to get everyone up early and to make our way to the airport, and they said they were pretty sure no one would actively try and prevent us leaving.

Next morning we were up very early; not difficult as I doubt whether any of us slept that well in the circumstances. There was no one about in the hotel as we quietly packed and made our way down the stairs and out into Red Square. I hailed a taxi and showed our air tickets, and he agreed to take us to the airport. When we arrived there we handed over all the rubles we had, which just about covered the fare, and made our way into the departure area, or so we thought; the only problem was there were different terminals like Heathrow and any other major airport, and we had deposited ourselves at the one for internal flights to Siberia. We had no more money and we had virtually no words of Russian between us. Somehow we got on an airport bus and although we should have paid, we somehow got a free ride, and got to the appropriate part of the airport. There was no announcement or display of our flight, but we did find two BEA stewardesses and they explained that the plane was waiting and it would take-off fairly shortly. Next problem, big Arthur, who like the rest of us had gone without his breakfast, insisted he had to get something to eat. He gave me his passport and joined a queue for some food. With that we were told to board the aircraft and we all did with the exception of Arthur. The captain told us we had to take-off quickly and there was no time for delay. Just as they were wheeling the aircraft steps away there was a commotion at the airport buildings, and Arthur could be seen pushing a couple of armed guards away and sprinting towards us. It was up the steps, and I think he had to jump from them into the plane as they were moving away. We were off, and all that trouble had got him just a couple of pretty awful hard boiled eggs. It was our "Retreat from Moscow".

It was at this meeting in Moscow that I came across something new in the athletic world. A new world record was set by a woman in the 800 metres, and she was literally taken onto the track and off it by men in white coats. As far as we could make out, hypnotism had been used on her to enable her to run beyond the pain barrier.

I do not think there was much artificial help for athletes in the 1960s; little was known about supplements and I know that there were only two substances that I ever used. One was glucose tablets, and the other was Redoxin vitamin C tablets that a researcher into the common cold advised me to take to avoid picking up colds after races. It is sad that some forty years later, the use of drugs has become almost commonplace, and athletes are always looking for that extra bit of help to reach the top, without perhaps training that little extra which might give them the edge.

More mud at Inter Counties Cross-Country with Tulloh in pursuit

The white police gloves come in handy,
chasing Basil Heatley at Brighton

In full flow with Mimoun chasing during the big race at Cardiff

The sprint finish gives me victory over the great Mimoun

At a Meeting of the Council

of the Royal Borough of New Windsor, held at the Guildhall, Windsor on Monday, the fifteenth day of December 1958:

RESOLVED – that congratulations be extended to Stanley Edward Eldon, a native of the Royal Borough of New Windsor, for his outstanding performances in athletics and for the contribution he had made to English Sport ~~~~~~~

The Common Seal of the Mayor, Aldermen & Burgesses of the Royal Borough of New Windsor, was hereunto affixed, in the presence of:-

John Proctor ... Mayor...

[signature] Town Clerk

A few of the headlines and cartoons that followed every race, win or lose

PETER WILSON—after seeing Ibbotson flop again at the White City—says:

ENGLAND MUST PUT FLYING COP IN 3-MILE SQUAD

WILL Derek Ibbotson run at all in the Empire Games at Cardiff?

The man who has—unofficially—run the fastest-ever mile, packed in after only two miles in the three-mile race at the White City A.A.A. championships on Saturday.

Apart from his woeful loss of form this season—excluding his mile victory in 4m. 5.4s. at Vancouver, Ibbotson hasn't run a really class race for months—last year's hero is suffering from a really bad case of "spiking."

NEEDS STITCHING

He sustained the injury at a small meeting last Monday. It really needs stitching, but obviously, with the necessity to practise, Ibbotson would immediately tear the stitches open again as soon as he put any weight on it.

It seems to me that Stan Eldon, who ran a magnificent three miles, leading by anything up to eighty yards after the first two laps, MUST be included in this event at Cardiff.

I know that he is already in the six miles, but one race is on the Saturday and the other is not until the Tuesday.

I believe the "Flying Cop" is strong enough to compete in both events.

And his meeting with the new three-mile world champion, Albert Thomas—the Australian who clipped 3.8s. off Sandor Iharos's time in Dublin last Wednesday—would be the highlight of the whole [illegible]

● Derek Ibbotson . . . is he fit to run at Cardiff?

Eldon is tough enough to tackle Games 'double'

courage to beat the highly-fancied Rae, from New Zealand, in the 100 yards.

How good it is to see the honours go round at athletics, spread across the face of all five Continents.

Back to the home scene again and a well-judged if slowish mile, won by the Scot, Graham Everett, in 4m. 6.8s.

NOT ENOUGH

In the 3,000 metres steeplechase, John Disley never quite got a long enough lead to compensate for the faster finish of Eric Shirley, who beat him by a fifth of a second with a new championship best of 8m. 51s.

A FINE CURTAIN-RAISER for the Games to come—and a nice touch when Prince Axel of Denmark, a member of the International Olympic Committee, presented the prizes.

For it was his grandmother, Queen Alexandra, who, almost fifty years ago to the day, presented the prizes at the 1908 Olympics when she was Edward VII's queen.

Today I'm off to Wales. As an Englishman I certainly hope we [illegible] our fair share of titles, but I [illegible] what a heartening thing it is to see the titles go round.

RESHUFFLE?

I wish that our middle and long distance runners could have sorted themselves out so that they could have given of their best in what is, after all, our greatest domestic sporting pageant.

I feel there must be some reshuffling in some of these events.

But I'm looking forward to a festival

Generous support from
Daily Mirror's
Peter Wilson

A selection of the many cartoons that were based on the 'running policeman' or 'galloping cop'

The introduction of the first road running shoes to the UK, Kitami and Onitsuka meet Eldon close to the start of the Windsor to Chiswick Marathon

POST
RACAL

VARIETY
CLUB
WALK

CLUB

Brian Bacon, Reading AC, helping another disabled youngster to enjoy the Reading Half Marathon

Facing page:
Top — Eldon and son leave Reading Evening Post *on Variety Club Charity Run to London in 1972*
Middle — Halfway with a 'backing group'
Bottom — Welcomed at the finish by the late Eric Morley (Miss World) and Jimmy Hill

Peter Hull, the man that inspired thousands

Waiting for the start of one of the smaller entries to the Reading Half Marathon

Epic race ends with runners in dead heat

By GUY HAYDON and JIM MURTY

THE eighth Reading Half Marathon became a tense battle for first place — and ended in a dead heat.

Runners Steve Brace, 28, and Nick Trainer, 27, were judged to have crossed the line together in a time of 63 minutes 32 seconds after an epic battle over 13.1 miles.

Originally Brace was told he had won. He said his first thoughts on the outcome were: "It was very close, no more than six inches in it."

The Post's photograph of the finish seems to support this view, showing Welshman Brace had pipped Trainer, from London.

Spectators packed around the finish line at Northumberland Avenue stood confused as Radio 210 told them Brace had won and the organisers then announced it was a dead heat.

Brace sportingly accepted the decision, admitting that it was difficult to choose a clear winner.

He said: "One step further and I think Nick would have been in front.

"It is a very unusual thing for a race to finish in a dead heat like this."

Nick, running in his first half marathon, was clearly happy with the decision.

He said: "It is very encouraging. It felt fast all the way and I managed to keep in there up to the end."

Brace's clubmate Greg Newhams, 31, was edged into third place just one second behind the winners with Gary Nagel from Valli Harriers fourth in 63 mins 34 secs.

First Reading runner was Tim Butler, 26, of Anderson Avenue who was sixth in a time of 64.12.

Commonwealth bronze medallist Angie Pain was the first woman with a time of 72.21.

The Whitbread-sponsored wheelchair race was won in a record time by defending champ Chris Hallam, of Cwmbran, Wales.

■ Pull-out race special inside. Colour picture special tomorrow.

The epic dead heat finish of Reading Half Marathon in 1990

The 'Chief Jogger' with Kathy Tayler at one of the early jogging events held in Prospect Park, Reading

A Stan Eldon Sports Fashion Show — daughter Caroline modelling

Another job for Stan, compere at the Fashion Show with goalkeeper Phil Parkes and athlete Donna Murray (Hartley)

Actor Robert Powell, a great supporter of SportsAid at one of the fund raising dinners at the Royal Lancaster

The agony and ecstasy of the London Marathon in 1985

Only 13K to go on my 176 mile run to France in 1992

Chapter Ten

Olympic Disappointment

Back home I did get back into winning ways within three days, when I won a three mile race in 13:48, running for Berkshire against the Army and the Universities Athletic Union. On the Saturday at the end of an eventful week, I retained both my Police National titles, winning the one mile in 4:14.3 and the three mile in 13:56.4.

I was signed up by the *Reading Standard* to write a column every two weeks in the build-up to the Olympics, and my first article was published on May 13th 1960.

The week after the Police Champs, it was the AAA Championships at the White City that were to be the main selection races for the Olympic team. In hindsight I was silly and ran both the six miles on the Friday evening, where I came fourth in 28:19.8, and the three miles on the Saturday afternoon, coming fifth in 13:39.4.

When the Olympic team was announced I was not in it, and I was on duty when I found out. I was not happy and telephoned Jack Crump at AAA's headquarters from a telephone box on my beat. He was very sympathetic and explained that it had been a hard decision, which had been discussed at some length by the Board, but that at the end of the day they thought that my problem with hot weather and my more recent health problem would prevent me from performing at anything close to my potential. He was quick to make me an offer, which did not make up for the disappointment of missing the Olympics, but was still acceptable. He promised me that I would be given the opportunity to go on any overseas trips that would come up after the Olympics.

I was told that I could still make the team if I performed well at a meeting in Glasgow at the beginning of August; and so, only a couple of days after my second child and first son was born, Jonathan Stanley, I was off on my travels again. The meeting was the Glasgow Rangers annual meeting at Hampden Park on 6th August. It was very hot and not ideal weather for me to prove myself to the selectors, but I was determined to grab my place by winning the three mile race. I had a good race and on the last lap I made sure by outsprinting my two nearest rivals, Alistair Wood the Scottish record holder at the distance, and Martin Hyman who was going to the Olympics in the 10,000 metres. My winning time was 13:39.6, not a fantastic time but I had won a tough race in my least favourite conditions, and thought as I crossed the line that I had my ticket for Rome. It was not to be, and when the final few places were filled I was not selected, and Gordon Pirie got both the 5,000 and 10,000 metres slots.

I flew home to see my one-week-old son, and within forty-eight hours I was running at North Shields in a two mile race, which I won in 8:49, the second fastest time of the season by a UK athlete, and beating John Anderson who was a selected runner for the Olympic 1,500 metres, so I was in reasonable form.

Other races in August included second place in an invitation 5,000 metres with 14:9.8, which was not very good but by then my Olympic dream had been smashed. I also got second in the annual London Fire Brigade meet at the White City, with 8:52.2.

I then had a month off racing and just trained modestly until the Welsh Games in Cardiff in the middle of September. On a wet and windy day, with a very soggy track, I had a very close race with Lazlo Tabori (exiled Hungarian), Dave Power (Australia) and Nyandeka (Kenya). At the bell, the four of us were running abreast, until Tabori took off with me chasing him, and it was a *tremendous race up the home straight* (a quote from the papers), and Tabori just got up to win by two yards with me taking second place, both with the same time of 13:49, and the Kenyan taking third place.

My racing programme started to warm up again, and four days after Cardiff I was second again in the Air Ministry Sports two miles in 8:55.8, followed three days later with a win over three miles at Welwyn Garden City in 13:43.8. The winning habit did not last, and four days later I could only finish fourth in the three miles, in a match between London and the Pan American Cities.

Jack Crump kept his word, and in October I was off to the West African Games in Lagos, Nigeria. This was an interesting and historical trip. The event was to be part of the celebration of Nigerian Independence, and the team was an international one, made up of mainly athletes who had attended, and in many cases won medals in the Olympics in Rome. The team included Americans, Commonwealth athletes and two or three of us from the UK.

Our first problem on the trip occurred in the air while we were flying across the Sahara to Lagos. Most of those on board the BOAC plane were asleep when we were awoken by the air stewards and told there was a problem with the plane; apparently the hydraulics had gone and there were no brakes or controls. As we flew south I remember seeing the camel trains going across the desert; it was a different world. We landed safely at Karno, an airport in the north of Nigeria, and had to stay there until the plane was fixed. By coincidence, forty years later, I was talking to my colleague in the Sports Aid office about the incident, and she knew all about it. She had been working at Heathrow at the time, and was responsible for despatching the aircraft engineers to Karno — a small world!

We did eventually fly on to Lagos, and were taken from the airport to the Games 'Village'. This was also a bit of a shock, especially for the team management and the girls on the trip. Our housing was concrete built units with no windows or doors. There were the most basic of facilities and we all had our mosquito net. The Nigerians had no intention of separating the sexes, but the women's team management had other ideas. They quickly decided that their girls could not stay in the same buildings as the rest of us, and before we knew it they had whisked the girls away to stay in a very nice area of large houses some way away from the rest of us. In the same area was a very nice hotel with a swimming pool, and every day we met up at this hotel to have a swim and to eat. I spent many happy hours in the pool with girls like Betty Cuthbert from Australia, the Olympic gold medallist sprinter, who sadly was at the opening ceremony at Sydney 2000 in a wheelchair. It was just as well that we had this special arrangement for eating, as the only other eating facility was back at the village where we shared the eating facilities with the local villagers.

The first morning we all made our way to this communal facility. It was a long building, open to the sky in the centre, and flowing through it was a trough or trench, and obviously food was thrown in there. It was open to the skies, so that when it rained it would be washed through. There was a long queue of the locals waiting to be served with breakfast. There was a huge black pot, similar to the cartoon type that missionaries were cooked in, and porridge was being cooked in large quantities. Fortunately there were cereals, which I think may have gone out with us, and we all opted for the 'safe' food.

Once we got used to our living environment, and the lizards running in and out of our 'rooms', it became tolerable. The organisers had a fleet of Mercedes cars and VW minibuses to take us and other VIPs about. They were driven by boys from the bush, who had literally been given a few minutes' instruction and then given their vehicle to drive. We had some hair-raising journeys, but in a few days they did grasp the rudiments of driving on the mud-made and very bumpy roads.

The whole team was taken to the stadium for the opening ceremony. There was a decent track, but the stands were mostly temporary, made from scaffolding. We lined up and marched into the stadium where we were announced as the team from the Commonwealth. This did not go down too well with the large number of American athletes, although most of them saw the funny side. The prime minister of the new emerging country was there to welcome us, but sadly within six months he was murdered when the inter-regional fighting started.

The fun really started when the athletics commenced. They did not have the right implements. They had a sledgehammer for hammer throwing, and there was no water jump for the steeplechase, which was to be one of my two events in the match. The meeting was very basic, but there was some good competition. The African nations were just emerging in sport and their inexperience was very evident. It seems a lifetime away from today when they dominate so much of athletics and other sports.

On the Friday, the first day, I ran in the 1,500 metres and came fourth in 3:54. A couple of the Africans had got in front of me as well as one of our team.

The next day it was the 5,000 metres and it was very hot. I ran with Max Truex, the US 10,000 metre champion and record holder for most of the race until he left me. I came second in 14:32.4, a very slow time, but we got the maximum points for the team.

I remember the actual handover ceremony that took place at midnight on 5th October 1960. Princess Alexandra was there to represent the Queen and I remember the Union flag being lowered and the Nigerian flag being raised to symbolise the changeover.

We were invited on board the warship that the Princess was staying on, and we were given passes and told to make our own way to the dockside where we would be taken on board. For some reason I made my way on my own and I will not forget the crowd, or what happened, when I arrived. There was a massive crowd between me and where I was going, so I showed my pass to a police superintendent and he immediately took action to get me through the crowd. He just walked through waving his swagger stick and hitting anyone who got in our way. There were barriers to keep the crowd contained and some people were trying to climb over them; down came his stick on their hands. I tried to stop him but it seemed that this was the expected police method of keeping control in Nigeria. I could not help thinking that there were times back home when I could have used such tactics, but rest assured this was not a serious thought.

My writing continued, and while I was in Nigeria the Wolfenden Report on Sport was published, and I sent my comments on the report to the paper.

A week after my return to England, I was selected to run against the East Germans in Berlin. It was the end of a long and rather disappointing season, but I decided I would take the trip because it was a little different. This was an interesting trip as it meant flying into Berlin, which was in the Eastern Sector of the city, and it was before the 'Wall' was built between East and West. We were to stay in the East and to compete there, but we did explore, and although there were armed guards on the border in the city, we ignored them and walked over into West Berlin. I remember the contrast was tremendous, with the new buildings and neon signs in the West, and the dereliction with bombed buildings still standing in the East. There was a great contrast in the people as well, with the Western Berliners smartly dressed and in bright clothes, and the Eastern people were drab and poorly dressed.

I ran the 5,000 metres, but only came third in 14:20; a very disappointing end to a disastrous season that could have been my greatest.

By now it was the middle of October, and into the period where I normally cut down on training and enjoyed the occasional race. For a few weeks my training did drop right down, and one week only had a total of sixteen miles in my training diary.

The last Saturday in October put me back into winning mood with a cross-country win over six miles in an inter-club race. Another win followed in an inter-police force race, and then it was off to the Le Soir race in Brussels.

This was one of the attractive races of the winter season, because there were good prizes and the runners were always well looked after. It was also an interesting and different event, because there was the *Criterium des Arcs* for the elite runners, but there was also several other races including a club race where there were thousands of runners. This was unique in those days, as there were no mass running events that we have come to see in the 1980s and beyond. I only finished fourteenth in Brussels, with a time of 32:46, for a distance of just over 9,000 metres or about 5.5 miles.

Back home I did manage to win four more races before Christmas, and my training crept back up to nearly seventy miles a week.

The New Year started off with my annual visit to South Wales and the Nos Galan races at Mountain Ash. I ran in the one mile again in the afternoon, which was won by Derek Ibbotson in 4:16.8, and then I lined up for the 3 mile 1,600 yard midnight race around the terraces of the town. As usual the race was started by the Mystery Runner, who was the winner of the afternoon one mile, Ibbotson. My main rival on this occasion turned out to be Martin Hyman, and as we came down onto the main street he was just ahead, and he maintained his lead through to where we turned right onto the bridge that would take us to the finish in front of the Town Hall. As we turned onto the bridge the crowd was so dense we had difficulty in making our way to the finish. I suppose I was less of a gentleman than Martin, and I fought my way through the crowd and arrived at the finish first. In one respect I suppose I was a gentleman as I refused to accept the win, and insisted that the winner's sash went to Martin Hyman because without the crowd he would genuinely have won by twenty metres or so. My time was 18:37, which was twelve seconds faster than in the previous year and it was in fact the fastest time I was ever going to achieve at Nos Galan over the years. Because of the crowds, the rest of the runners were allowed to finish on the other side of the bridge to avoid any further disputes.

Back in Berkshire I did manage to win the Berkshire title yet again.

Around this time I had started to teach Marion to drive, and on Friday, 13th January 1961, while we were having a short drive very close to our home, she took a corner too wide at the same time as a biscuit lorry was also over the white line in the middle of the road. We collided and the car was thrown some way up the road, and the lorry ended up in the ditch. The car had spun around and I was thrown out onto the road, landing on my head. We had our two young children in the car; baby Jonathan was in his carrycot on the back seat and narrowly missed being hit by the fire extinguisher that fell off the back shelf, and Caroline, who had been sitting on my lap, came out of the car with me. Fortunately I hit the ground and she didn't. There were no seat belts in those days. Marion was taken to hospital but did not have any serious injuries, which was surprising when we later saw the damage to the car which was a write-off.

I had just got my training back to a reasonable level and had run fifteen miles the day before the crash, and as a result of my bang on the head I then lost four days, but I then got back to training the following week. I trained quite hard and that is why I probably had such a lousy run on the Saturday in the Inter-Counties race, where it took me 47:07 to run the eight miles and finish in 106th position. I took time off on the Sunday and started training again on the Monday, and clocked up a total of 100 miles, including a six mile cross-country race on the Saturday in the Police against various Army units match. I finished fifth, but according to my notes on the day, I and others got lost and ran off the course. The week following I clocked up 101 miles in twelve training sessions, followed by seventy-seven the next week, when I won an inter-club race. The next week it was seventy-one miles, and this included two races. The first one on the Wednesday I won. It was an inter police force match, but on the Saturday it was the Southern Counties where I had always performed well. This time was not one of them, and I finished ninth in 45:32 for the nine miles. Then I was back to 100 miles of training and a win in a small inter-club match. On the evening of Wednesday 1st March I did one of my favourite runs; I ran to Windsor from Reading via Twyford, a distance of nineteen miles, which I did in one hour forty-six minutes.

I had some shorter steady runs on the next two days, before lining up in the Thames Valley Harriers Relay, again at Cranford. The course had been changed and was now slightly shorter than the one where I held the record, but I still came out on top with the fastest time of the day, 20:18 for the 4.5 miles.

A steady week of training followed, and at the end of that week I ran what, looking back now, was a race that signalled the coming to an end of my international running. It was the English Championships, and I came thirteenth in only 51:05 for the nine miles. This was outside the automatic place for the international where they selected the first nine, and it did not even get me a reserve spot. It was a great disappointment after my first, fifth, and tenth positions in the international race of the previous three years.

Shortly after this I did win the Police Cross-Country Championship for the last time, and a few days later ran in a new event for me, the Swindon Road Relay. I loved the road and once again I clocked the fastest time for the 4.5 mile leg.

Over the next two weeks I was to win or set the fastest times in four races. The first was in Northampton, a six mile cross-country race, and then the Watford Road Relay, 6 x 3 miles where my time of 13:41 was the fastest. Then on Easter Monday it was another of my special events, the Maidenhead '10', and I won again in 51:34, just one second slower than my time in winning the previous year. At the end of that week it was the Uxbridge Road Relay, and I was fastest again with 26:47.

By now I was just getting back into track training and had some good sessions, and so I thought I would have a go at the AAA Ten Mile Championship to be held at Motspur Park. One of my old Army friends and rival, Basil Heatley, was entered and I knew that he wanted a world record. We ran together and we took the lead in turns and reached the three mile mark in 14:16, which was well on schedule, but then on the sixteenth lap disaster struck as I was running down the back straight. All of a sudden my left leg seized up with cramp and I struggled for the rest of the lap before dropping out. I remember the AAA physiotherapist telling me that my problem was caused by running on too many different surfaces in a short time; cross-country, road, and then rapidly onto the track.

I wanted to get over the disappointment of dropping out of that ten miles, so a week later I lined up for the Finchley twenty mile race. I knew my basic fitness was good in spite of my trouble at the AAA 10, and I set off in the '20' in my usual way, leading from the start and clocking off the five mile laps in twenty-five minutes a lap, but after three laps and around fifteen miles I paid the price for my enthusiasm and I slowed rapidly, and my last lap of five miles took around thirty-eight minutes. I suffered and my final time was only 1:53. All I wanted to do after the race for about twenty-four hours was eat and drink. I packed in sandwiches, fruit juice and anything I could get my hands on. I found out what it was like to be totally dehydrated.

Just four days after that twenty miles, I was back on the track for the annual AAA v Oxford University match at Iffley Road. This time I did not win and had a terrible run, finishing sixth in only 9:23. I was still being asked to run all over the place, and only another four days later I was in Hanover in Germany, running an invitation 3,000 metres, where I was sixth again in 8:30.2.

I was really on the slide now, and things could not get much worse, or could they? All I won over the next couple of weeks were a few club races in unspectacular times, and I did manage second place in a three mile at Portsmouth where I recorded 14:12. I then ran the three miles again in the Inter Counties at the White City. Absolute disaster, seventeenth in 14:29. Form was very much up and down from then on. I won the Berkshire titles at one and three miles again, in 4:16.4 for the mile, and 14:11.9 for the 3 miles. I won a few club races and managed to make the first three in several invitation races, including one at Farnham where I managed 8:51.8 for two miles.

At the end of June I ran for my second claim club Reading AC, in their match against a Swedish Club, Idrottsklubben YMER. I won the mile in 4:20, and the two miles in 9:9.2, and even managed to get fourth place in the 1,500 metres steeplechase in 4:40. The erratic form continued, and at the end of that week all I could manage was a fifth place in a mile race at Nottingham in 4:16. The following week I had two contrasting results, with second place in the Paddington 1.5 miles, in a time that was close to my best for the race, 6:27.5, and then back to a modest run at Oxford, where I ran two miles in over nine minutes. This was followed by a win for the Berkshire AAA v Army v University Athletic Union in the mile. My time was 4:11.6, which was quite respectable for me.

I sharpened up in the rest of the week with some short fast running, and then ran the AAA's six mile at the White City on the Friday night. I had to be content with third place and 28:13.4, but this was only eight seconds outside my British record, so it was not a bad run and showed that I was not quite finished. I then won the Police Championships at one and three miles for the last time, with modest times of 4:20 and 14.02. An invitation 1,500 metres in 3:58.3 followed, and in the Welsh Games I had another poor performance, fifth place in the three miles in 13:46.4.

I did start to think about my future, both in terms of running and career. I was approached by the Chairman of Lex Motors, Rosser Chinn, and offered a job, but it was a bit vague what my job would be.

During August of 1961, training and races fell off. This was the year that my time in the police was going to come to an end, but before I quit I saw an advert for a selling job with Caxtons, who published encyclopedias and sports books. I got the job and had the training; then it was out to sell sporting encyclopedias.

During the summer and autumn of that year I was doing two jobs. I was still in the police force, but I was earning more part-time with the selling than the police work. I was still pounding the beat, but I had also started this new job as a door-to-door salesman for Caxton Press, so I was working up to fifteen hours a day, which left very limited time for training. I resigned from the police but, that was not easy for three reasons. First of all I had enjoyed police work and the people I had worked with; I also had a young family, two children at that stage; and thirdly the police did not want to lose me. Within minutes of me typing my resignation, the news had reached the chief constable who summoned me to his presence the next morning. I reluctantly went to see him and we had a very frank discussion, which ended up with me being offered any job I wanted within the force, and promotion as I had already passed my promotion to sergeant examination. We parted on good terms, and he said that I could go back any time and he would take me on again, even if I had passed my thirtieth birthday, which was the age limit in those days.

I left the police in November, and there was an adjustment to my life to be made. The cost of the removal firm to convey us and our goods from the police house to our new home in Plough Lane, Wokingham, just £6.10s.

By now my serious running career was over; not by choice, but by circumstance. I suppose I was typical of athletes of the era. We could not afford to concentrate on running for too long, as there was not any real money to support life and family. I had enjoyed both my hobby/sporting career of running and my career in the police. I had held British records, won several AAA titles, and I had won the big one, the International Cross-Country (now the World Championship). I had won quite a few very good international and other races at various distances, and although I never quite held a senior world record, I did have those two 'Junior World Bests' to my credit, and I had ranked top or near the top in the World or Europe Rankings at several distances, at different times, from 1958 onwards. I had beaten most of the best distance runners in the world at that time. Running in those days was challenging and fun, but life moved on.

Life was pretty tough once I had quit the police, and Marion was often waiting for the eight shillings (40p) family allowance on a Tuesday, so that she could buy some meat. I had my money from selling sports equipment, and the *Reading Standard* had asked me to write a column for them, and after getting permission from the AAAs, they gave me a portable typewriter which I still have, although it is not used these days. The *Standard* also agreed to pay me £3 a week, and this paid the mortgage on our little house in Wokingham.

While out selling the book one night, I met a very good amateur footballer with Woking FC, and he introduced me to a man in Wokingham, Ken Berry, who was just setting up a sports shop. Ken was the least sporting man you could imagine, but we got on well and he agreed to pay me £10 per week, plus a commission.

After working for Ken Berry and KC Sports for a while at Wokingham, I decided to go it alone and start my own retail business. I had a good stock of Puma shoes from my freebies supplied to me by Puma, and as I had good contacts with the Dasslers. I wrote to them to see if they could help. They certainly did and told me that they had just appointed Mitre Sports (the football manufacturers) as their UK agent, but they had put in a word and they would supply me with whatever I required. Mitre were very helpful and I was in business, even though I had no money and an overdraft of several hundred pounds.

Chapter Eleven

Business Life Begins

Before I could go into business I had to get further permission, and I wrote to the AAAs again; this time Harold Abrahams (of Chariots of Fire fame) dealt with my request to trade under my own name. No athlete had done this before me, and there was a fear I could be infringing my amateur status. Harold however gave me permission, and I was up and running.

During this time we had to survive on little or no income, but this did not stop Gordon Pirie and his wife Shirley coming to visit on a regular basis, so that they could get something to eat during their hard-up times. Years later I found out that we were on their circuit; Bruce Tulloh and Mary Rand were both invaded as well. But I liked Gordon and he did give me some ideas about going into business, and it was he who suggested that I might like to be the UK agent for Puma shoes, as he assured me they were looking for a distributor. He also introduced me to Norwegian Ski Pants that he imported, and from these I was later able to develop the slimline trackster, which we sold so well in the 1960s and 70s.

During the time in Wokingham our income was helped by my egg round. I had around sixty laying chickens, and these produced about thirty dozen eggs a week, and I had regular orders for supplying eggs to family, friends and others; and this produced around an extra £5 a week. In our last Christmas there these chickens turned in their last profit, when I had to kill, pluck and draw them before they appeared on many Christmas tables.

My first shop was at the back of a grocery store, the Roundshill Bakery in Bracknell. I did a deal with the man who was then Chairman of the Wokingham Town Football Club, to rent a small space in his premises. It did not last long as he had forgotten to tell his landlord, but it had got me started and there was then no turning back.

I was only running around twenty miles a week, and mainly only club races. It was back on the road in September and another fastest time in the Highgate Harriers Road Relay; the lap was over 4.6 miles and I had a time of 22:55. In the middle of the month I had a couple of third places in invitation two mile events; one just under nine minutes, and the other just over. I was still doing very modest training for me, but at the end of the month I went to Wales to run in another Bernard Baldwin special; the Wattstown Road Race. Not an easy course in the valleys, but I won in 21:45 for the four miles. Another fastest time in the Ealing CC Relays, with 13:04, and some Chiltern League cross-country wins followed, but my lack of training over the past few months was taking its toll, and proof of that, if I needed it, was my usual trip to Mountain Ash for the Nos Galan race. No win this time and not even a high place; just a miserable thirteenth. The race was won by Eddie Strong, and John Merriman was the Mystery Man.

What would 1962 bring in terms of success or otherwise in my running career? The first six days in January I did a total of forty-eight miles, double what I had been doing in a week for the previous few months, and the final day of that week, the Saturday, I won the Berkshire Cross-Country title again in 43:43 for 7.5 miles. My training was edging up again, and the following week I won a five club race against some good opposition, but in the Inter Counties a week later I only finished sixty-sixth; probably the result of upping the training after doing very little.

I immediately took my training back to something like my usual winter level, and ran between ninety and 100 miles over the next three weeks. This included good wins in three cross-country races, and in the fourth week it was the Southern Counties again. I eased off the training and finished thirteenth, which according to my running notes, I had run well. It was a ten mile course on this occasion, and I recorded 50:59, so I suppose it wasn't bad.

A week later I won the Berks, Bucks and Oxon Championship, and followed this up with my annual run in the Thames Valley Road Relay. For once I did not set the fastest time, but I did a respectable 20:35 for second fastest time. It was then back on the track for sharpening up, although I did have a couple more cross-country races to end the winter season. Then I had the usual round of road relays, including Watford, Leyton to Southend and Uxbridge.

On Wednesday 30th May, I was involved with something that I did not realise at the time was going to set me on a path for the future. Along with others, I helped to set up the first of a series of Gala Nights of Sport in Reading. They were sponsored and promoted by the *Reading Chronicle* who I wrote for at the time. The idea behind the Gala Night was to bring top sport to Reading, and it was to be a combination of cycling, athletics and football. The star of that first 'Night of Sport' was former world mile record holder, Derek Ibbotson, who ran the mile. He had a go at running the first four minute mile in Reading, but the opposition was too far away to help him, but he stormed home in 4:4.6. The two mile race was won by Derek Haith (Thames Valley Harriers) in 8:52.6, from Mel Batty (Thurrock) and Martin Hyman (Portsmouth). I took part and just avoided last place. The programme for the evening was quite simple, with a selection of athletic races and cycling events, and a five-a-side football match. This match between Reading and Aldershot was won by the away team, who scored four to Reading's three goals. One of Reading's goals came from Maurice Evans, later manager of the club.

I remember arriving at Palmer Park in Reading, the venue for the event, about two hours before the start and there were already queues at the gate to the stadium. The total number who attended that night was around 5,000. They packed into the small stadium, and all but a few hundred were standing around the outside of the cycling track. It was an instant success and was to be repeated for a number of years.

If 1961 had not been a good year for me, 1962 was a disastrous one. I won a few club races, and had one or two wins in invitation events, but nothing earth shattering.

In October I went to Wales and ran the Gilwern Harriers Road Race. I could only manage fourth place, one minute behind the winner T. Edmunds from the home team. I had to wait until November for a reasonable time in a race, and that was close to home at Bracknell, where I finished second to Martin Hyman with 50:40 for the ten mile road race. In December I ran the famous Hogs Back race in Surrey, and recorded 46:50 for fifteenth place in the fifth running of the nine plus mile race. Looking back at the results of that race is like looking at a directory of British distance runners; they were all there.

I revisited the Nos Galan races, and finished fourth in the one mile, and eleventh in the four miles; an improvement on the previous year. This was one of those winters when it was a difficult journey to the event. There was very heavy snow, and as well as digging ourselves out from snowdrifts on the way, when we approached Mountain Ash we took a wrong turning, went down a terraced road, got stuck at the bottom and could not get out onto the main road again. We managed to get help from the police and they took us onto the races, leaving my car to be collected, hopefully, the next day.

In January 1963 the Inter County Cross-Country Championship was held at Emmer Green, Reading. The strange thing about this race was that there did not appear to be a county championship to select the team; presumably the county race could not take place because of the very heavy snow. The winner of the Inter County race, that was run in very heavy snow and very cold conditions, was Tim Johnston (Cambridge), with Gerry North second and Basil Heatley third. The first Berkshire runner was Don Stevens (Reading AC), who ran one of the best races of his career and finished in the high position of twelfth. The press reports at the time kindly said that Stan Eldon failed to make the first twenty places — in fact I was ninety-fourth.

I believe the reason there had been no country race, was due to the very heavy snow that was on the ground from Christmas to late March. Training during the rest of the year was only at the level of twenty to fifty miles.

I ran in the Inter County twenty mile race at Victoria Park, London, for Berkshire, but after reaching twelve miles in sixty-five minutes, I eventually dropped out at seventeen miles.

My first marathon was on 15th June 1963, when I ran the Poly Windsor to Chiswick Marathon. It was in the middle of the track season, and I was really training for track races with average mileage of only about forty miles a week. I had always wanted to run the marathon, and I remember lining up in Windsor Castle with great anticipation. I was in nineteenth place at ten miles with 55:55, and twenty-sixth at fifteen miles in 84:51, and I reached the twenty mile mark in just 1:59. I was quite pleased with the result considering my lack of mileage training, and ran into the finish at the Kinnaird Stadium in Chiswick in 2:47:32 in fifty-fifth place. Oh how I would settle for running that time today. The race was won by American Buddy Edelen in 2:14:48, a world best at that time. A whole four minutes behind him, in second place, was "Mr Marathon" Ron Hill (Bolton United Harriers), and a further four minutes back, in sixth place, was another running legend from the same club, Jackie Haslam.

Although my greatest achievements were winning that cross-country championship against Alain Mimoun, and also the record runs on the track, I think that my real enjoyment came from road racing. The road race season used to come as a natural break between cross-country and track in April, and the reverse at the end of the season between track and cross-country. As my track running diminished, running on the road became more important to me.

By 1963 I was more and more involved in business, but still did a little running. I ran in the Reading Borough Police ten mile in August, and managed to get eighth place in 51:47. The race was won by the Cooke brothers from Portsmouth, and the winning time was 50:30.

In the same month I ran in the AAA Marathon at Coventry. I was in fourth place at five miles in 26:19, same position at ten miles in 53:47, but I was in a bad way by fifteen miles, reached in 83:52, having dropped to thirteenth place. I then did something that I did not do very often, I dropped out as I had in the Inter County twenty mile earlier. I was suffering from the lack of mileage. The winner was Brian Kilby (Coventry Godiva) in 2:16:45, and Basil Heatley from the same club was second in 2:19:56.

Later I ran in the second Bracknell ten mile, but it was no repeat of the previous year, as this time I was only twenty-fifth in 52:28.

In November I took a team of five from Windsor Slough and Eton AC to compete in the Le Soir cross-country races in Belgium. This trip was memorable, not for the running, but for what happened that weekend on the wider stage. We arrived in our hotel on the Friday afternoon and I met an American runner, Buddy Edelen, who had been living in the UK and had won the Polytechnic Marathon in 1963. He was in great distress, and when I enquired what was the matter, he told me about the assassination of President John F. Kennedy. The Windsor and Eton team won the team race for non-Belgium teams. I had run in the main international event and finished twenty-seventh, but this was added to our other team runners in the mass event, where Peter Yates was fourth, Robert Graham nineteenth, Dave Bignal fifty-fourth and Ron Smith 272nd. On Monday we caught our ferry back to England. It was a very rough crossing and there were not many people on board. Many of the team were sick, but there was a television room on the ship and we watched the funeral of Kennedy for the whole journey home.

The next step was to find a more permanent home for Stan Eldon Sports, but to be able to afford this it meant selling our little house in Plough Lane, Wokingham. This gave me my first insight into estate agents and the property world. The house was put up for sale at £2,150 and several people came to view. An offer was received at the asking price and then a slightly better offer came in, the only trouble was they were from a husband and wife who were retiring, and both liked the property but had not told the other what they were doing, and had come through two different agents and the estate agents certainly did not tell them. In the end a compromise was reached with the purchasers agreeing to pay more to us, and the agents agreeing to split a commission.

The search for property took us to Caversham on the north side of the Thames at Reading, where we found a small terraced shop, with a reasonable flat over and a small back yard. The rent was £500 per year, so we took it on and moved in March 1962. It had been a cold winter and the snow was still on the ground from Christmas but the shop had to be fitted and we had hungry young mouths to feed.

In those days sports shops sold everything, and so we were into fishing tackle as well as football kits, boots, tennis rackets, running shoes, hockey sticks and anything else that was needed by the local sporting populous. The shop was not really big enough to carry the wide range, and it rapidly extended into the downstairs kitchen and hallway, with the family totally contained upstairs and on the first and second floors.

The business grew, and I went out selling to schools and football clubs, as well as visiting local running tracks, including Windsor and Bracknell, selling running spikes and clothing; frequently on the 'never, never'; in other words I gave my customers credit and took a few shillings a week off them.

Life was not easy, and living above the premises you never knew when someone was going to call on our services, either in person or on the telephone. I remember late one Friday night, having a call from a well-known athlete who wanted a pair of shoes to run in on the Saturday, and on a Sunday morning, a visit from a major at Arborfield Garrison who was desperate for medals for a sporting event at the garrison that day. We really were 'Open All Hours'.

About a year after opening, it was decided we should become a limited company, and so Limited was added to the Stan Eldon Sports name.

I wanted to expand into my home town of Windsor, and all I could afford there was a shop that was due for demolition in Oxford Road in the town. It was only about 200 yards off the main street and did have parking close by, so it was a good place to start, and the local council only charged me a small rent of £28 3s. 4d. per month (£338 per annum). The shop was pretty dilapidated and mice, if not worse, were in evidence, but we made the best of it, and after a couple of weeks customers started to appear.

After a short while, I was able to find another shop nearer to the centre of shopping in Peascod Street, Windsor. It had been a well-known bakers, Dennys, in the town, but had been empty for some time. This did not stop people walking in the shop to buy a loaf of bread, and even walking up to the counter surrounded by fishing tackle, sports shoes and clothing, and only realising their mistake as they asked the question. The shop was also only three hundred yards from Windsor's long-established sports shop E. J. Harding.

As we outgrew our shop, another door opened. A new shopping centre was being built in Caversham with a mixture of shops. I dived in quickly and got one of the largest units, but because someone had just beaten me to first choice, I had a downstairs unit of 1,600 square feet, but the upstairs above this unit had been let, so we had to take the upstairs of the next-door unit which was only about 800 square feet. We set about designing a modern open-plan sports shop. Instead of everything being pushed behind counters, as with the traditional shops at that time, we opened everything up and had displays all along the sides and in the middle of the store.

Two big names from football joined the Stan Eldon team. We were expanding and I needed staff, and the advertising brought two top ex-footballers to work for me. One was Bobby Ayre, who had played for Charlton and been an England 'B' international player. As well as being a good footballer, he was also a very good golfer with a handicap of one or scratch. The other was Sylvan Anderton, who had played for Chelsea under Tommy Docherty, and like Bobby had finished his playing career with Reading.

In 1968 we moved into the new premises with what was then a large rent. In the June my family had grown by one more, when daughter Joanna Elizabeth was born at 26 St Peter's Hill. This brought my tally to four, and three had been born in Olympic years. No wonder I never made it to that big event in an athlete's life.

In 1969 someone walked into the shop and made me an offer I couldn't refuse. The man was Derek Baylis, a local grocer who had himself created a unique business, and had sold out a short while before for around £1 million. He was impressed with my modern shop and concept, and he offered to put £10,000 cash into the business for a minor share. There was no formal agreement and he handed me a cheque for that amount within days.

He had some ideas for the business, and wanted to introduce some of his supermarket techniques into the sports trade. This included trading with Green Shield Stamps whose redemption shop was next door to our sports shop.

Very rapidly he decided we should expand, and he asked me for ideas, so at Easter 1969 we went off in his Rolls-Royce to Windsor and called on a long-established sports shop, E. J. Harding. We walked into the shop, spoke to the manager and found out that Mr Harding was at home and unwell. A quick phone call and off we went to his home at St Leonards Hill in Windsor, where he was in bed. A quick conversation, and Derek had done the deal with Harding. He would not return to the shop and we could take over at once, which we did. A few days and the stock was assessed and everything else was tidied up.

It was an interesting acquisition. The shop was very old-fashioned, and some of the stock had been there for twenty years or more. The only way up to the stockroom was up a ladder and through a small gap into the roof, where out of season sports equipment was stored. This included cricket bats and pads, as well as a good stock of Hornby railway stock. Some of the cricket pads had been there so long they were wrapped in brown paper, which along with the pads was disintegrating into dust. The cricket bats also told their own story. There was a stock of about forty, and when the sales rep from one of the leading manufacturers came around for his order, he told me that Mr Harding had always ordered the same quantity of bats; around ten, each year; we concluded that he did not sell many cricket bats. The previous proprietor did not believe in reducing the price of anything to shift it, and would rather it wasted away in the upstairs loft. All that changed when we took over, and I had to change the attitude of the manager who I took back after the takeover.

We never suffered too much from break-ins at any of our shops, but on one occasion I did get a phone call about 1 a.m. in the morning at home in Caversham, to say the window had been smashed and some stock grabbed from our shop in Peascod Street in Windsor. The police had telephoned and wanted me to attend at once, but when I arrived at the shop barely twenty minutes later, they wanted to know how I had got there so fast. It was not a serious theft and the felon was quickly apprehended. The only thing missing from the shop window were a couple of sheath knives, and they had obviously been grabbed by the blades because there was a trail of blood. It did not take Mr Plod long to realise that it was probably a soldier from Victoria Barracks, not more than a few hundred yards from the shop. A quick trip to the barracks and the offender, with his hand still dripping with blood, was in custody.

The relationship with my sleeping partner Derek Baylis was rather strange, and was not without its problems. He did literally write a cheque and give it to me without any formalities being agreed or signed. We did move over to his London accountants and they gave useful advice. Using his muscle, D.B. and myself went off to see the local Barclays Bank manager, and an overdraft of £20,000 was agreed so as to finance the purchase of Hardings in Windsor. That was OK with me and the bank, until after only a few weeks, D.B. decided that he could then take back his £10,000. Once the bank found out they were not happy, and it affected our relationship from then on.

Derek Baylis kept in touch and very occasionally appeared in the shop. These appearances and any contact at all gradually disappeared, and after about six years he decided he wanted to be released from his commitment to the bank, where he was still securing the overdraft. This was a very difficult period, and it got more than a little heated, with the bank refusing to release him and the threat of liquidation hanging over our heads. I was determined not to be beaten, and I consulted with an acquaintance, who was himself a successful businessman and who was in the Rotary Club I had fairly recently joined. With his help I was able to secure an accountant who was an expert in liquidations and the like. The whole attitude changed very quickly, and both the bank and the Baylis family came to heel. The bank accepted a payoff of the overdraft, but not the full sum from Baylis, and I moved to Lloyds Bank. I learned a lot about banks and banking from that incident.

In 1970 I advertised for a shop manager for Windsor, and was amazed when I received an application from my older half-brother Bernard, who had worked for the Borough Council since leaving school and was now in his mid-forties. I thought he was a permanent local authority mandarin. He insisted I treated him like every other applicant, but he did get the job and stayed with me until he eventually bought the Windsor branch from me. Most of the time the shop could manage with one full-time manager and some part-time staff for busy times like Saturday. We did advertise for a full-time school leaver on one occasion, and I interviewed several young applicants before selecting what appeared to be a bright young lad who was very keen. We had a semi-automatic till that could do some calculations, and the lad soon picked up how to use it, until after a few days someone bought twelve football studs at 3p each. He got confused because the till would not do such a simple calculation for small items. The adult with him in the shop at the time explained that you just did that in your head. Then the truth was out, he could not muliply the simplest sums or do any other adding up. We had a chat and he explained his problem, which had not come out in either his job interview or in the report from his school. We had to let him go and it was a lesson for me; I was always a lot more careful when appointing staff after that.

Over the years this shop had some interesting customers, including Michael Parkinson, Mary and their two sons, who were regular visitors for cricket and sports equipment. They lived in Windsor at that time, just a few hundred yards from the shop. I served them personally on many occasions, but one personality I missed, who was served by my brother when he was later managing the shop, was Joan Collins, she called in and bought a tennis racket for her daughter. There was another customer who sent someone to the shop, especially around the time of Royal Ascot each year. Her Majesty ordered tennis balls for her guests attending and being entertained at the Castle for the special week. Our Reading shop did not miss out on personalities, and George Cole and his wife, who lived at Henley, were regular shoppers; as was cartoonist "Mac" and his first wife. At the Caversham shop, I got involved in some bartering with a rep for a record company who used to pay me regular visits and bring me the latest hit records. The arrangement was more for his benefit than mine, and we used to exchange his records for squash rackets and other sporting clothing and equipment.

In 1964 my track running had continued to decline in quality, although I still ran regularly for Windsor, Slough and Eton and for my second claim club Reading AC. In April I did run the Finchley 20 again, and although I was nowhere as fit as when I had run the race the first time, I did set off with the intention of having a serious run. I ran the first lap of five miles in twenty-six minutes, but this was one minute behind the race leader and eventual winner Mel Batty. I went through ten miles in 52:13, and fifteen miles in 80:42, before finishing in 1:57:58. I was thirty-seventh and it did earn me a First-Class Diploma. In fact 1:58 was the cut-off point for these awards, so I was the last in the list.

By now Windsor had quite a good team of road runners, and I lined up again for the Poly Marathon in June. I had learned a lot from the previous year, and finished much higher up the field in thirty-fourth place with 2:34:04.

My family was growing, and on 18th October 1964 our third child was born, Neil William, and this time I was not off on my travels as with the earlier births.

At the end of 1964 I was back at Nos Galan, but this time as the Mystery Runner, but I did join in the race after I had sent the runners on their way and finished thirty-ninth in 20:41.

By 1965 I was really back to being a club runner with no international ambitions, but in some ways it was a successful year, as our club road and cross-country team did have some successes. My training had really dropped off, as I was busy trying to run my business and bring up our young family, which was now three. My training mileage was only thirty to forty miles a week and sometimes very much less, with just a couple of weeks in the first half of the year when I touched seventy miles.

In the thirteenth running of the Maidenhead 10, which was won by Gerry North in 51:37, I only finished thirteenth in 54:38, but the Windsor team easily won the team race; in fact the 'B' team won and the 'A' team were second. The teams were Peter Yates third, Roger Collins ninth and Robert Graham eleventh, making up the 'B' team, and the 'A' team was D. Collins sixth, Eldon thirteenth and Bernie Allen fifteenth.

I ran the Finchley twenty mile race again, and surprisingly improved on my performance of the previous year, by finishing nineteenth in 1:53.59.

The season's top cross-country races were the Southern at Brighton and the National at Parliament Hill, but I did not feature in the results.

I again ran in the Poly Marathon, and with the experience of the two previous years, I ran a good race. I reached twenty miles in just about two hours, which was slower than the previous races, but I managed to finish twenty-eighth in 2:36:31.

Riding on the back of this modest success, I decided to go to Holland in August to run the International Marathon at Enschede. I travelled alone by train and it was a very pleasant journey. I say I travelled alone, that was the intention, but at dinner on the train in the evening I was invited to join an elderly lady at her table and we found plenty to talk about. The company was good for me as it helped me to stay relaxed and it was a bit like being on the Orient Express.

As we lined up for the tenth running of this international marathon, I felt quite confident I could crack two hours thirty minutes for the first time. The race started in the stadium at Enschede with a couple of laps around the track. This was perhaps my undoing, as I could never resist running fast on the track. I was in the leading group as we left the stadium for the flat and fast out and back course of 26.2 miles. I was running well and had been maintaining a place in the first three or four. I started to slow slightly before the point where the race turned back, but at the halfway stage I was in seventh place with a time of 74:14. I was in a group of four and we were just two minutes behind the leader Vandendriesse of Belgium. Those ahead of me included a German, two Czechs, two Dutch, and I was in fact the leading English runner. It was a warm day and that was never good for me, but I was still OK at twenty-five km, which I went through in 87:22 and still in the same position. Within the next five km I was in trouble; it hit me suddenly. I had seen other runners, quite good runners, taking a short walk, and I could not understand why. It was unusual to see runners in leading places having to walk, but it caught up with me, and I remember one runner, who I had flashed by a few kilometres back when he was going though a bad patch, suddenly doing the same to me. I did walk quite a bit and never really got going again, and could not wait for the stadium to come in view. I finished in sixty-sixth place with 3:9:43. There was an official England team competing, and they won the team race with 7:41:43. Interesting to note that the team result was worked on time, something which I thought did not happen until the switching to computers for results in the 1980s. The first English runner was Ron Franklin (Thames Valley Harriers), in seventh place with 2:31:58, someone I knew well as he had the largest stock of running shoes outside of a sports shop; at times he would have over forty pairs of shoes in use. Just one place behind was G. Dickson in 2:33:57. The third member of the team was G. Winchester who finished in 2:35:48. The race was won by the Belgian who had led at halfway with a time of 2:21:16, and he was over five minutes ahead of his nearest rival V. Chudomel of Czechoslovakia. There were some interesting names from England running in the race. There were runners from the Metropolitan Police, whom had I run against frequently in my days with the police. Also running was Stan Jones (Polytechnic Harriers). He had finished in seventeenth place in the 1948 Olympic Marathon, and on this occasion finished eighty-eighth in 3:26:52. Stan, along with Len Runyard, the Windsor secretary, were the two people who had helped me through my running career.

My family were growing, and we had to look for something larger than our flat above the shop. Having no money to speak of, I had to get a mortgage if I was to buy a property. As we thought my mother-in-law was going to have to live with us, I approached Reading Borough Council for a mortgage, and they agreed they would lend me £4,000 for a suitable property. One of the very first houses we looked at, was an Edwardian five-bedroomed semidetached house in a very good position; not far from the shop at St Peters Hill in Caversham. It was a large house; over 2,500 square feet, and stood on a plot of land 440 feet long and about 40 feet in width, but it needed a lot of work on it, as it had not seen any decoration since before the war. I made an offer to the owners, the Millward Shoe family, of £4,250 which was below the asking price of around £5,000. They did not agree, but did accept an increased offer of £4,500.

Huge cracks started to appear in my training in the next year, 1966; although I did have some weeks of consistent decent training, there were large patches when I could not find the time to run. I occasionally had a race on the road, country or track, but nothing like my schedules of the past. When I did find time for a run I usually made it a long one, and this usually fitted in with some other activity like a family visit to see friends and family in Windsor. On one of these runs I ran from Twyford to Windsor, about thirteen miles in seventy-two minutes, and on another run I clocked eighty-seven minutes for about fifteen miles. That run was on the Sunday, and on the Wednesday I ran back from Windsor, a measured distance of nineteen miles in 1:50, but my training notes say it was run into the wind all the way, so it was not a bad run. This was a fairly regular feature during March and April in this year, as I did the same on the next three Wednesdays; all of these were runs from Windsor, and the first of these I ran in 1:42, the second 1:47 and the last in 1:41 (with a following wind).

On the 23rd April I again ran in the Finchley 20, but after passing five miles in 25:50, and ten miles in 52:50, I dropped out at fifteen miles. I must have taken a little while to recover from this, as training fell away to very little, although I did have another run from Windsor, which took 1:43 for the nineteen miles again.

After a couple of modest track races, I ran in the Portsmouth to Chichester 16.5 mile race, and the Inter County twenty mile, which took me 1:58.

This was followed by another run in the Poly Marathon, but this time I dropped out at twenty-two miles, having gone through the ten mile mark in fifty-seven minutes.

As that year progressed my training disappeared, and by the 1st October even my training notes and diary stopped. I was only thirty but I was now busy with other things.

Looking back on my 'life on the run' between 1957 and 1962, it was strange that I never had the opportunity to run my favourite distance on the track, the 5,000 metres, where I had been ranked in the top three in the world, in a major international championship. I ran in international races for GB at the distance but never in the Olympics, European or Commonwealth Games (Empire Games in those days). I always got pushed into the longer 10,000 metres where I was never as highly placed in world rankings. A classic example of this was my selection for the six miles and not the three miles at the Empire Games in 1958. But I suppose that was my fault, as having been selected for the three miles, I broke the British six mile record and that immediately got me put into the six miles.

My greatest victory was the win over Alain Mimoun in the International Cross-Country, and I had other good wins over the country, but in many ways I was not a good cross-country runner. I could not fly over muddy fields like Gerry North in his prime. My win at Cardiff over Mimoun was on a flat, fast, frozen surface which turned the race into more of a road race than cross-country (if you ignored the fences).

I liked track running, and the challenge it presented, especially at 5,000 metres, but my favourite event was road running, where I was able to excel and break records even after my other performances had started to decline. Maybe I should have stuck with my early ambition from 1948, and taken up the marathon seriously.

Regrets, I have a few. Not being selected for the 1960 Rome Olympics has to be one, but perhaps the missed opportunities for a world record were more important. The lesson I learned, and would pass on to any athlete today, is never let an opportunity pass you by. There were three races in my career, where I was in such good form that I should have picked up a world record at three miles, six miles or 5,000 metres, but on each occasion I won races so easily and probably did not push myself to the limit which would have given me those records. Always grab the opportunity when it comes, and do not leave it for another day, because that other day may never come. I suppose that applies to everything in life.

In those days of the late 1950s and early 60s there were no specialist road running shoes. There were heavy trainers, like the Adidas Rom, but the racing shoe for me, and for many others, was a pair of Woolworth's plimsolls; cost about four shillings and sixpence, or 22.5p. They were normally brown, and I used to put black polish on them, partly I think to smarten them up and partly to make them slightly waterproof. I think this failed on both counts, but as racing shoes they were successful as they were lighter than trainers. There was no heavy padding, just a thin runner sole, but they never gave me any injuries despite running up to 100 miles a week.

In June 1964 I lined up at Windsor Castle again for the Poly Marathon and this time I was thirty-fourth in 2:34:04.

Later in that year, my old training and racing partner Bruce Tulloh, went out to Japan for the Tokyo Olympics. While he was there he was given a pair of revolutionary shoes called Tiger Marups; a superb lightweight shoe with a special thin sole, but with some cushioning and light leather uppers. When he met the Onitsuka Company (now Asics) who made the shoes, he told them he had a friend who was big in the sports business in the UK. He was referring to me with a small shop on the outskirts of Reading. He brought the shoe back and I was very impressed, as I had never seen anything like it before. It was very light and comfortable, and was completely different to anything I had seen before. I wrote to Japan and introduced myself, and very quickly I had a response offering me the sole UK rights to the shoes and their other products. I had to set about finding out how to import the shoes, and this was not easy as there were no agencies around in those days like now, and the banks did not know very much either. Somehow I got the information I needed, and the first shoes were ordered.

When they arrived, runners were queuing up to buy them at sixty-five shillings a pair. These first shoes were called a Marup, but others followed including a cheaper canvas version of the Marup, and Marion came up with the name Cub, Tiger Cub, for the cheapest shoes in the range, and this sold for just twenty-nine shillings and sixpence.

To help finance the new venture I formed a new company, Stan Eldon Wholesale Limited, with an old school friend John Hatton, who lived in Windsor and worked in financial services. We rented a warehouse under the railway arches in Windsor, the scene of many "Carry On" films, and that was our base for the importing and distribution of the new Tiger shoes and other products.

We invited the Onitsuka Company over for discussions about expanding the business, and Mr Onitsuka himself came along with the finance director

Mr Kitami. We hired a limousine and collected them from Heathrow, and took them to lunch at Skindles Hotel, then a very up-market restaurant on the Thames at Maidenhead. In the car on the way to Maidenhead, the conversation somehow got around to the war. Colonel Onitsuka had served in Burma and by chance so had our chauffeur. As the conversation progressed I thought 'Oh dear this will blow it' especially when the two decided they had been exactly in the same war zone at the same time, and could have fought against each other. On the contrary, when we arrived at the hotel they were getting on so well we had to take the chauffeur with us into lunch. The business discussions with the company were very interesting, as they used an abacus for their financial calculations. The Japanese were not using electronic calculators in the early 1960s.

About this stage in my business life I was approached by Mr North from the Kit Kat Cafe at Blackpool, to see if I would employ his son Gerry. Yes, it was my old running colleague from Army days Gerry North. His dad gave me £500 towards the business so that I could afford to take Gerry on. Gerry worked on selling the Tiger shoes to shops and individuals for some time, before leaving me to start up his own company, where he carried on selling the same products.

We were then responsible for another new product. I had seen something called track pants, lightweight cotton tracksuit-type bottoms; baggy but light, and with the idea of the ski pants that Pirie had given me. I set about redesigning them, and had a large quantity made up in Hong Kong. These were a slimmer fit, and I called them Tracksters. They were a great success as they sold for just under £1. I never did register them and another runner, Mr Marathon himself, Ron Hill, made them a little more sophisticated and has sold them ever since. My loss his gain.

I did not get the opportunity to take advantage of either the imported Tracksters or the great Tiger shoes, as a few years after I started importing, the Wilson Government introduced an import restriction which required the putting up of half the value of the imports in cash in this country, as well as funding the letters of credit to pay for the goods in Japan. It was crippling for small businesses like mine, and I had to get out of the wholesale/import business quickly. I did and the retail business survived.

Our business was all about innovation, and we were first in the market place, not just with special products like the Tiger shoes and Tracksters. We got involved with Fashion Shows, which we did on a regular basis, often to support charities, these were good fun and I enjoyed my behind the scenes job of helping the attractive models disrobe and prepare for their next catwalk appearance; the trouble was it all happened so quickly, and there was never enough time to take in the beautiful scenery. The girls were all local and came from a local agency, and their performances were always very professional. We started up 'Football and Cricket' evenings, and at these we would show the latest clothing, footwear and equipment to invited people from the particular sport. On the football side we often had the help of West Ham goalkeeper Phil Parkes at the football shows, and at one of our cricket evenings we had almost the whole Hampshire County Cricket Club team, along with some very special cricket bats we had borrowed from the bat manufacturers, like a bat used by the Edward VIII when Prince of Wales, and another used by the great Jack Hobbs. They were very successful evenings and helped us to build up a strong customer base with the local sports clubs.

I spent a lot of money on advertising, especially with the *Reading Evening Post,* who had a very persuasive salesman, John Madejski, the multimillionaire owner and chairman of Reading Football Club. This was before he had started his Auto Trader empire that brought him the great wealth.

The birth of all my children was planned, that is up to 1971, when on 29th June, Alexandra Michelle came along. She was our fifth and final child, and I missed her birth by a few minutes. As it was Marion's fifth she had to go to hospital for the birth, and I was at home looking after the family and waiting for news. On the day she was born I went to bed at about 11 p.m. and tried to sleep, but the phone rang and it was the Royal Berks. Marion had just gone down to have our baby. I drove across Reading at lightning speed and arrived at the Royal Berkshire Hospital maternity unit, which was in semi-darkness and appeared to be almost shut down for the night. I found a gown and mask and made my way through to the delivery room just after the birth, with wife and baby still on the trolley. All was well, and after a short stay it was home to catch up on sleep, get the children off to school next morning, and open up the shop. I could not complain, because on previous occasions prior to our other children being born, Marion had worked up to the day of birth, sometimes in the shop and on one occasion she was paperhanging and decorating up to a couple of hours before going into labour. The birth of our fifth child changed our life. Up to that time we had never had a television in our home, but after this latest addition to the family we added a TV and had no more children!

Chapter Twelve

176 Miles for a Joke (and for Charity)

I ran the first of my long charity runs in 1973, when the Variety Club of Great Britain invited me to walk or run from Reading to the Sportsman Club in Tottenham Court Road, London. Various sports personalities took part, and were to travel to London by different methods. These included Freddie Trueman who travelled from York by stagecoach, and then rode on a horse from Hyde Park to the Grosvenor House; Jimmy Savile who walked into the final destination from Broadmoor Hospital in Berkshire; Jimmy Hill walked from Haringey; Stanley Mortenson (footballer) walked part of the way from Blackpool accompanied by the Mayor of Blackpool and 2.5 cwt of Blackpool rock. There were boxers, a former Miss World, and many others from different walks of life, and all were sponsored for a minimum of £1,000. The total raised from the walk was over £89,000. The lunch was sponsored by Sir Jack Cohen, from Tesco; there were around 500 present and the bill was £5,000. The special guest was HRH Duke of Edinburgh.

My run started from the *Evening Post* offices in Reading, and the newspaper were my main sponsor along with Racal. I ran the first stage of twenty miles to Windsor in two hours. I ran to the castle and arrived in time to walk out from there ahead of the band of the Coldstream Guards, who had been changing the guard. A rare privilege which is not normally allowed. After the band turned off to head back to barracks, I turned right out of the castle and started to run and walk again down the hill and through Datchet for the final twenty-five plus miles to the finish at the Sportsman Club in Tottenham Court Road, where I was met by Eric Morley, the Chief Barker of the Variety Club, and footballer Jimmy Hill, at about four o'clock in the afternoon.

The next day we all attended a Variety Club Dinner at the Grosvenor House in the presence of the Duke of Edinburgh. It gave me my first insight into large fund raising, when Billy Butlin and Fred Pontin were trying to outbid each other for a very large stick of Blackpool Rock. Their bids went up to thousands of pounds, and after one of them had secured it, they immediately put it back to raise even more money.

There was a long hot, very hot, summer in 1976, and to keep the family cool and amused I erected a large above-ground swimming pool in the garden at St Peter's Hill. It was well used that summer, as I was very busy with fashion shows and other promotional activities for the business. It was great to get home at midnight and dive into the pool for a swim and cool off.

In 1977 I helped to set up a Superstars Competition in Reading, with the help of Robin Sharp, a local school teacher and tennis coach. The name we used for the competition was Skillmaster, as Superstars was a registered name used by the televised competition. The event was staged each summer for a number of years, and some of the best sporting talent from within the Borough of Reading took part. The first event was staged in 1977, as part of the Reading Silver Jubilee celebrations, and the funds raised by the event went to the Queen's Silver Jubilee Appeal Fund, which earned me a certificate from that fund. The competition was organised by the Reading and District Sports Council and my company, Stan Eldon Sports, who were also the sponsors. The competitors had to compete in a wide range of sporting activities, so that talent in one sport would not necessarily be an advantage. The major events were swimming, running, cycling, archery, goal scoring, and a number of special events to test the skill, as well as the physical ability of the competitor.

Later, one of the regular participants, Alan Taylor, a professional footballer with Reading, wanted to take up athletics where he had shown more than a little talent. Because he was a professional I fought his case with the athletic authorities, so that he could take part in the then amateur sport of athletics. He got the permission that was required and joined Reading AC, and I became his coach. His best event was the 880 yards where he improved very rapidly and quickly got down to a respectable 1:55. He learned fast and was a very good prospect. He had sprinting skills as well, and could kick from 300 yards before the finish, and leave any field behind him. I went to his wedding and he and Shirley were a very happy couple, but tragically within months he was in a car crash with another ex-Skillmaster competitor at Arborfield near Reading. He was killed and his colleague was badly injured, losing a foot. I don't think any other sad event has had a greater impact on me, and I suppose that is why I have never got directly involved with coaching a talented athlete again.

In the same year I was carrying out a speaking engagement in Reading, at the lunch of the Federation of Master Builders. Something always triggers the memory about events, and my memory of this occasion is very clear. I was just reaching the end of my talk, and a buzz went around the room. I didn't think it was anything I had said that caused such a stir. No it was the news that Harold Wilson had resigned as Prime Minister which had come as a complete shock, but I think it was welcomed by my audience of builders and developers. Later in his retirement I was to meet

Lord Wilson when he attended the opening of a community centre near my home in Caversham.

In November 1977 I received a copy of *Punch* magazine from an old school friend, David Stone, who lived in Switzerland. He sent it to me as there was a story about the police in it, and the photo used was one of me in my days on the beat. Solicitors had just started to advertise their services, and it was a comical skit on what the public could expect from other professionals by way of advertising their services. These included nurses, judges, clergy and the police. I wrote to the editor of *Punch* and received a reply which effectively said they thought they were using an old library picture of a policeman who was a long time dead!

After a period away from running, I had started back having a weekly run in the early 1970s. In 1975, while working in one of my shops at Tilehurst, Reading, I had a visit from a Tony Holden who was a DJ on the new commercial radio station for the Thames Valley, Radio 210. He was running a sports show on every Monday evening, and wanted someone to talk about sport, and so he had found his way to me. Just before the Easter weekend in 1976, we had a chat on air about the new jogging craze that was big in the States, and almost as a joke we challenged Reading people to turn up in Prospect Park, Reading, across the road from the radio station for a run around the park on the Tuesday after that Easter Monday. The radio station promised everyone a T-shirt who turned up.

On that Tuesday evening I went along to the park and Tony Holden also turned out. We thought that we might be the only people there, but as the appointed time of 7 p.m. approached, we were amazed to have a couple of hundred people there in their plimsolls and training shoes ready for a run. Needless to say the supply of T-shirts did not last long, and we had to promise to get more for the following week. The group kept going for the rest of that year, and some decided to meet on a regular basis; and that was how the Reading Joggers was born. After their running together they decided to become a club, and about one year later they were formed into the Reading Joggers, and that club is still alive and kicking today.

I continued to work on 210 every Monday night until they discontinued the programme. It was great fun and I enjoyed taking along guests and interviewing them about their sporting activities. My broadcasting days were not over even then, as when the half marathon was up and running, I was always on the air talking about the event and those taking part. In many ways this radio station was to be one of the keenest supporters of the event in coming years.

In May of the same year I was invited back to Windsor for the opening of the new track. The local council had been persuaded to finally put down a quality all-weather running surface to replace the grass track on the Vansittart Recreation Ground, where I had run many races and carried out much of my early training with the Windsor club. I ran a ceremonious single lap of the track before it was officially opened by the then Mayor of the Royal Borough, Kit Aston (later Sir Kit Aston). The athletic match was won by Southampton AC from the home team, with Surrey Beagles third, followed by Newbury, Reading and Maidenhead.

The 1970s were a busy time, with the family growing up and the business growing as well. It was difficult to find time for holidays, so I bought a new large on-site caravan at Wimborne in Dorset. Most weekends during the summer I would dash away from the shop at 5.30 p.m. sharp, and by about six o'clock everything, including the kids, were bundled into the car and it was off to the caravan. It gave us a break, if it was a very hectic and short break from the working week. We would arrive on Saturday evening around 8 p.m., and would leave about the same time or earlier on Sunday evening, and very occasionally very early on Monday morning. Then it was back to school for the family and back to the shops for me until the next Saturday evening.

Through the Joggers a number of Fun Runs were started in the area, and because of my involvement with them, I was invited by the Sports Council in 1978 to be part of a steering committee to look into forming a National Jogging Association.

That original committee was made up from a number of high-profile people who were into 'jogging' and running. They included John Disley, who later started the London Marathon, along with Chris Brasher, Harold Evans (Editor of the *Sunday Times*), Andy Etchells (the first editor of *Running Magazine*), Ted Dexter (England cricket captain and later selector), John Whetton (one of our most successful ever UK milers and 1,500 metre runners), Tom McNab (athletic coach and author of the book *Flanagan's Run*), and myself. Funding was provided by the Sports Council, and the NJA was formed and was very active for a number of years, helping to promote running for fitness and health.

I was still running my sports shops and employing quite a few of my family; my brother Bernard, his son Philip and three of my own children, Caroline, Jonathan and Neil. We had always led the way in the sports trade and I had written articles for the trade magazine. So when a computer was shown to me that could control stock through the till, I jumped at the chance and invested the £3,000 to £4,000. It was a good system and I spent nearly a year putting every item of stock, including shoelaces and football studs, onto the data base. It worked and I got hooked on computers.

But there was trouble ahead, and not of my making. The system I had was from the Finnish company, Nokia, and after we had been running with it for about a year, they came back to me and insisted that I sell the whole system back to them. I never did know the exact reason, except that it was to do with software they had used which I believe was owned by Digital, and they Nokia, only had licence to use it in Finland and not the

UK. I negotiated with Nokia and finally settled on a price around twice what the system had cost. I could possibly have got more, but the system went and it was back to pen and ink for stock control. The time and learning had not been wasted though, and stood me in good stead when I got involved with Digital, and a race results development programme using computers.

In November 1980 I took over a small shop near the centre of Reading, and opened up a branch specialising in sports footwear. It traded under the name of Sporting Feet, and was managed by my eldest son Jonathan; the shop was doing quite nicely, when in July 1981 the landlords of the property gave us notice under the lease to leave the premises as they wanted to redevelop their corner site, which included our little shop. I was going on holiday to France with the younger members of my family and left eldest daughter Caroline in charge of my shops, with the help of her brother who was a little younger. Just before we went off to France, I appointed a local commercial estate agent to handle the matter for me, and while we were away I received daily reports by phone on the state of the negotiations. I had paid just £1,750 for the short lease, and the first offer from Abbey National was just a few thousand pounds. Each day the figure went up as they wanted a quick decision, and when the figure reached £30,000 I gave instructions for my agent to accept, as I had fears they might withdraw their offer. Telex messages had to be sent to give authority for the agent and my young daughter to complete the deal. By the time I arrived home a few days later, the money was in the bank and the shop had closed and been cleared of stock. The kids had done well and the rest of the family had all had a good holiday.

Having seen the success of the Nos Galan Midnight races in Wales, I persuaded Reading Athletic Club to celebrate the dawn of their 100th year by having a race through Reading at Midnight on 31st December 1980. The race was started from Portman Road on the east of Reading at 11.50 p.m., by a club member who was current President of the English Cross-Country Union, Cyril Parr. The 100 plus runners ran through the centre of Reading to Palmer Park Stadium, where they had run for nearly all the 100 years of their existence. The winner reached the stadium just after the strike of twelve that brought in the year of 1981. At the end of that year the race was repeated, to end the celebration of 100 years of the club; one of the oldest in the country.

I did eventually have part of a world record, when I ran for the UK vets in the 100 x 1 mile relay at Crystal Palace on 29th June 1980. The total time for the 100 mile relay was 9:58:16. My contribution was on the thirty-third lap with a mile in 5:37.

A year later on 31st May 1981, we had to repeat the run as the San Diego Track Club broke the record we had set one year earlier with 9:15:44.34. Our new total time was 8:45:21, so our team had got the record back. It was great fun, and in the team were some old athletes like myself, but there were some who were the new breed of runner, those that had only taken up the sport in later life like the Managing Director of a newspaper in Chesham, Bucks, Dick Askew.

Over the years my business sponsored many sporting events in and around Reading, and one of these was a special rugby match between Reading Abbey Rugby Club, who were celebrating twenty-five years of rugby at the club in 1981, and Henley Rugby Club. Another event was a golf day at Calcot Park Golf Club in Reading, which I sponsored along with the *Reading Evening Post*.

In 1982 I was invited to take a look at the Borocourt Hospital in South Oxfordshire, with a view to persuading me to take on the position of Chairman of the League of Friends of that hospital. If I was shocked when I met poverty just off the town square of Wokingham, I was more than shocked by some of the things I saw at this special facility for those with mental problems. There was a public view of the hospital, and a view that was kept from all but the staff.

On this, my first visit, I did see the non-public side. I saw a young man, really only a boy, in a toughened glass cubicle which was totally secure. He was naked and was eating off the floor, and there were other things in that 'room' which made it disgusting. It was not the fault of staff, who frequently went in two at a time to see him and clear up the best they could. He was violent and would not keep clothes on or care for himself. I then went to another room where the light was switched on as we entered, and saw a couple of pram/cots with people laying in them. They were very seriously disabled and could not talk, see or move. Most of the time they were in the dark, as there was no point in them being in a lighted room.

They were the extreme cases, and at the other end of the disability scale were those who probably should never have been in an institution at all. They were the elderly, who in some cases had been there since the First World War or even before. They were the 'not so bright' sons and daughters of aristocratic and well-heeled families, who were disposed of by putting them into an institution.

After that first visit I did take on the chairmanship of the league, in the hope that perhaps I could make a small difference. We had a dedicated ex-hospital matron as secretary, and we worked together until her retirement. She ran the hospital shop which always made a handsome profit, and with other fund raising we were never short of money. The biggest problem was how to do things to help the patients, and at the same time not remove responsibility from the authorities for providing the necessary care and support. We provided a therapeutic pool, televisions, washing machines, decoration, seating and anything else that would improve the quality of life for those whose home was the crumbling baronial mansion, set in beautiful countryside with splendid views.

There were many rumours about the potential closure of the hospital, and then finally, in 1995, the final decision was made and the hospital closed. A sad day for many, as friends who had spent their lives there, were moved to all parts of the country. We were left with a substantial bank balance and had to wind up the charity. All the appropriate action was taken, and we were able to distribute moneys to charities with similar aims and objectives. Between £6,000 and £7,000 was passed on to six charities working with disabled people. All the tens of thousands of pounds worth of goods supplied by the 'Friends' just disappeared when the facility closed its doors.

In the latter years the hospital had a secure section, which housed violent and very disturbed people, and this was closed along with the rest, only a few years after the special facility had been built at great expense.

With all its faults, Borocourt did provide a home for many who could or would not be able to exist in the community. What has happened since has proved that the closure of these special facilities was a terrible mistake, and very costly in terms of money, and more important, human life and quality of life.

In late 1981, almost as a joke at a Rotary meeting, someone suggested I could run from our twin club in France to our own club in Reading, as a way of cementing our twinning. In an unguarded moment I must have said yes, and a few months later my friend Ted Brazil, who had suggested the run, took me to one side at a meeting and said "When do you want to do this run from France?" A date was agreed for the end of April, and work then started on the logistics of putting such a run together. First of all we had to convince and explain to our French colleagues what we were going to do, and also explain that it was to be a sponsored run for charity; something that they did not understand at that time. Ted and I went off to France to convince the French it was a good idea and to look at a route.

We convinced the French that it was a good idea, and with their help a route from Meru, near Beauvais, north of Paris to Reading was chosen. Our target was to raise over £8,000 for a new high jump area at the athletic stadium for the disabled at Stoke Mandeville, near Aylesbury.

On the 28th April I was in the square of the small town of Meru. I had been accompanied to France by a small squad from the Rotary Club of Caversham; two of whom were going to cycle back with me. A friend of mine from the French club, Alan Hau, was also going to cycle with me as escort, and lined up with me in the square was a French gendarme, a very fit young man who worked for Interpol. I think they thought it would be good for me to have someone to run with, but the only trouble was that he was twenty-five years younger than me and very much fitter. Instead of the slow start to my run that I had hoped for, it was more like a race, as we ran at about seven minute mile pace. It was made even more difficult as he spoke some English and I understood very little French, and we chatted and ran for nearly ten miles. Fortunately he then had to drop out to return to work, and I could resume a more leisurely run for the rest of that first day.

At the end of the day after some breaks, I had run twenty-five miles (forty km) and arrived at Entrepagny. I was then taken back to the start so that I could be hosted by my friends in Meru. I remember getting up on that second day and feeling pretty stiff, but we went back to the finishing point of the first day and set off again on the road to Duclair. It was very warm and John London and myself found that second day pretty tough going, not least because of the fast running the previous day. It was also a fairly hilly stretch and plenty of liquid was needed. For the runners this was water or Origina. Our cycling escorts were enjoying themselves with their wine and French bread while we kept running. We did get a break at midday, well what would you expect in France, and had a good lunch before running on in the afternoon. At the end of the second day we had covered another forty plus miles (sixty-three km), and we stopped at a small hotel at Duclair, just outside Rouen, for the night. A pleasant meal, quite a lot of wine and a good night's sleep, and up early next morning for the final stage to Le Havre.

Even on a run like this it was necessary to do some stretching and warming up to try and ease the tired sore muscles. After jogging up and down outside the hotel, it was off on the run again. Another warm day, but I was beginning to feel fitter and stronger as the runners and entourage made their way towards the venue for that day. We ran into Le Havre and up to the Yacht Club for a shower and rest, before attending a special dinner in our honour in the evening, put on by the Rotary Clubs in the area. Another forty miles (sixty-two km) had been covered. Another boozy enjoyable evening before staggering onto the overnight ferry for Portsmouth. It sailed at 11 p.m., and I had a good night's sleep.

Next morning, it was now Friday, we awoke at Portsmouth and my old Army colleague and international running partner, Gerry North, was there to meet me and to run with me for the ten miles to Petersfield. This was also a bit like the old days, and we had a bit of a ding-dong as we ran over this ten mile stretch. From Petersfield we ran on to Alton, and then Basingstoke, and on the way I passed a group of school children who had been taken to the route to cheer me on. Seeing them helped me to make it into Basingstoke, where we finished for the night. A total of thirty-five miles for the day (fifty-four km). By now I was feeling tired but elated that we had nearly done it. It was Friday evening, and I was staying with a Rotarian friend Claude Fenton, a great man who had been a prisoner of the Japanese and worked on the Burma railway and survived. I remember laying in his bath having a good soak, and he sat in the bathroom with me, and the bottle of Scotch we both enjoyed. This was followed by a superb dinner with a few bottles of wine, and off to bed to get ready for the final nineteen miles to Reading next morning.

Claude brought me a cup of tea, we had a good breakfast and then he drove me to the Basingstoke Civic Offices, where the mayor was to send me and the escorts on our way. I was greeted there by a squad of around twenty from the Reading Joggers, who had come to run with me on that final run into Reading. It was a great thrill to have so many of the 'Joggers' running with me. The mayor sent us on our way at about 9.30 a.m., and I remember feeling very good, and in fact some of my running colleagues could not believe how well I was running, after four days of running the equivalent of 1.5 marathons a day. The final eighteen miles (thirty km) took only just over two hours, and we nearly arrived at the finish too soon. We swept into Reading, with a police escort, and over Caversham Bridge and onto the Porsche headquarters building just around the corner. It was just before midday on the 1st May and my forty-sixth birthday. What a welcome; my mother Ivy, the Mayor of Reading, the local MP Tony Durant, the Rotary District Governor and many friends from Rotary. I remember sprinting into the finish; it was a wonderful feeling and Porsche had pushed the boat out; although they did not give me one of their products to sample. They had laid on a great reception for me and the others. I was given a glass of champagne just after I finished and was very light-headed. Then they told me the *Sunday Observer* was on the phone and wanted an interview about the run; somebody pushed another glass in my hand and I gave an excited review of my run to the reporter, who I am sure thought I was quite mad. There was a large cake with the map of my run on it, and it was a great party with my friends, and especially John London who had run a lot of the way with me, David Watts and Roy Lambert who had cycled all the way, as well as Alan Hau my French friend and his family who had come all the way with us. It was over and I think I said never again; BUT it was not the end and more about that later.

The final climax to that run was a day at Stoke Mandeville, where I handed over a cheque for £8,000 as a result of the run.

In early 1982, just after my run from France, I ran the Paris Marathon. It was an experience but not very successful for me. I was still very tired from my marathon effort and never really got going. It was a very hot day, and the Paris Fire Brigade were out all around the course spraying the runners with cold water. It was not the best organised event and it seemed that anything went, including taking short cuts if you were so inclined, or even jumping on a bike. It was great fun though and totally different to running events I had previously taken part in. Runners would suddenly stop by the side of the road and a wife, girlfriend or friend would cycle up with a supply of wine and bread, and the runner would join them for a snack before rejoining the race. The annoying thing was that some of these people had the cheek to beat me to the finish, but I am not sure they all ran the full distance.

Chapter Thirteen

Does He Take Sugar? — Not Any More!

Six years after my first run from France I developed a health problem. It was 1988, the year one of my daughters, Joanna, got married at St Peter's Church in Caversham, where we had attended since moving to Caversham, but I did not remember too much about it as I was not feeling very good at the time. I thought it would pass and went off on holiday to the Algarve with Marion. We had a great holiday and I thought that whatever it was that I had been suffering from had cleared up. I was wrong, and on my return I was persuaded to go the doctor by my then secretary who had suffered two very serious bouts of cancer. She said that whatever it was, it would be better to know and to be able to deal with it. I made that appointment, and at first the doctor thought that I had picked up a viral infection, but he decided to take blood samples and it was August Bank Holiday.

On the Tuesday morning after the holiday, he telephoned me to say he had bad news; he quickly realised that was not the right thing to say and changed it to "I think you have a problem, and you had better come back for more tests." The tests revealed that I was diabetic; type 2 Diabetes; not a disaster, but it was to change my life slightly in the future, although not to any great extent. Research has shown that exercise helps fight off the problem, but I had been exercising all my life and had never been a heavy drinker. I suppose the other two main causes of diabetes I did suffer from. If you compare my racing weight of between nine stone twelve ounces and ten stone, to my weight when I had not been exercising very much of around thirteen stone, I suppose I was overweight. The other cause I certainly suffered from, diabetes in my genes. At least one of my maternal grandparents were diabetic and so was my oldest sister. So I suspect this was my main problem.

I was put on some pills, and not much happened for a long time, and I kept on running. This included another 175 mile run to France in 1992, and another London Marathon in 1997.

In 1999 my diabetes had deteriorated, and my doctor at Didcot, where I now lived, had sent me to the Diabetic Clinic at the Radcliffe Infirmary in Oxford. They started to take care of me, and when they were looking for some patients to act as guinea pigs for a new treatment they asked me to take part. A doctor and a senior nurse came out to my home to talk me through what it would mean, and I immediately volunteered. It was going to require my presence in the hospital for an overnight twenty-four hour stay, once a month for four months, from May until August. I also had an extra twenty-four hour stint in the September to help further with the experiment.

In each of my stays I had blood taken from me twenty-seven times over the twenty-four hours, and sometimes I was given a new drug made from the saliva of a lizard, and other times a placebo. I was very well looked after by some very special nurses, who visited me all day and all night to take my blood samples. I also saw some of the difficulties that hospitals had to put up with, including a shortage of basic things like pillows; if you got a real pillow you were lucky and if you got two, you hung on to them. I also saw some of the more difficult patients, like the elderly lady who had probably previously been detained in an institution. She was a real handful and would hit the staff with her walking stick if she did not get her own way. She would also wander off and they would not know where she was, and sometimes she would get herself into the wrong bed, whether there was a patient in it or not.

I found the research fascinating, and after my first twenty-four hour stay, I was invited to join a lunch time seminar with the consultants, doctors and nurses from the Diabetic Department for a talk about the subject. Having been invited to attend, I then got a phone call to tell me that the speaker could not make it, and before the end of the conversation Dr Hisham Maksoud had asked me to take over the speaker's spot and give a talk myself. He left it to me to decide the theme of my talk. I decided to talk on the subject of "Does Diabetes Change Your Life?". I explained that with sensible lifestyle, an individual could continue life as before.

After that final visit to the hospital, I went back to see my friendly Doctor Hisham Maksoud. The pills were no longer controlling my blood sugars, and he suggested I should take the next step and go on to insulin. On one of my journeys by taxi to the hospital, I had listened to my taxi driver explaining how it was so much better to be on insulin, so in a way I took his advice and agreed to start what I knew was to be a lifetime decision, twice a day injections. This created its own problems, as I rapidly put on weight and found it very hard to run even short distances. The discipline of injecting did not prove difficult and in many ways it did make me feel better.

I have become fascinated by diabetes, and I have learned and I am still learning much about it. I believe there will be drastic changes in the treatment of the disease over the next few years.

The year of 1988 was a traumatic one in various ways. I had my diabetes and Joanna had got married, but later that year there was a family row that resulted in the disappearance of our middle child and second son Neil. He got himself involved with a girl and they both attended the wedding, but shortly after that they found themselves homeless. Our eldest daughter Caroline and her then boyfriend, took pity on them and allowed them to share their new home. Things rapidly deteriorated due to the two 'lodgers' not working, and not doing anything to keep the house tidy either. They were asked to leave by Caroline, but Neil and his partner started legal proceedings by issuing a writ against his sister, claiming some right to the property. It was quickly dealt with, but at some considerable cost to Caroline and her other half. As a result of this, the children closed ranks and said they did not want to see him again, and they haven't. His parents kept out of it, and we did not actually fall out with him, but none of the family have seen or heard anything from him since the end of 1988.

Chapter Fourteen

The Reading Half Marathon

Over the years I have organised, or been part of, many different events. Organising any event, whether sporting or otherwise, requires the same dedication, direction and enthusiasm if it is to succeed. The largest of these events was the Reading Half Marathon, and many of the other running events mentioned elsewhere. Other activities have included large Celebrity Dinners for SportsAid at the Royal Lancaster Hotel in London, from 1995 to 1998. These dinners were a highlight of fund raising for SportsAid, and there were some interesting speakers, including Jeffrey Archer who came more than once, and on one occasion helped with the auction which raised a lot of money. He had come direct from a meeting with Margaret Thatcher, and had persuaded her to give him her autobiography to auction and this raised a four figure sum. He also auctioned his latest book, but that only raised £50. Each year we were able to auction a special print of Grand National Winner Bob Champion on Aldaniti, signed by both the jockey and the artist Bryan Organ. This always raised four figure sums for the charity with the help of Bob Champion himself who often attended. Other regular supporters at this and our golf days, were Nicholas Parsons, Robert Powell, Henry Cooper, Jimmy Hill, Phil Parkes, Michael Barratt, Sally Gunnell, Steven Redgrave, Matthew Pinsent and many more stars from stage and sport — the stars were always introduced by Paul Dickenson from BBC Sport, himself an ex-athlete. Refereeing It's a Knockout and Reading Top Team Competitions; organising Golf Tournaments and a Corporate Challenge, again for SportsAid; the Gala Nights of Sport in Reading, and the town's Skillmaster (Superstars) Competition; all these activities have called on me for help, as well as the many running events mentioned. But the very big one turned out to be also the most traumatic and wearing on my health and temper.

In 1982, after the success of the first London Marathon in 1981, suggestions were being made that Reading should have some sort of marathon like the big event. A lot of people in the media, and in the running clubs, suggested to me that I should start something big in the town. I had already organised a number of fun runs and had a high profile at the time because of my marathon run from France, so I think this is why I was approached to set up this special event. Little did I know what a battle it was going to be, or what the eventual financial burden was going to be for me. I spoke to Reading Borough Council, and a young lady in the Leisure Department had been pushing them to start a similar event, with the idea of raising money to plant trees in Broad Street, Reading.

After a couple of meetings, it was decided that the matter should be put through the town's Leisure Committee. The suggestion was put to that committee, and I remember waiting outside for the verdict. I did not have to wait long before the young lady came out from the meeting crying and very upset. They had turned down the joint proposal, BUT if I wanted to go ahead they would give the event its blessing, but no money.

I quickly started work on finding a sponsor, as I had been told there could be no financial support from the Borough. My first conversation was with Courage, one of the major companies in the town. I had put out some publicity about the proposed event and within days I was being pursued by various people from Digital Equipment, a company who were growing very fast in the area, and their finance director was a man with a very apt name, Martin Ranwell. Digital would not let go and rang me daily for a decision. A meeting was arranged and they quickly agreed to sponsor an event, at this stage not knowing whether it would be the full marathon distance like London, or something that was still very new on the running scene, a half marathon.

With the guarantee of £5,000 from the sponsor, work started on the first event. A committee was put in place which included a representative of RBC, Terry Harding, the sponsors Digital, Marcus Palliser, and two from the running scene, John London a new mature runner, and myself as chairman. A little later a representative of Reading University, Ian Moir would join us, along with Ken Bridges, a former Chief Officer of the Berkshire Fire Service, who agreed to be responsible for the marshalling of the event. A few years later that position was taken over by a new chief marshal, Bernard Patterson, who before his retirement was the police superintendent in charge of the police for the first few half marathons. The chief marshal from the late eighties was Lieutenant Colonel Malcolm Bryant, who had himself been a very good runner with Reading AC. Very quickly the decision was made that a full marathon was going to be too complex to arrange in the town of Reading, and the half distance was settled on.

Then a route had to be found, and at this stage the police were brought in for their comments. It was decided that the university would be a good starting and finishing point, but where should the runners go in between? Everyone agreed the race should cover all points of the town, and hopefully incorporate the river and its bridges. One of our exploratory visits arranged by the council was to Caversham, and we looked at running along the Warren and up through the woods by a narrow path to Upper Warren

Avenue, a residential area. It was the first indication I had as to how difficult it was going to be to convince the local mandarins what a big event it was going to be, and what was required to make it a success. The suggested route was totally impracticable even for a small field of a few hundred runners. A number of other suggestions were looked at, including a run along the towpath and under Reading Bridge; again fortunately rejected in view of what was to happen when the event was launched; thousands of runners and not the few hundred some people expected. Finally a route was found that satisfied all the requirements of the time.

In October 1982 Digital held the first launch of a half marathon in the town. It was to be held from the university at Whiteknights on Sunday, 13th March 1983. The entry forms were put out with an entry fee of £2.50, and by the end of December an entry of around 5,000 had been received.

At the launch the *Reading Evening Post* decided they would like some 'guinea pig' runners — people to run who had never run in their lives. These were a married couple from Winnersh, Christine and Maurice Shackleford. She was a thirty-six-year-old ward clerk at Reading's Royal Berkshire Hospital, and he was forty-one years old, and a bricklayer. The third one of these brave three was Eileen O'Neill, who was already fifty-three years old, and who would be the first to admit she was not the shape or type of person to take up running. They all trained hard and were ready to go on their big adventure on 13th March 1983. The three volunteers had been selected from others to train and run the 13.1 miles. All were totally new to running, and they took on a training programme so that they could cover the distance. Eileen O'Neill, the fifty-three-year-old, who six months earlier could not run more than a few yards, finished in two hours fifteen minutes. The husband and wife couple, Maurice and Christine Shackleford, both finished in good times; Maurice in 1:42 and Christine in just on two hours. These three people were guinea pigs in every sense, and proved that people who were unfit with no experience could run a half marathon in reasonable time.

Everything was new about the event. Where do you go for a results system, time clocks, marshals, special medals and all the other things now associated with the big event? Today organisers have it easy, especially at events like Reading, where the hard work was done on research and the setting up in those early days.

As the event got nearer another challenge was thrown at it, and it was something that was going to have a lasting effect on the race and on me personally. The committee were approached by the British Sports Association for the Disabled, to see if we would allow competitors in wheelchairs to take part. The two officials from BSAD who pushed for this, were Philip Lewis MBE, and Alan Crouse, and they were so keen that they persuaded us the organisers to accept wheelchair athletes. This presented another problem, was the route suitable, and what to do about the finish where it was intended to run the last few hundred yards on grass? We took the challenge so seriously that we even tried to persuade the Army to lay a temporary hard surface on the grass. In the end we opted for the cheaper option, and the wheelchair competitors finished on the road opposite the 'real' finish, but accurately measured so they did complete the full distance. It was a great success, and their participation added a special dimension to this big new event, and I have maintained an interest in sport for disabled people from that time until the present day.

The excitement built up around the event in the following months and the media got very interested, especially Radio 210 as it was then (now 2TenFM).

On that big day, Sunday, 13th March, around 5,000 runners lined up to take part in an exciting experience. Many of them had never run anything like 13.1 miles before, and at 10 a.m., the Mayor of Reading, Councillor George Robinson, sent them on their way. It was a beautiful day and warm for the time of year. As the runners ran around the streets it was not without a few problems, as the motorists had also not experienced anything like this before either; road closures and single lane operations.

There were no obvious big names in the race, and no one had any idea who would triumph in this first Reading Half Marathon. The hour passed and then at about sixty-five minutes the winner came in sight and entered the university grounds. He was a very fit young runner from Reading University itself, twenty-one years old Mark Couzens, and he crossed the line in 67:45, to be adorned with a wreath of flowers by the Mayor, George Robinson.

It was a great triumph for local runners, with the team from Reading Athletic Club winning the team trophy for the first time. Their first runner was Paul Lanfear in second place, with Ron Tyler third, Peter Mitchell seventh, and Robert Love eleventh. They had many more in the first fifty places, including Bob Allden in twenty-third place, the second veteran over forty behind the winner Malcolm Moody (Burnham Joggers).

The runners then flowed in and kept coming for over three hours; some fit, some struggling, many in fancy dress and all enjoyed the experience of the finish and receiving their medal, even if the getting there had been tougher than they thought. There was a great carnival atmosphere as the runners wandered around after they had finished eating their Mars bars and having a drink in the sun.

It had been a great success, and not least of all financially, and BSAD benefited by around £17,000 in that year from the self-sponsorship of runners, and a £5,000 donation from the event organisers.

Apart from the success of the race, there was another big surprise for me at the presentations. I had arranged the production of all the trophies but, unknown to me, John London had worked behind the scene to add an extra trophy, the Stan Eldon Trophy for the first wheelchair athlete.

Reading had not seen anything like this sporting/community event before, and the local media were ecstatic and lavish in their praise with banner headlines and leader columns. One article was by journalist Shelley Alexander, who ran the distance in 2:24, encouraged by her then boyfriend and later husband, international and Manchester United footballer Neil Webb.

There were many interesting stories created around the race that bright sunny day; most were happy, but there was also one sad result. A runner from Burnham Joggers, Stan Tugwood, who was seventy-two years old, the oldest runner to complete the first ever Reading Half Marathon, who had been a runner all his life, collapsed at the finish. He had run the London Marathon twice, and the New York Marathon, and was using Reading as training for another London. He had some chest pains before the Reading race, but did not want to let people down by not running. He went home with the help of Dr Bob Green, who was the founder of the Burnham Joggers, but died of a heart attack at Wexham Park Hospital in Slough in the early hours of the next morning. He made one last request; that his last medal should be buried with him, and that request was carried out when he was buried at Marlow a few days later. It was pleasing to me that the media treated the whole matter with decency, and there were no scare headlines to put people off running after such a successful day.

The other stories had much happier endings. The vicar of a local church, Reverend David Evans, ran for his church roof fund and raised over £1,000. Perhaps the biggest story of the race was the first appearance of a young man in a sporting event who was to go on and compete in many London Marathons, as well as become a Paralympic Gold Medallist. The seventeen-year-old was Peter Hull, who although without arms or legs had taken part and completed the 13.1 miles. He received the Douglas Jacobs Special Award for his achievement. Later at his school, the Hephaistos School at Arborfield, he was presented with a new state of the art racing wheelchair, donated by the manufacturers C. F. Hewerdine Ltd., from Egham in Surrey. They had decided to give him the special 'chariot' after his story appeared in the *Reading Evening Post*. A local prison officer ran with one of his previous charges, who had only left prison two days before the Reading race, and there were many more human stories around that first very special event.

A *Reading Evening Post* photographer, Ian Pert, won a Kodak Picture of 1983 award for his photograph of a runner applauding a wheelchair competitor as he worked hard on the climb up to Whitley Street.

The trophies and medals had all been specially commissioned, and made locally by Paul Ranson of Nash and Co, a local jeweller and W. H. Ryder and Son (Reading) Ltd., architectural woodmasters, who did specialist work in cathedrals, on cruise ships and at top of the market hotels. Ridd Ryder was a member of my Rotary Club at Caversham, and we had worked together on many major Rotary events together.

The first big after-event reaction to the race was regarding the inclusion of wheelchair racers. The London Marathon in 1981 and 1982 had refused to accept them into that event, but the *Sunday Times* now took up the story and had a full report on how successful their inclusion at Reading had been, and urged London to do the same. In fact Tony Banks, then with the GLC and later sports minister, said in the article *"No wheelchairs, no marathon."* It worked, and Chris Brasher relented and wheelchair athletes were admitted to the 1983 race that followed a couple of months later. A few years later I was to find myself as Chairman of the London Wheelchair Marathon Committee. It was an interesting experience and one that was not without some controversy, and I refer to this later in this book.

Later in the year, after the first Reading race, the mayor did invite me to one of his mayoral lunches which he held several times a year. It was a very enjoyable occasion, with other guests including Robert Morley the actor and raconteur, the Bishop of Reading Graham Foley, and a few others from the commercial life of the town. It was at a time when all mayors of the town were able to hold these very good special events. I was to be invited to a few more of these special lunches, but I think that first one is my favourite memory.

In 1983, John London, my partner in Running Management Services, and myself decided to try and open a branch of the famous Athlete's Foot running shoe shops that were growing very fast in the United States. They were a franchise organisation, and we thought that we could make it work in this country after the modest success of my Sporting Feet. Senior executives flew into Gatwick in their private jet, and we had a meeting to discuss the possibilities. They were very keen, but unfortunately had a legal problem over the registration of the their trading name in the UK. Another UK business had registered the name some years before, and although it was not being used, the advice was that Athlete's Foot and ourselves would not be able to extend the franchise into this country, so it never happened.

After that first Reading Half Marathon, there was a lot of fine tuning to be done, and there was much discussion before the 1984 event could be up and running. I remember a quote from Terry Harding, who was the Reading Borough Council representative on the committee after that first event, it was "If the Borough had given its full support, the event would have been much better." These words had a ring of truth for many years.

Work started straight away, and the support of Digital was again confirmed.

People had been so impressed with the first event, that they were waiting for the entry forms to come out for 1984, and when the launch was held in September of 1983, there was a rush of entries that was only held back by the lack of entry forms. By the beginning of November 5,000 entries had been received, and within a month the 6,000 mark had been passed. The route had been confirmed as the same as for the first year. The total entry for the 1984 event was a staggering 6,801.

The office for the race was above my shop in Caversham (now a branch of Boots), and the workload of dealing with this number of entries was enormous. In particular the mailing out of race numbers and programmes a month before the race. On one occasion there were twenty large mailbags packed with the packages to be collected by Royal Mail. My own staff helped when they could, but there was only one person to carry out much of the work, and that was a newly-retired member of Reading Joggers, who had taken up running in his sixties; Dave Hutchins was the father-in-law of the late Alan Taylor, the footballer who became an athlete.

By now Digital had been working on their own results system instead of using a bought-in service as in the first year.

The huge field lined up at Whiteknights for the start of the 2nd Digital Reading Half Marathon, on Sunday, 25th March 1984. The weather was not as good as that first year and there was a lot of rain, but the race not only attracted a large field but it also started to draw in better class runners, following the success of the first year. It also attracted some undesirable youngsters, who kept creeping under the side of the large marquee that housed the various giveaways including oranges, and in particular the Mars bars. Fortunately we had some good stewarding and they did not get away with very much.

The winner Mike Hurd, from the RAF, set a new record of 64:39. The women's race was won by Karen Goldhawk, who was coached by Hurd, in a new record of 73:56; and so was the wheelchair event which was won by Gordon Perry in 87:24. Reading AC repeated their team win of the previous year with a great team result, which included Rob Watt in second place with 65:21, and Peter Mitchell third with 66:37, Ron Tyler fourth in 67:30, Pete Sugden fifth 67:39, David Gilbert seventh 67:46. In 108th place there was an Eldon; son Jonathan ran in with 76:07. The race had attracted some big names from the world of athletics, including Ron Hill, Britain's most prolific and successful marathon runner, and John Whetton the UK's most successful miler and 1,500 metre runner. They had their own private battle for the vets' prize and Whetton won by finishing in tenth place in 68:25, with Hill in thirteenth place (and second vet) with 69:15. Bob Allden (Reading AC) was third in 70:39 (twentieth in the race). The winner of the men's fifty plus group was Albert Patterson in 75:16.

Some of the other local characters and runners included Kathy Tayler, the Reading girl who was a former World Ladies Modern Pentathlon Champion and later a TV Holiday programme presenter, and Roger Smee the then Chairman of Reading FC and his sixty-five-year-old father Don, who went on running until he was nearly eighty years old. One of my running contemporaries from the 1960s, Brian Bacon, a long-standing member of Reading AC, ran the race and finished in 78:01. This was to be the last time he ran the race without pushing a disabled young person, which he did for the next fifteen years, as he was to continue running with a wheelchair until he was well into his sixties, and still recorded very respectable running times of around ninety minutes. A local police sergeant, Michael Burgess, had entered the race but was injured before the day, and was pushed around by Brendan O'Dowde. Everyone wanted to be there and take part whatever the circumstances.

As the *Reading Evening Post* put on its banner headline after the race *"WET, WINDY AND......WONDERFUL! Marathon Mania gripped Reading yesterday. Six thousand ignored bitter wind and driving rain to run in the Digital Reading Half Marathon..."*

A new results system had been developed by Digital and it had a good test. The system depended on bar codes, but when they had to be read after the event, the wet conditions and the sweat on the numbers made reading difficult. So 7,000 numbers were put to one side for a day to dry out before they could start to process the results. A large number of people were involved, probably about thirty, in producing results that a few years later could be produced by one or two people.

In 1984 we started training sessions for new runners at Palmer Park. Most of those attending were new runners who wanted to have a go at the half marathon, or wanted to improve their times. They were interesting sessions and I recall that even when the track was covered in snow, at least fifty people would still be there to carry out some sort of training. John London and myself developed a training programme and structure which helped many runners improve their times in subsequent half marathons. After we stopped running the sessions in 1987, many of the runners stayed together and kept up their training at the Park, and it was from these sessions that the now very large and successful Reading Roadrunners was formed.

There were problems before the third race could take place in 1985. In July 1984 there was a row between two Reading Council committees. The Leisure Committee wanted the event to continue over the route used for two successful years, but the Transportation Committee wanted a new route, which may have excluded Caversham which had always given the event massive support. The matter went to the Policy-making Committee and rumbled on for some time until a slightly revised route was found, but the race was the last to be held at the University of Reading before it moved to a leisure centre to the south of the town, which required another rethink. Even if the council were playing about with the event, the success of the event was now assured with the continued backing of Digital, Barclays Bank and other powerful supporters, including the media, even though the battles with the local council continued as they did right through until 1994, when they suddenly decided it was a good thing. Before the final decision was made about the route, I had to address a full meeting of the Borough Council, after detailed discussions with the leaders of all the political parties to convince them of the importance of the event to the town, and why some of their options would be no good for the wheelchairs. I won that battle and the event continued to grow.

The entry was huge again, and there were over thirty wheelchairs entered.

The third winner of the Digital Trophy was Kingston Mills (Shaftesbury AC), who took the winning time below sixty-four minutes for the first time with 63:55; in fact the first three all beat sixty-four minutes in the very close race, which was only settled as the runners hit the grass at the finish. Second place went to Keith Penny (Cambridge Harriers) in 63:56, with Mervyn Brameld third in 63:59. The winner from the previous year, Mike Hurd was fifth in 64:09 and Steve Brace (Bridgend), making his first of many appearances, was seventeenth in 66:28. Veronique Marot won the ladies' race in 72:56. In the wheelchair race, Mike Bishop took a huge chunk off the record with 76:31, and Basildon AC prevented Reading from taking their third team title. Aldershot Farnham and District were second with Oxford City AC third, and Reading AC next with Pete Mitchell (twenty-second), Pete Sugden (twenty-eighth), Rob Watt (thirty-eighth), Dave Gilbert (thirty-ninth), all under seventy minutes, and the team results were very interesting in retrospect. London Irish, a future winning team, were fifth, Maidenhead sixth and Reading Joggers seventh; their team included Dave Lancaster who would feature in the race many times over the years, but running for other clubs. The Maidenhead B team which finished ninth included Duncan Hurdwell. The individual age category winners were, David Clark in the over forties men with 66:48, from Taff Davies (Aldershot) 67:34 and John Whetton (the vet winner in 1984) 68:34. Brian Shave took the over fifties with 80:32 and Paul Norman the over sixties with 94:49. In the women's race, the thirty-five to forty-four years winner was Margaret Lockley in 77:02, the forty-five to fifty-four years Esme Thompson 84:28 and the fifty-five plus Joyce Smith in 101:22, with 'guinea pig' Eileen O'Neill runner-up.

Looking back fifteen years later, it is amazing to see how many runners, especially local runners, were able to beat seventy minutes and a whole host more sub seventy-five minutes.

There were a total of fifteen team categories in those early years, and hundreds of teams took part. There was a separate category for Jogging Clubs, and in 1985 Reading Joggers B team took the trophy here. The Gurkas took part in the race and their band provided musical entertainment on the day; their team won the Sports Clubs category from Palmer Park Plodders, which was the forerunner of Reading Roadrunners. Reading FC were sixth in this group, with Ian Branfoot, Brian Roach, Stuart Henderson and Glenn Hunter. The Motor Trade Trophy went to Reading Garage, who were led home by Reading AC's Ron Tyler. Slough Casuals won the very large category for Civil Servants and Local Government. The Banking Category went to the Co-op Bank; Courage took the Industrial; *Reading Chronicle* the Media; the Computer/Electronics award went to Burroughs

Education Centre; Helen House, Oxford, won the Charity; the pub winner was the Pig and Whistle; and the family team winners were the Bookers, from the Gosneys and the Smees. I mention both these latter families as they continued to support the event very strongly in different ways over the years. Advertising category was won by Fericon Press; Transport by Cab Running Club; and Retail by Heath and Watkins.

When races like Reading started up in the early 80s little was known about computerised results, and Digital put a lot of resource into developing a satisfactory system for the Reading race. Working with their software company, Cambridge Online, and with a hand-held Psion Organiser that had been specially programmed by Will Chapman of Serpentine Runners, the work of producing fast results became much easier.

From the start we had used tags on our race numbers, and these were carefully collected at the end of each funnel where the runners finished, and put on spindles (knitting needles with corks) in strict finishing order. This still required race times for all these finishers, which was a massive job for those on the finish line, and it was also very time-consuming transferring these times into the results system. The Psion saved all this and cut down on time and manpower.

At the finish a couple of confident people would each have a Psion, and as a runner approached them before the line, they would punch in that runner's number; as the runner crossed the line he would hit another key, and that runner had an accurate time. Obviously in a race with 7,000 runners coming across the line at over 200 a minute, not every time would be taken. The Psion handlers would then look at a group of four, five, six runners coming towards them who were very close together, and pick the simplest number to read from that group and use that number for the accurate time; if he had time he might put a plus four or five runners in with the identified runner. This did not matter very much as the accurate finish tag collectors would provide the finishing position, and the computer was clever enough to allocate times to runners between the clearly identified runners with sufficiently accurate times.

I lined up for the London Marathon in 1985, and Digital had progressed to producing the results for London in that year. I had a reasonable run on inadequate training, but finished in the first 10,000 with an official time of 3:45; but allowing for the few minutes to cross the start line, this was probably a couple of minutes faster.

It was around this time that I got involved for the only time in a campaign. It was to save the grammar schools in Reading, and my youngest daughter was a pupil at one of them — Kendrick Girls' School. I joined a protest with banners and hundreds of other supporters at the Berkshire County Council building, Shire Hall, where we made out feelings known to the county councillors as they attended a meeting there. We won the day and the schools still exist at this time.

In the same year I got involved more and more in the organising of other running events. One of the first of these was the Courage Half Marathon, that ran from their Brewery in Reading. The company itself organised the race, and my involvement was producing the results on the Digital computer system designed for the Reading Half Marathon. It seemed strange that Courage set up their own race, when they could have had the main Reading Half in 1983 before Digital emerged as a sponsor. I remained involved with this race until Courage finally gave up the event in about 1990.

Chapter Fifteen

Launch of the Nabisco Fun Runs

In 1985, Huntley and Palmers, for which Reading was famous, had been taken over by Nabisco, and the new company wanted to make its mark in the town. My next-door neighbour, Mike Paxton, who had been Army Champion at 440 yards, and nearly made it to the 1948 Olympics, was the PR Manager there, and after some discussion it was agreed we would organise the Nabisco Family Fun Runs. These were to be age-related runs, similar to what had become very popular each year in Hyde Park, the *Sunday Times* Fun Runs.

Runners were put into age bands, from as young as under elevens to over sixties. Everyone over eleven ran a two mile lap, and the youngsters ran just one mile. Based on the numbers of entries in each category, runners would be awarded a gold, silver or bronze badge. This was a successful formula that encouraged people to come back and try to move up a grade in the following year. I now think that it would have been much better to have this type of grading for medals in mass events such Reading and London. It might encourage people to try for better times, and perhaps our standards would not have slipped so low.

The events were very successful and ran for a number of years. Younger age group runs were introduced in future years, and these ran just 800 metres.

Organising and seeing the great success of the Reading Half Marathon and other events was a great pleasure, but there was an unsavory side to running which I know existed in many other events, and still exists into the third millennium. These were the running cheats; in some cases just mild cheating that really harmed no one but the pride of the individual who was cheating, but sometimes it was and is much more serious.

The first sort of cheat was the one who joined in the race part way round the course, or maybe, and this could happen at Reading, cut out a loop and rejoin the race. These silly people did no more than cheat themselves unless they were very well up the field.

The second class of cheat were those who would run wearing a false number, normally a photocopied or made-up one. They avoided paying for their entry and therefore were cheating on those who had paid their fee. As results systems improved it became much more difficult to cheat this way.

Then of course there are the more serious cheats, some of whom have been caught and been dealt with by the law. These are the ones who have been sponsored for a charity and do not hand over the money, or all the money collected.

There are also the 'smart a...s' who join in a race and pay nothing because they say "You cannot stop me running on public roads". Many of these problems have now been eliminated from the running scene.

The local radio station 210FM and the then Chairman of Reading FC, Roger Smee, and his company Rockfort, wanted us to organise another event in 1986. We approached the Duke of Wellington and got permission to run a 10K at his estate, Stratfield Saye, near Reading in March 1986. The star celebrity at this event, apart from the Duke and Duchess who presented the prizes, was Erica Roe, the first female streaker.

Then it was onto the 1986 Reading Half Marathon, and the race was memorable for a number of reasons. The entries were received as usual and it was a particularly good year. The main list of entries was handed over to the local newspaper who were going to print the list of runners, and I then received a phone call. What did I know about an entry from Marina Victoria Ogilvy? I had not noticed that the daughter of Princess Alexandra, and seventeenth in line to the throne at that time, had actually entered the Reading Half Marathon. She did not run in the end, mainly due to security implications, but we did correspond on a number of occasions. Another entry was Graham Taylor during his first stint as manager of Watford FC, and there was a total of 7,089 runners, with many turned away.

The race was run for the first time from a new venue, the South Reading Leisure Centre, and the first race there produced some great results. The winner was Paul Davies-Hale, who took over a minute off the record set the previous year, and recorded the new figures of 62:39. He received a cheque for £2,000 for his great effort. It was a comfortable win in the end, but up to the eight mile mark he was chased by Eddie Herridge (Aldershot), who took second place with 64:06. Philip O'Brien was third in 64:10, and Chris Buckley fourth in 64:13. The winner of the Barclays Bank Trophy for women, and £1,500, was Ann Ford who set new figures of 72:09; a record, that at the time of writing, has not be beaten. Her husband Bernie Ford (Aldershot), was fifth in 64:18. The team winners were Westbury Harriers, with Aldershot as runners-up, and Birchfield Harriers third. The third record of the day was set by Mike Bishop who took the wheelchair record even lower to 72:00. Another outstanding performance in the race was that of Mike Hurd, the winner in 1984, who had now reached the veteran age of forty years. He finished in sixth place and won the veteran age group in 64:26, a vets' record time, and also ten seconds faster than his winning time two years earlier. This was the only year that records were set in four different categories. Glynis Penny won the women's vet group with 74:08, and was second in the women's race for the second year, while husband Keith took ninth place in 65:02. The man who was to play a major role in the race in future years, Steve Brace (Bridgend), finished twenty-fifth in 67:40. Two Reading AC runners had good runs; Steven Fenney thirtieth in 68:12, and Pete Sugden thirty-third in 68:36; but their team could not make it into the top six on this occasion. A runner who was later to join the club, Tim Butler, was running for Bournemouth this year and finished eleventh in 65:12.

In the summer of 1986, Running Management Services, the race organising company set up and run by John London and myself, were invited by Nashua Copiers at Bracknell to organise an Executive Relay. The Nashua company had already run successful similar events in South Africa. The idea was for relay teams of eight runners to run the total marathon distance of 26.2 miles. The longest leg to be six miles, and the shortest just two miles. The teams would be from companies and all had to work for the same company.

A great deal of work went into planning a marathon route around the Wokingham and Bracknell area. There was great support and enthusiasm in the area, and a launch was held at Wokingham Town Hall where David Moorcroft was the main attraction. Other personalities were present, and the details of the first event of its kind in the UK, to be held on Sunday, 14th September 1986, were announced. Entries started to come in and everything was going well, and then out of the blue while I was on holiday, John London got a call from the company to say they were pulling the plug and there would be no event. It was one of those strange company decisions that did not make much sense as they were already into expense. But the decision was final and they did the honourable thing and paid us for our work. It was a pity as the event could have been as great a success as the London Marathon or Reading Half.

In June there was the second running of the Nabisco Fun Runs in Reading. I sometimes think that the formula for these events regarding awards should have been used more widely for many of the mass running events, like the London Marathon, Reading and other half marathons. Instead of everyone receiving a medal for just competing, there were awards based on achievements. The top fifteen per cent in any age group getting the gold award, the next thirty-five per cent a silver, and the rest a bronze award. This gave everyone something to aim for; if you did not achieve gold this year, it gave you the opportunity to improve and have another go the following year. This system was also used by the very popular *Sunday*

Times Fun Runs in Hyde Park, run in the late 1970s and 80s.

In October the second Yellow Pages 10K was run from the university. The individual winner was Hamish McInnes (Old Gaytonians) in 30:45, and the ladies' winner for the second successive year was Diane Wildash (Basingstoke) in thirty-five minutes. The Old Gaytonians won the team race from Aldershot and Reading.

Before the next half marathon there was another 10K at Stratfield Saye by courtesy of the Duke of Wellington. There was also a special event staged to raise money for the 1988 Olympics, the Grant Thornton 10K.

This was followed by the 1987 Reading Half Marathon, which was now a very large event and also a quality race. Many of the problems of the new event had been resolved, and with a good sponsor, Digital, who had now become DEC, were now investing well over £25,000 each year into the event, and with a large entry the future of the race looked secure. Runners from overseas started to show interest, as well as some of the best names in British road racing. The Reading Borough Council were beginning to see the benefit to the community of the event, and they offered to sponsor a mini marathon for those below the age for the half marathon, that is under seventeen. The first winner of that new event was Dean Putt and the first girl was Ingrid Kinch.

There was a good entry of first-class runners, including previous London Marathon winner Hugh Jones, and twins from Czechoslovakia, Pavel and Petr Klime. The winner of a very exciting half marathon was Kevin Forster, who took the record down yet again to a very good 62:07. It was a great run and he reached the ten mile mark in about 47:20. The Klime twins were second and third; Pavel in 62:30 and Petr in 62:38, both just ahead of Hugh Jones in 62:42. The winner of the women's race was Paula Fudge, the twin sister of record holder Anne Ford. She had a go for that record, but just failed and ran 72:45 to record the second fastest time in the history of the event at that date, and to win and set a new record for the vet category. Mike Hurd returned to take the men's vet prize for the second year, and still in a great time of 65:01. In the wheelchair race Chris Hallam made his first appearance, and shattered the record with 65:04. The team race went to Birchfield Harriers, with Bournemouth the runners-up. A future winner of the race, Steve Brace (Bridgend AC), finished eighth in 64:54.

Around £60,000 was raised for charities, including the BSAD, Helen House Hospice, Royal Berkshire Hospital and St John Ambulance. There were lots of runners in fancy dress and even the police were happy. The police officer in charge of the 111 officers on duty on the day, Superintendent Eyles, said after the race "I was very pleased with the way it went.." There was a problem on part of the course when barriers had been put in the wrong place, which would have led to the runners going the wrong way. I had to leap out of the lead car and race on foot to sort out the problem ahead of the runners. I had not run so fast for years, but just managed to keep ahead of the field and jump back into the lead car still in front of the race.

In May there was another new event organised by Running Management Services, that is John London and myself. Permission had been obtained from Peter de Savary, the owner of Littlecote House at Hungerford, to use that great facility for a run for charity. The new event was to be a 15K, starting and finishing near the House, but going out around the country roads including some very hilly terrain.

The race was sponsored by Isostar, the energy drink, and the benefiting charity was the British Sports Association for the Disabled. The race was an instant success and a complete sell out. It was surprising that even then, a veteran forty plus athlete Shel Cowles, was able to win the race in the very good time of 48:40. He had a very big margin over second runner Stephen Miller in 50:26. There were many runners in that event who have remained on the running scene until the present day, including Ray Stevens, John Cullingham and Richard Disney from Reading AC, Robert Taylor Newbury AC, and many who were to form Reading Roadrunners a little later.

The race was to continue there for a number years, and several different charities were the beneficiaries. On one occasion Peter de Savary, the owner of Littlecote House at the time, invited one or two of us into the house early one morning for a drink; he was still in his dressing gown, and we sat and drank champagne.

In the same year I was asked by Reading AC if I would take on a role with them as Commercial Manager; my main function to raise money for the club by sponsorship and events. It was a challenge, but the club had a long history and some considerable success since its formation as one of the first clubs in the country in 1881. One of the greatest individual triumphs for the club was when Ann Packer won the Olympic Gold in the 800 metres in Tokyo, thus achieving for Reading what I had failed to do for my club Windsor and Eton. I had also known their chairman, Derek Bradfield, for many years as a very successful team manager for the club. He was their manager when they were in National League Division 1 in the 1970s, before taking on the job as chairman. I persuaded Digital, the sponsors of the Reading Half Marathon, to become club sponsors, and for four years, from 1988 to 1992, they supported the club with £10,000 a year sponsorship as well as other support which totalled around £60,000. In 1992 that sponsorship reduced, but they entered a new agreement and gave the club £7,500 per year for a further two years. The club had major sponsorship that should have lifted them to a high position in the sport, but the money really achieved very little and the long-established club continued to decline.

In September there was the annual Courage Half Marathon, and under my arrangement with Reading AC, I took on the management of their annual ten mile race that they had taken over from the Reading Police in 1983. There were nearly 400 runners, and included some very good runners and teams. The individual winner was Graham Payne (Basildon AC) in 49:45, and the first lady was Ann Ford (Hounslow) the Reading Half Marathon record holder, who finished thirty-fourth in the race with 58:14. Aldershot won the team race from Fleet and Crookham and Reading AC. One of the winning team was Martin Duff, now well known through his reporting of athletics in the *Athletics Weekly*.

Like many events at that time, including the Reading Half who had rejected a potential 2,000 extra entries earlier in the year, the Courage race was sold out well before the day, and a special slip had to be sent out rejecting many runners.

In October I was asked to help with the Great Sam Run Half Marathon which had been running since 1981. I had run in the event in 1984 when it was held at Virginia Water in Surrey, and I had a rival in the race that day, my fifteen-year-old niece Lucy Dancer, running the race although she was under age. We both did around 1:40.

My first duty with the event was to act as starter, and the programme said they could not get Diana Dors but had someone far less cuddly, Stan Eldon. The race was now run from Easthampstead just outside Bracknell, and four of the key people involved with the event were related to me by marriage; Les Webber and Jackie, and Reg Morton and Patricia were relations of my sister's husband.

For the next ten years Marion and I were to enjoy working with the team from the Bracknell, Wokingham, Ascot and District Samaritans, who organised the event to raise money for their very worthwhile cause. Our function was to produce the results using the very good system that had been developed for use at Reading. Like so many events, circumstances surrounding them demand changes, and in 2001 the half marathon changed to a 10K race at Wellington College.

The build up on events continued into 1988, and I was involved with a large number that had started the previous year and some that were new. The first event of the year was a new one for us, when we took over an established event, the Burghfield ten mile near Reading. It was sponsored by accountants Grant Thornton, and was run to raise money for the 1988 Olympics.

The next event was the Reading Half Marathon, and on this occasion just one record was broken, and it was again in the wheelchair race. It was not Hallam this time but 'the new kid on the block' David Holding, who took the record down to 63:57. The sun shone on the race this year; it was a very fine day and it brought out very large crowds all round the route. The team winners were London Irish, and Paul Cuskin won the Digital

Trophy with his win in 63:16. The Klime twins returned and again took second (63:21) and third (63:22) places but in the reverse order with Petr getting the upper hand this time. The winning lady was Karen Macleod from Bristol in 74:09, a personal best time by over a minute, and a new vet winner emerged, Ernie Cunningham, who lived in Reading but ran for Aldershot, Farnham and District. His time was 65:13, so the outstanding veteran times were being maintained. Veteran Martin Duff, who had previously been a member of three Berkshire clubs and well known for his contributions to *Athletics Weekly,* was also running for Aldershot and finished twenty-second in 68:10 and fourth placed veteran. The over fifty winner was Ron Pannell with 73:36, with Reading AC's Brian Fozard third in the category with 78:19. The over sixty men included some runners who are still running today, including Patrick Phillips (Reading Roadrunners) and Bernard Dembo (Maidenhead). The winner was Tom Shilling (Basingstoke) in 93:54. The winner of the women over forty-five, Karin Downs, 80:47, was way ahead of the first over forty woman Jackie Clark in 87:04.

In the mini marathon Mathew Lockey was the winner, and the first girl was Vicki Stevens. A runner with a fine pedigree from the Stevens family in Reading. Father Don a very good cross-country runner, and uncle Gerry a former British record holder for the steeplechase at both 2,000 and 3,000 metres.

It was either in this year or the following year that a problem occurred with the police. They did not turn up on time for the road closures on an important part of the course. A group of about eight turned up in a minibus at the start/finish venue well after the time they should have reported. I noticed that the sergeant in charge of sending them to their points did not say much to them, so I enquired why they were late and why he had not at least drawn their attention to their poor timing. I have not forgotten his reply "Oh they are a special group and we have no control over them; they do their own thing." I was not amused or impressed.

This was the year I had another strange incident, which I really did not understand until a few years later when I had time to reflect. I was approached by an Italian about bringing a few of the runners he managed across to Reading for the half marathon. We got permission from the then AAAs, and agreed to provide a hotel and pay for their air fares. I collected the three from Heathrow on the Saturday morning, and one of the runners from the start insisted he 'had to get to London'. After we had got them to the Post House in Reading, this one individual could not wait for me to get him to the station and a train to London. He was very vague about his 'mission' or where he was going. He arrived back later that evening and turned up for the race next morning, but he did not get very far; was 'ill' and dropped out. It was all a bit strange, and it was only much later that I put two and two together. I now think he had gone to London to collect some drugs, either performance enhancing or recreational. Either way he did not get it right, and whatever he did certainly made him quite ill.

I have always been surprised that the drug testing, that is carried out on track athletes and in major marathons like London, has never been introduced into these other events where there has been fairly substantial money rewards for the winners and others.

In May there was a 10K race at Cantley Manor in Wokingham; this was a new venue for the race that had been held at Stratfield Saye on the previous two years. In the same month the Littlecote Challenge 15K was held again, and this time for the benefit of the West Berkshire MacMillan Cancer Care Appeal. The event was again a sell out, and was proving to be very popular at the attractive Littlecote House.

I had been asked by my Rotary District to use my knowledge and skills to organise a major half marathon in the City of Oxford. The purpose of the run was to raise money for the Rotary International Polio Plus Campaign. The object of which was to eradicate polio and other diseases from the world by the turn of the century. There was a lot of work involved in putting together a race on the streets of a city like Oxford. We had all-round cooperation, and in June 1988 the race was on. Over 3,000 runners took part, and perhaps the most interesting feature of the race was that a woman, Paula Fudge, took second place, in the very good time of 72:59, behind the winner Bill Domoney from Oxford City AC in 71:14. This must have been one of the highest placed women's positions in any mass running event. The race raised a total of £15,000 for the very worthwhile cause.

The race was run four more times, in 1989, 1990, 1991 and 1992, and although the numbers were never as great as in that first special year, the event did raise worthwhile money for the charities that were chosen in each year by the Rotary Clubs of Oxford who were responsible for the event. The only reason the event finally came to an end, was the ageing of those who had worked very hard to make it a success.

The Nabisco Family Runs took place again in the same month in Prospect Park, Reading.

In September there were two races; the Courage Half Marathon again, where I provided the services for receiving the entries and producing the results; and also running the Reading AC ten mile race sponsored by Claude Fenton at Reading University again.

The year 1989 saw the Reading Half Marathon move into a newly-set up Star Ranking. It was also the first year that the race was run without the major sponsor Digital, although they still gave support to the race by providing the computers and technical support, and the sponsorship was shared between six companies. The other five were headed by Barclays Bank, who had been involved in the race from the start, and four other companies; Clark Whitehill, Horncastle Ford, who always did a great job of providing the lead vehicles all very smartly decorated with the event logos each year, Dunster and Morton, Surveyors, and TNT Printed Leisurewear, who provided T-shirts for several years. The race became one of the Star Rank HOT 100 races, which were set up to give individuals a personal ranking in their own category. The event produced a first back-to-back winner, when Paul Cuskin returned to win again in a slower time of 64:11. It was also one of the wetter race days. There was another huge entry, and the team race trophy went back to the 1986 winners, Westbury Harriers. The Barclays Bank Trophy for women went to a local girl, Marina Samy from Bracknell (the third twin to win that trophy), who won in 73:43. Chris Hallam took the wheelchair race for the second time, although he could not match the record time set by David Holding the previous year. The winning male vet was previous race winner and veteran winner Mike Hurd in 66:20, and the first lady vet was a local runner who had taken up running later in life, Jackie Jeffery.

This was the Stars and Stripes race, as we received three guests from Reading; England's twin Reading in Pennsylvania. The three had won their trip to our race as they had won or finished second in their category, in what was known as that town's Historic 10K Run. The team of three was led by their race winner, twenty-five-year-old Randy Haas, who had a best time of just over thirty minutes for the 10K. There was a last-minute replacement for the women's entry; Donna Anderson replacing Shelly Steely who had won the Historic Reading 10K, and the third team member was Tim Whitehead, an eighteen-year-old wheelchair athlete. In exchange, the Reading UK race was to send three athletes to compete in the US event later in the year. Randy Haas ran a very good race to finish thirteenth in 66:36, just one place in front of Tim Butler the first man from Reading to finish and earn his trip to the US. He was to be joined by the first Reading woman to finish, Caroline Hughes, 78:29, and the wheelchair winner Chris Hallam. Donna Anderson finished 270th in 83:38, and in the wheelchair race Tim Whitehead finished sixth out of twenty-four in 78:29.

The Mini Marathon winners were Russell Trimmings and, for the second successive year, Vicki Stevens.

The pre-race Pasta Party was held at the Three Men in a Boat at the Caversham Hotel, and to accommodate everyone the event started at 4 p.m. As always the leading race entrants attended and mixed with the 'also rans'. This was another established tradition that disappeared from the event in later years.

There was a huge entry of over 100 people running for the Imperial Cancer Research Fund, and they were motivated and led by Alice Gostomski from Reading, who turned out masses of runners for the charity every year. In this particular year the race hit the national headlines again but perhaps for the wrong reasons. It concerned a cancer victim, twenty-three-year-old Karen Still from Reading, who was one of the squad from the charity. She had been determined to make it around the 13.1 miles, even though like many she had never done anything like it before. She completed her challenge in close to three hours forty-five minutes, but when she arrived at the finish virtually everyone had gone home, and there was no one around to present her with her finisher's medal. The *Daily Star* presented her with their own 'Gold Award', and I arranged to meet her at her home along with some friends who had run with her to present her medal and other 'goodies'. It would be easy to list reasons why this happened, but the story did have that happy ending and all was forgiven, and both the event and the charity made national and local headlines yet again.

A very popular T-shirt for the 1989 event was produced with the Reading Gold Lion leaning on the event medal.

As in all the earlier years, the official on-street collection was carried out by the Rotary Club of Caversham, who with a large army of volunteers, collected around £5,000 from the spectators around the route; a task they took on for a number of years, raising a very considerable sum for various charities.

At the end of April that year, Digital brought someone from their Belfast office to see me to discuss how the results system worked. They had just taken on responsibility for producing the results for the Belfast Marathon, to be held on 1st May. After a quick discussion, it was decided that it would be better if I went to Belfast and did the results myself. For a couple of years I made the trip to Belfast on the early-morning shuttle from Heathrow, on the early May bank holiday. It was always a very enjoyable experience, even with the security that had to surround me and the event. After two years a young local man had learned enough about producing quick and accurate results, and he was able to take over.

Producing the results swiftly was not easy in Belfast, as there was not only the full normal marathon, but a marathon relay of the same distance run at the same time. The very small office, almost a cupboard, where I had to work my magic, was also used to store the emergency stretcher and medical equipment, so at times it got a bit cramped. I always arrived early in the morning, and was driven from the airport and through the various check points, before arriving at the leisure centre to find that the sniffer dogs and Army personnel were checking out my 'office'. Despite the limited facilities, I always managed to get the full results out and with the *Belfast Telegraph,* before I caught my shuttle flight home in the evening.

My most vivid memory of these race days, was the occasion when towards the end of the race (bands were playing and everyone was enjoying the day, including the ample supply of Guinness), the commentator, a mature man, a local journalist, got very emotional. He went away from his commentary on the race and said "What a wonderful day. Why, oh why can't we always be together like this?" Within days, when I had returned home, the violence that had been missing on Marathon weekend returned and people were dying again.

There were three races as part of the Reading AC Grand Prix Series run in July. The first was a 10K along the Thames, south of the river to Tilehurst and back, and then two races were run on the attractive Mapledurham Estate, north of the river; one a 8K and the other a full 10K again.

In October 1989 I helped with the organising of a 10K race in Guildford for the British Heart Foundation.

The three representatives from the Reading, England race, who ran in the Historic Reading 10K in Pennsylvania in October did very well, with Tim Butler from Reading AC winning the event. Chris Hallam won the wheelchair race and Caroline Hughes (now Stevens) from Reading AC, was second lady.

By the late 1980s the Reading race was being organised almost entirely by Marion and myself, with the help of fewer volunteers. A lot of the previous key people had gone from the scene for one reason or another. These included Terry Lewins, who had been a great help in setting up the finish each year and helping with the timing. He had tragically died at a young age and was missed, not just by the Reading race, but by other events where he was involved. Terry Harding had moved from Reading to a new post at Strathclyde, and Ian Moir had left the university at Reading. John London had also retired from the scene.

It was a tremendous workload. Apart from the actual organising of the race itself and all the setting up work, which included printing and delivering notes to all business and private premises on certain parts of the route, both as a courtesy and to ask them to keep vehicles off the road. We even made special parking arrangements for people who had nowhere else to keep their car but on the road. We received and dealt with all the entries, and this in itself was a major job that in many events would be handled by another agency. We did get valuable help from a few good volunteers with the mailing out of the race programmes and numbers, etc. One of these was Janet Robson, who along with husband Mike, had set up the International Spinal Research Trust Runners Network. They did, and do, great work for the charity, persuading runners to run and raise funds for them. They honoured me by making me their patron. The media were kept fully informed on the entries and stories as they emerged, from months before the race right up until the day. Entries would be received right up until the event, and team declarations would also arrive in the last couple of days, so that on the night before the race the computer would still be going at 3 a.m., putting in all the data and running off final print-outs for the media. By 5 a.m. I would be up and away to the venue to supervise the setting up of the gantries and barriers around the route.

The day of the race would last nearly twenty-four hours, as after the event we would be at home producing the results until they were accurate and ready for publication.

The first event to organise in 1990 was the second running of a Reading AC event; the Claude Fenton 10K run at Theale on the outskirts of Reading. The winner in 32:51 was Kevin Flavin (Reading AC) by just one second from Ernie Cunningham (Aldershot Farnham and District), a previous winner of the veteran category in the Reading Half. Tom Munt, also from Reading AC, was third in 33:16, and a runner from Holland was fourth.

The next race was the half marathon held on 1st April 1990, again from the South Reading Leisure Centre, for what was to be the last time. The race from that venue had drawn the biggest entries in the history of the event, and in many ways was a great venue, but it had one large problem, it was on a large housing estate and there were a lot of children in the area who could find nothing better to do on race weekend than climb all over the marquees and cause damage. They were particularly bad on the day before this final event from South Reading, and to get help to restore order and clear the site, I had to get the mayor out from an event so that she could put pressure on the police to do something so as to prevent further damage. We managed to keep the tented village in place and it was the usual 5 a.m. start next morning. There was a foggy start to the day, which later turned out to be very warm which brought the crowds out in the largest numbers since the race was first run in 1983.

The race started in spectacular fashion with the release of thousands of red and white balloons. This race was to be one of the most memorable, as it was to be not only the closest race in the history of the event, but also one of the closest half marathon finishes anywhere. Four runners finished within two seconds, and the first two could not be split. The referee was Derek Bradfield, a very experienced man from Reading AC, and after some debate and discussion Steve Brace (Bridgend) and Nick Trainer (North London) were given the joint first place in 63:32, with Greg Newhams third in 63:33, and Gary Nagle fourth in 63:34. The race winner was in doubt right up to the last 200 metres when they came around the last roundabout side by side. In that final dash the two eventual winners just edged ahead of the other two, but it was some race and is probably one of my lasting memories of that great event. The photo of the two winners crossing the line was to be used on race medals for events all over the country for some years after the event. The women's race went to Angie Pain in 72:21, still the second fastest time recorded by a woman in Reading, and the twelve seconds that she missed it by cost her an extra £1,000 that had been put up for a new course record. The wheelchair race saw Chris Hallam back in the driving set with his third win and a new record of 62:06. The veteran over forty winner was Ernie Cunningham for the second time in 67:54. Steve Brace led his team of Bridgend to victory in the team race for the first time. Reading AC were second with Windsor and Eton third, and Reading AC "B" team fourth. Reading Roadrunners were fifth. Accountants Ernst and Young won the Company team award.

In the Mini Marathon, which was being run for the fourth time, Craig Siddons ran the fastest time to date; 13:41. It followed on a good cross-country season for him, where he won a Berkshire title and finished forty-fifth in the English Schools Cross-Country. A new face won the girls' race; Claudia Lawrence in 16:40.

Some runners found the going a little hot, including Reading Jogger Arthur Abbott who was dressed in a red lion outfit for the race. A total of fifty runners were treated for heat exhaustion by the St John Ambulance. Reading girl and TV presented Kathy Tayler ran to raise money for the British Sports Association for the Disabled. They had a bonus on the day as an event sponsor who had put up the prizes for the course records on this occasion and did not have to part with the money, gave a special donation of £500 to the charity as a thank you for the excellent performances by the wheelchair athletes. Blind runner Bill Gulliver ran the course in ninety-nine minutes, and staff from the Special Baby Unit of Buscot Ward in the Royal Berkshire Hospital, raised over £2,000 for their good cause.

It was a very successful event, and as one local newspaper put it *"The course was well marked and traffic well controlled by police. By early afternoon, the runners, plastic cups, all the usual debris from a race had gone, and the wonderfully supportive Reading population was left to enjoy the unexpected 'summer afternoon'."*

In November it was back to Reading University for the annual Reading AC ten mile race, which attracted one of its largest entries, with over 400 taking part. The race had the quantity but perhaps not the quality on this occasion, and it was won by Mark Cooper of Southampton AC in 51:34, from Ian Van Lokven (Burnham Joggers) in 52:38, with Tom Munt third in 52:57. The team winners were the home team of Reading AC from Aldershot and Reading Roadrunners A and B teams. This was a time when the decline in running standards was beginning to notice for the first time.

Before the next half marathon could take place there were more changes to deal with, and the course had to be measured yet again. I had got quite used to working with various course measurers over the years. The first person I worked with was John Jewell of the Road Runners Club, an ex-long distance man himself and one of the characters of road running. John was still measuring courses on his old cycle up to around eighty years of age. He was meticulous and had passed on a lot of his skills to others. One of these was Richard Whybrow from Reading Athletic Club, who was now responsible for measuring the more recent half marathon routes. In a busy town like Reading this was not easy, as the course had to be measured on the shortest possible route a runner might take on the closed roads on race day. Normally the measuring was done at first light with Richard on his bicycle, and if we were lucky a police escort to assist, especially when he was cycling on the wrong side of the road. There were always some hair-raising moments covering the 13.1 miles around Reading.

The slogan for 1991 was "Everyone's a Winner", and out of an entry of over 6,000 there were 4,425 finishers. The race had moved to a new venue; the Rivermead Leisure Complex near the Thames at Caversham. It was a very windy day and not conducive to fast times, but Steve Brace had another win, this time in 64:28, not a fast time but he had a good margin over second runner Greg Newhams, 65:09, and Gary Nagle third in 65:22. The race was used as an inter area competition by the AAAs. Pete Marsh from the Army was the winning vet in twentieth place with 69:49. Tom Munt (Reading AC) in twenty-second place with 70:09 was the first local runner. The winning lady veteran, Celia Duncan, was well back in the pack in 139th place with 78:59. The team race went to Bridgend again, with Bournemouth second, and Norwich Road Runners third. In the women's race it was one, two, and three for Reading Roadrunners, who also won the award for first vet men's team. There was the now familiar sight of the Essex Police regular runners at Reading. Group Ten as they were known, were running as usual in police uniform, except on their feet and legs that is. This year they were aiming to raise £10,000 for research into leukaemia and kidney disease. Another uniformed runner was fireman Steve Beard, who found the going 'hot' over the 13.1 miles. Three other runners made running tough on themselves by pushing wheelchairs around the course. Brian Bacon (Reading AC), fifty-six years old, pushed nine-year-old Daniel Cooney and finished in 1:40.26. He pushed many youngsters from the Avenue Special School in Reading, where his wife Stella was a teacher, in all the half marathons from 1985 to 2000. With his faster runners taking under ninety minutes. While thirty-two-year-old Joe Gregory pushed friend Karl Hodgson round in 1:49.

The wheelchair race again attracted a great field of entries; twenty-six in total, with David Holding winning in a time of 59:50 to leave Chris Hallam, the winner of the previous year, well behind in 67:58. Rose Hill again won the women's race in the slightly faster time of 75:42. Chris Hallam's comment after the race was "The b.....r took it from the start racing past me at nineteen-twenty miles an hour; there's always next year."

The largest of the charity groups was the Imperial Cancer Research team, with sixty-eight runners raising around £6,000 for their charity.

The winner of the Mini Marathon was someone who a few years later was to feature in the main event; sixteen-year-old Steve Smith from Newbury won the three mile event in 15:5 from over 300 young men and women. Claudia Lawrence repeated her win of the previous year with a time of 15:45.

The Reading AC ten mile was run again from the university in November, and over 200 runners took part. The first three runners all came from the home club, with former Bournemouth AC runner Tim Butler first to finish in 50:48. Dave Ramsay was second in 51:20, and Andy Neatham third in 51:53.

There had been some eventful and frantic moments around the half marathon since its inception, but nothing so dramatic as what happened just prior to the start of the 1992 race. We had always been aware that there could be some sort of security incident on the day of the half marathon in any year. I had discussed it with the local police chief on more than one occasion, and I remember what I said to him when he asked whether the runners would stop if asked after the race had started. I told him nothing would stop them and if they put cars across the road they would probably run over them! To his credit he agreed and we just hoped it would not happen. But this was the year when something did happen; as all the runners were lining up on Richfield Avenue, the wheelchair athletes were ready to be sent on their way by the mayor. Suddenly I got a message to see the police superintendent in charge of the policing of the event. He was very close by so I was able to meet him at once. He told me that he had just been notified of a suspicious car left abandoned outside the Army Recruiting Office in the St Mary's Butts, Reading, right on the route the runners had to go. They had called in the bomb experts and the whole area had been cordoned off so the runners could not go that way. I had to make one of those instant decisions; delay, postpone, cancel or go over a shortened route? I did not feel I could keep the runners hanging about, and what do you do with 6,000 people waiting to run? So the race was started and the runners did not run a full half marathon that year. I estimated afterwards that it was about 750 metres short. It was announced to the runners before the start, but in the excitement waiting for the start few heard the news, and when they returned to the finish many thought that they had run personal best times; some may never have realised and have kept their times as PBs. The winner of that eventful race was Steve Brace for the third successive year. His time 62:20, probably equated to about sixty-four minutes for the full and correct distance. His team Bridgend also got their hat trick of wins, by carrying off the Sweat Shop Trophy for the third time. Gebriye Tsegay (Reading Roadrunners), finished in twelfth place, with a time of 65:57, to be the first Reading man home, but because of the shortened course his time was probably worth about sixty-eight minutes for the full distance, but still a very big improvement on his 1991 time of 72:05. David Holding won the wheelchair event again, with what would almost certainly have been a new record, 55:30, and Rose Hill won the women's wheelchair race for the third successive year. The Arlington

Business Trophy went to the Whitbread Beer Company, Gloucester. The first athletic/jogging club for women winners were Ravishing Rampert Runners.

In the mini marathon the winner of the Reading Leisure Trophy was Jonathan Cooper, and Claudia Lawrence took the trophy for first girl; her third successive win.

Yellow Pages 10K; Grant Thornton 10K; Rockfort 10K; Littlecote 15K; Stratfield Saye 10K; Courage Half Marathon; Oxford Half Marathon; Okehampton Half Marathon; Claude Fenton 10K and ten miles; Mapledurham Grand Prix; Fulham FC Fun Run; Nabisco Fun Runs; National Children's Fun Runs for SportsAid; New Year Midnight Runs through Reading; New Year's Day 10Ks for National Playing Fields Association in Hyde Park; and even some one mile road races in Milton Keynes —these were all good events that helped to encourage people to take up running.

During the early to mid 1980s John London and myself set up a race organising company, Running Management Services, which organised a large number of these running events, and some of the latter ones were run by myself. The first of these events was the Ron Hill Sports 10K run on 21st October 1984. It was part of a nationwide series, and the Reading race, which was run from Palmer Park, the home of Reading AC, attracted 452 runners; the largest event in the series. The first three runners all beat thirty minutes, and the first across the finish line was Martin Philpot (Hillingdon AC) in 29:36. The first sixteen runners beat thirty-two minutes.

The following year the sponsor of the 10K changed to Arrow, a shoe company wanting to promote itself in the UK.

In October 1985 we organised the first race for Yellow Pages, when they took over as sponsors of what had become an annual 10K race in Reading. It continued to be a good event, but the new sponsor went overboard with the promotion of itself; something that was to be repeated nearly ten years later in the Reading Half Marathon, when they took over as sponsors. This event continued for a further two years under the Yellow Pages banner. For the first two years the race was run from Whiteknights Park (Reading University), and in the final year the race moved to Palmer Park. This actually brought races from that venue to an end, as the police said they would not allow another race from Palmer Park because of traffic conditions. A great pity, as the running track and facilities provided an ideal location, and many races are run from local running tracks. Nearly 1,000 runners lined up for this final race, and it was another good quality field with winner Chris Buckley (Westbury Harriers) clocking 29:11. The early leader had been an "American at Oxford", Paul Gompers, who had a previous best time of 28:24, but finished up in third place with 29:36 on this occasion. Mike Cadman (Wolverhampton and Bilston) was second in 29:32, and there were fifteen runners inside thirty-two minutes. The outstanding run of the day was by the man who finished in eighth place, Taff Davies (Aldershot), who recorded 30:35; the fastest time in the world by a fifty years plus veteran. Westbury Harriers won the team race, with home team Reading AC taking second place, and the other new local team Reading Roadrunners fourth place behind Aldershot. The surprise in the women's race was the defeat of the two 'Samy' twins by Alison Gooderham (Bournemouth) 33:48, and Lynne Harvey (London Olympiads) 34:41. Marina Samy was third in 34:48, and sister Shireen, who had won the race in the previous year was fourth in 35:29.

The following year, 1988, we could not get permission to go back to the same venue, so we moved the event to Cantley Park at Wokingham. It was Olympic Year and the usual request had gone out for fund raising, and we persuaded Accountants Grant Thornton to sponsor a fund raising 10K in March.

After John London decided to retire from race organising I continued, not just with Reading, but with other events as they came along. These included New Year's Day 10Ks for the National Playing Fields Association in Hyde Park. I organised these in 1995 to 1998. Hyde Park was a good venue, but New Year's Day was not the best day to be organising a road run around the Royal Park. We had high winds, heavy rain, snow and frost, which made the task of producing quick results more difficult than normal.

In 1997 I was approached by Ian Branfoot, the former Reading FC Manager who was now at Fulham, to organise a fun run from the football ground, as part of an open day at Craven Cottage on 6th April. It was a nice event, and the race went along the towpath on both sides of the river; most of the Fulham team took part and some of them were very good runners.

The quality of races was lifted by the likes of my partner John London and myself during the 1980s. Time clocks were introduced; prizes were improved; many more category prizes were given, and the overall management of events was much better, with proper marshalling and water stations. Proper full results were also possible with the help of special computer programmes. Sadly by the end of the 1990s things were drifting back to the old sloppy ways, except in the larger events. Races were being run by well-meaning amateurs, some in charities and others in the athletic clubs where time had stood still. Some events have started to use technology to produce results swiftly, but others are still struggling with quills and ink. Having said that, the way that results were produced forty or fifty years ago did have some merit. In events like marathons, the results always included the times at various stages like five, ten, fifteen and twenty miles, not just for the lead runners, but for all those taking part.

Chapter Sixteen

France — The Return Run

In 1992, just ten years after my first run from France, I was persuaded to run the 175 miles in the opposite direction, finishing at the French end. On a very wet Saturday morning we were outside the old Town Hall in Reading, ready for the start. A small group of us were sent on our way by the mayor, including some Rotaractors in fancy dress. Well-known blind Reading runner Bill Gulliver was there, and he was going to run with me to Portsmouth; also in the line up, an old friend, Kathy Tayler, television travel presenter and former world modern pentathlon champion. She was there to support me by running the first few miles with us. There were also five French runners, including my old friend Alain Hau, who had cycled with me on the first run, but had now taken up running. Dominque Zitouni from the Meru Athletic Club; Monique Spiguelaire, a thirty-eight-year-old mother; René Bollé, a veteran runner in his sixties, and José Antonio Santiago, all from the Meru Athletic Club. Before we left a lady rushed up and gave me a St Christopher medallion. I said thank you, but that was all, and do not know who it was. It may have been someone I should have known, or it may have been a complete stranger, but in the excitement of the moment it did not register with me. I hope one day I will find out who she was.

Off we went with our escort runners, cyclists and vehicles. We ran out from Reading for a few miles, and said goodbye to Kathy as we left the town. In my diary of the event I describe the run and how I felt on each stretch. The first 14.5 miles, run in two hours nine minutes, I wrote 'going well'. It really was raining hard, and the water was pouring down the side of the road as we ran towards Basingstoke. I like the rain, and I could see to avoid the water, potholes and puddles, but for Bill Gulliver it was very tough. The minders and myself tried to help him as much as we could, but he got very cold and wet. The second section of 13.5 miles took two hours twenty-eight minutes, and the last four miles were described as 'tough'. Eventually we arrived at our first stop, Faringdon in Hampshire, and we had all had enough. We were wet, cold, and I had a bit of jogger's nipple, even though I had given myself the Vaseline treatment. My main problem however was my diabetes. I ended up very low on blood sugar (2.4), and the doctor who was accompanying us decided I would need some help to get through the next and subsequent days. Total distance on that first day in the rain, twenty-eight miles or 47K in 4:37.

We all returned to Reading that night; it was the plan, as there was no point in putting up at a hotel only twenty-eight miles down the road. Alan Hau and another of my French companions came back to my home, where Marion had the washing machine going to wash all the socks and T-shirts that we had used on the first day. We had a good roast beef meal and some wine and an early night. There was some disappointment however when Bill Gulliver confirmed he would not be able to continue next day.

The next morning it was up and back to the finish point of the previous day. The weather was a bit better, and the entourage set out for the thirty miles to Portsmouth. Dr Borthwick had been to the local Savacentre and bought up their stock of glucose tablets, which were to be my life-saver over the next few days. The weather was better and there was a following wind, and I ran 14.6 miles in 2:30; but the next section of 6.3 miles was not so good, and it took me seventy-five minutes. We made our way south, and had a good run into Portsmouth with the help of Portsmouth Joggers, running the 5.7 miles in just an hour, and arrived at the Mountbatten Sports Centre in Portsmouth in the late afternoon, where we were welcomed by Portsmouth North Rotary Club and others. Total running distance that day 26.6 miles or 43K, and total time 4:45. A shower and meal followed before boarding the cross-channel ferry for the night crossing to Le Havre.

I slept well on the boat; I have always been able to sleep anywhere, and arrived refreshed in France at 7 a.m. next morning. A slight hiccup here, as we had been told that the Rotary Club were to meet us and take us to a breakfast meeting. This did not materialise, but arrangements were made by our escorting French to have breakfast before setting on our way towards Meru and Chambly; our final destinations. We had left the wet and windy weather of England behind, and in France it was quite warm again, like my first run in the opposite direction. The target for the first day in France was Norville about 35.5K from Le Havre. We set off at 9.10 a.m., and my legs were very stiff and it took time to get running properly. The first section was just over eleven miles (18K), which was reached in just over two hours, but we made good progress and my legs were easing as we ran the next 10K in sixty-five minutes. Finally it was just 7.5K to finish the day, and we all grouped together those that were running all the time, and those who were running in stages, and although very tired it was a 'sprint' finish for a bit of fun. That final stretch took just fifty minutes, and the 35.5K (22 miles) had taken four hours of running time.

The mayor of the small town of Norville, where we finished that day, suddenly found out that we were arriving and sent his wife off to the hypermarket to buy drinks so that he could entertain us! He was very generous and took the instant decision to give us a cheque.

We were now well into the run, and I had stopped taking my pills for the control of my diabetes and instead was taking dextrose tablets very frequently, as well as sweet drinks to keep me going. It was the reverse of my normal lifestyle of avoiding all things sweet.

Next morning, Tuesday, we left Norville at 9 a.m.; there was a following wind, and the first session went well with 21K covered in just over two hours. I seem to remember lunch followed and a glass of wine or two, and at 1 p.m. I had to start running again. I was stiff as I started running, but it improved and I covered the 8K in forty-seven minutes. Another short break outside of Rouen, where fifteen from the local athletic club joined me and the others for the final run to the Hotel de Ville in Rouen. It was just about rush hour as we hit Rouen, but that was not a problem as the gendarmes were there to provide a motorcycle escort into the town. They rode in front and stopped all the traffic at every junction to give us a free run. We had a good final 5K to finish in front of the Town Hall, where there was a huge banner welcoming me and the others to the town. The last leg was run in just twenty-six minutes. A total for the day of 34K (twenty-one miles or so) in 3:17. There were speeches, champagne and presentations, before we called it a day and retired to recover for the next day.

It was now Wednesday and very hot, and we started running at about 10.30. We ran a first section of 13K in eighty-one minutes. Followed by two more legs of 12.5K in eighty-nine minutes, and a short run over only 4.5K in thirty minutes, to finish the day with 30K (nineteen miles) run in a time of three hours twenty minutes. Again I had been met by about thirty-five youngsters from the local school at Entrepagny, who ran with me to the Town Hall for yet another presentation and reception. It was a hot day and the running had been tough, and as I ran into the finish there was a funeral going on next door to the Town Hall; not the best welcome when I felt shattered anyway.

I had a good night's sleep, and 10 a.m. next morning we lined up for the first run of the day. It was a short run of 10K, which we covered in fifty-eight minutes, followed by just 2K (eight minutes), before arriving in Gisors. We then ran on to the Golf Club, a further 6.5K, where we stopped and met runners who were going to escort us for the final run of the day. This was an interesting part of the run, as we were joined by a large group of young children and a local farmer; not a young man, who was determined to run with me. TV Picardy joined us for some TV coverage, and they seemed to have the camera set on my feet most of the time. It was as my diary said 'very, very hot'. I wrote at the end of the day 'a very moving experience, more than anything previous'. I added 'Tomorrow is it! Lots of bits aching but OK'.

It was now Friday, and the only thing left to do was to run to Meru via Chambly. The day started with 10K, run in fifty-two minutes, which took us to Chambly where my wife and others met up with us for the final run in. The next 7K took thirty-six minutes. We met up on a roundabout with about thirty school children a few miles from the finish, and then the final leg began. We were all running together; the two runners who had run all the way with me, and the others who had run sections of the run with us, plus the youngsters who had now joined us. We joined hands as we turned into the square at Meru. What a sight greeted us; there were lots of people; a stage, band and flags and bunting. It was fantastic and I was, I admit, very moved that the French had gone to so much trouble. There were speeches; the national anthems were played, and there were presentations to all of the runners. Then the champagne flowed. I was interviewed by the local press and media, and when asked if I would do it again, I said not before 2002, and added that I would be an old-age pensioner before then.

The total raised by us and the French was around £30,000. Our contribution went again to Sport for Disabled People, through a Trust that was set up for the purpose. The French raised their money for heart equipment at their local hospital. Much of the money raised was by selling buttonhole pin badges; very popular in France. These had the flags of the two countries, the Rotary Wheel and a picture of a runner who had a moustache, and had a close resemblance to the man who had run the distance twice! These two runs had been very hard work for the runners and all concerned, but they were great for international relations, one of the reasons they were set up, were great fun and helped others by our efforts. There were speeches, presentations and the national anthems; it was like a mini Olympic Games ceremony, and perhaps it made up for missing my Olympic chance thirty-two years earlier.

Chapter Seventeen

The Last Two Years in Charge at Reading

Then it was back to work on the 1993 Reading Half Marathon. There was no major sponsor forthcoming, although a great deal of work went into trying to find one, but it was the height of recession and so the race had to go ahead without one. The entry was not quite as large as in the past, but it did produce a really great race.

Sitting in the lead car, which I always did on race day (mainly because I could not trust that the course was going to be correctly directed), I watched a tall blond runner, Paul Evans from Belgrave Harriers, stride around the 13.1 miles. It was obvious from the first couple of miles that something special was going to happen, and as each mile rolled off in something like 4:40, and the ten miles went by in forty-seven minutes, it was obvious the record for the course was going to go, and there was no easing up on the pace into the final 3.1 miles, which he covered in 14:38, to arrive back at the finish in the excellent time of 61:38. It really was a superb run, and it was a pity that the whole race was not televised or videoed. Paul was well rewarded for his splendid run with a cheque for £1,000 and a new Ford Fiesta. It really was a great run, and it was my privilege to be one of only three or four people to see the whole of that great run.

The first twenty-one runners beat seventy minutes. The runner-up was Peter Whitehead in 63:32, with Joseph Keptum (Kenya) third in 63:46. Three times winner Steve Brace was fourth in 64:43, with a Russian Vladimir Shtyrts fifth with 64:55. The event winner from 1988 and 1989 Paul Cuskin, was sixth in 65:37.

The wheelchair race also produced two other records and two new winners, when Ian Thompson won in 59:23, and Tanni Grey (Grey-Thompson) won the John London Trophy as first lady in the new record time of 67:18.

The first local runner was again Tsegay from Reading Roadrunners; this time with 69:48 (nineteenth); and Tom Munt (Reading AC) featured for the first time, finishing just behind Tsegay in 69:50 (twenty-first). The team race was won by Bridgend AC for the fourth successive year, with Reading Roadrunners just grabbing second place from Les Croupiers

Running Club (Wales). But the Welsh club picked up two of the other team awards; the Women's and the Athletic Club Veterans. The Royal Mail team won the companies category, which gave them fourth place overall in the team race. The Kempton Children's Ward at the Royal Berkshire Hospital won the Charity Team award, and the men's over seventy category winner was Ralph Batten in 101:26. In the Reading Leisure Mini Marathon, the winner was Daniel Getliffe in 11:58, with Jo Winterbourne first girl to finish in 13:51.

The battles with the police and Reading Borough Council, that I had during the life of the event, continued. They did not seem to appreciate the importance of the event, either as a race, a community activity, or as the major fund-raising event that it was; or at least that was the impression they liked to give. These battles continued throughout the history of the race up to 1994. There were good years and not such good years, with regard to relationships with the council, and those connected to the event had to be strong-willed not to give in to pressure from these bureaucrats to abandon the race. I remember John London saying to me one day in the early years, that he would have to walk away from the event because he could not stand the attitude of the council. Even the council employee who sat on the original organising committee stated on one occasion, that the event would be much better with proper support from the council. John London did eventually do just what he threatened to do, and walked away from the event. I carried on for a number of years, striving to make the event one of the outstanding running events of its kind.

The media as well were difficult to please, although they were coming round to giving the event the support it deserved. We always had a battle with the local papers because they both said that only one could be officially involved with the event. This remained a problem throughout the history of the event. These problems were sent to try us, and we sometimes wondered why we were doing it. It was certainly not for the money, as none of us were being paid in the early years. It was something that I think the Town Hall mandarins could not understand in their cosy little world of well-paid jobs.

The hot and cold attitude of the local council built up from the time we moved to Rivermead, and came to a head in 1994 after a couple of difficult years. First of all they started to charge for the use of the facilities there, and the cooperation was almost nonexistent. Then the police brought in charges for their services, based on the fact that if we were paying the council, we could pay them. There were other ways in which they did not cooperate with the event, that made the task of keeping it going even harder. This was not the fault of the staff of the council, as the individuals I had dealt with over the years had always been friendly and cooperative. The problem was the policy makers and senior management, who resented the success of an event they could have controlled from day one, but chose not to. First of all they started to charge for the use of the facilities and many of the small things that they did around the event. Prior to the 1994 event, I had a lot of problems with the police. Instead of dealing with someone of senior rank, like a superintendent or above, the race came under the control for policing purposes of an inspector, who turned out to be not very stable and totally inadequate. He did not understand, or did not want to understand the event, but I did try to work with him, and everything possible was done to meet their requirements. Reading Leisure Services promised to supply marshals from their Over 50 Club and to give us other help, but this help did not materialise, and it became obvious that this was all part of their plan to grab the event. As a result of a public appeal, we did man all the crucial points of the route. In fact their whole attitude was to be very unhelpful to an event that was well established and brought credit to the town.

In spite of all the problems and lack of cooperation the race went off well, and as in all the twelve races I controlled, there were no hazardous incidents. The race was held on a difficult date; just one week before London; which did effect the entry quite considerably. Both the running entry and the wheelchair entry were well down on normal, and the event had an air of a local run like that first event in 1983.

The winner was not local though. Andrew Leach, a thirty-year-old from Bingley Harriers in Yorkshire, headed the field of 2,500 runners to the finish. His winning time of 66:46 was the slowest to date for the race, but that still gave him a two minute plus lead over second placed runner, John Matthews (Bracknell AC), who was running on this occasion for the Imperial Cancer Charity Team. Bob Treadwell (Redhill and Surrey Beagles) was third in the race and first veteran, in 69:42, to repeat his category win of the previous year, with Ian Van Locken (Burnham Joggers) fourth in 71:22. The winner of the ladies' race at last was Tanya Ball (London Olympiads AC) in 84:40. It was her fifth attempt at winning the race, after finishing in the frustrating position of fourth in her previous four runs.

In 1988 we had set up a Reading Half Marathon Supporters' Club, and the members of this exclusive club had helped to keep the event alive by their annual subscriptions and support each year. I was sorry when this club had to disappear with the changeover in the management of the race.

Things really came to a head after this race, even though the race went off well as usual. There had been increasing problems with both the police and Reading Borough Council from when we moved to Rivermead Leisure Complex at Caversham in 1991. First of all the council started charging for parts of the administration around the event that they had previously covered as part of their sponsorship. These costs included those related to the road closures, cleaning up after the event, and a charge for the use of the leisure facility. Somehow the problems snowballed, as the police found out that the council were paying for nothing, they did not see why they should provide their services free of charge, so they passed on a charge to the event of several thousand pounds. I don't think that I even realised then what dirty tricks were being played, and I had no idea what was to follow.

After the race it was agreed that we would have the usual 'wash-up' meeting, and I duly went along to the Civic Offices to the meeting. Normally these meetings would have representatives from the police, Reading Transport, St John Ambulance, Reading Leisure Services, the chief marshal and myself. I duly arrived at the Civic Offices at the appointed time, only to be kept waiting quite some time. I then went into the room where we were due to meet, only to find people there I did not expect to see, and what was worse, it was very obvious that a meeting had already taken place. It was equally obvious then, as now, that the two main people responsible had only been involved in the town for a very short time, and both left within a few months of this meeting. They were the Chief Executive and the Chief Superintendent of Police. In fact the police chief had his own problems with his officers, when some of them complained to the local paper about poor morale, and he did not last long in the town after that. At this stage it was clear that the Reading Borough Council were going to get more involved with the event, and not necessarily to the advantage of the event. In the room was Roy Brown who ran the Reading Leisure Services, and the meeting concluded that I should talk to him about the future. I could still be involved and I could sort the details of how it was to work with him.

Over the next few months there were to be a lot of meetings between him and myself. The negotiations went well initially, and we had talks about a joint venture where I would carry out some of the work on the event for a set fee. Part of our negotiations were around the overdraft of the event, which I had guaranteed for around £15,000. I gave permission for Brown to speak to Barclays Bank, but instead of doing any good it actually made things worse. While these discussions were going on, I agreed to let him have a list of the previous year's runners for a sum of £1,000. Promises were made by him but were not kept, and in the end I lost control of the event, and was left with a direct debt of around £18,000, and an indirect linked debt of around twice that amount. The loss of the event in this way cost me around £40,000; some of which was paid out by me over a period, and a sum of £18,000 that I had to pay Barclays Bank to clear my guarantee on the sale of my home in Caversham in 1998. The loss of this total sum was more than any money I had received for the administration of the event by me and my staff over the twelve years.

No satisfactory announcement was ever made about the change, and to this day I know that a lot of people think I still have a connection with the event that I set up and ran for twelve years, but my only connection in recent years has been as a columnist for the *Reading Evening Post* and writing for and about the event. The only money ever received from Reading Borough Council was that £1,000 for a list of runners which they could target for 1995, when Yellow Pages had been taken on as sponsor of the event. Something I have never understood till this day is, why they, Yellow Pages, could not have been part of the event in the really good days. The unsatisfactory situation was never resolved, they stole the event and left me with the bill. I was entitled to Legal Aid, and I tried to get some legal support and did spend money on legal advice as well, but it was all to no avail. Legal Aid would not touch the case, because they thought the chances of winning a case against a large council was not good, even though it was accepted there was a case. In fact on one occasion a prominent local councillor was heard to remark that they did not care what action I took, no one could win against them. I learned just how hard it is to get help and support when you hit hard times. Even my own solicitors, although sympathetic, would not help to pursue the matter, because they also had Barclays Bank as their clients.

Within months of the chief superintendent disappearing from the scene, the Chief Executive of Reading Borough left for pastures new. This left just Roy Brown from that stitch-up squad, but in 1999 he finally disappeared from the 'Reading Mafia' as well. I think he was the unfortunate who was left to do the dirty work of the council.

Since the council took over the event, no accounts have ever been published and no one knows where the money goes, or how much the sponsors put into the race. With income each year of up to £80,000, without the sponsorship, there are some questions to be asked about the current structure of the event. The total income, with free services provided by support sponsors, must now be well in excess of £120,000. The costs of staging the event should not be any more than half that, as they still do not pay many of the volunteer helpers, and the prize money at the event has not increased. So where does the rest go? I believe that the sponsors share the responsibility for this, as they do not declare what resources they actually contribute to the event. They are not the same quality sponsors as Digital were in the first six years. They were very straightforward sponsors, and there was a very good working relationship with all levels of management in that company, and they worked hard with the organisers to build the foundations for the great success it was to become.

Chapter Eighteen

A Fresh Start

After a very difficult year following the 1994 Half Marathon, I started to rebuild my life and interests, and in March 1995 I took on a role with SportsAid Foundation (Southern) in Reading. I had carried out a little work for them before when I organised the Reading part of the National Children's Fun Runs.

The Reading Half Marathon of 1995 was the first time that I had not been involved with the event. It was difficult in one way, as for twelve years the race had been my life and I had taken it from nowhere to a major event over that period. In another way I suppose it was a relief not to have all the worries of organising a major event, especially as it was with a hostile Borough Council.

The first three places went to runners from East Africa, who running as team Damji were on a three-month tour of Europe. The winner from Tanzania was a seventeen-year-old civil servant Baha Tulumbo, who won quite comfortably in a comparatively slow time of 64:49, from Robert Naali in 65:56, and Paul Sigei in 65:59. In the slower run race it gave many local runners the chance to make high finishing positions, and these were led home by Howard Grubb (Reading Roadrunners) in eighth place with 69:24, which was just one second ahead of Bracknell runner Paul Daly in ninth place with 69:25. Andy Neatham, a Reading AC runner, better known as a 1,500 metre man, was eleventh in 71:31, and Chris Mason (Reading Roadrunners) also made it in the top twenty, with eighteenth place and 74:09. The veteran prize for the forty to forty-nine year age group went to Robert Treadwell (Redhill Surrey Beagles), for the third successive year, who finished tenth in 70:39. The wheelchair race provided another spectacular time, when Chris Madden set new figures of 56:06. It was a good year for the green vests of Reading Roadrunners, as they collected team trophies for both the men and women.

The fourteenth Half Marathon was run on Sunday, 31st March 1996. There was only a modest entry that produced just 2,528 finishers. On this occasion it was good to see a victory for a British athlete over two Kenyans. The winner was Garry Staines (Belgrave Harriers) in 63:31, and he had two minutes to spare over the two Kenyans, Yatich and Kipchumba, who both finished in 65:38. Several of the top awards went to local clubs, including the first vet over forty, Dave Lancaster (Reading AC), with 74:01. In the ladies' race, Caroline Horne (Crawley) received the trophy as first lady with 79:08, and second place went to Lesley Whiley (Reading Roadrunners) with 80:53. The first vet male fifty/fifty-four went to J. Sheridan (London Irish) with 74:42, and the next age group, fifty-five/fifty-nine, was another local win with Brian Fozard (Reading AC), the headmaster of a local special school, who recorded 84:37. The winner of the over sixty was Alf Toomer (Vets AC), a sports shop owner from Southampton, with 88:41; and the over sixty-five went to Paddy Phillips (Reading Roadrunners), with a time of 108:30. The first two in the ladies' race were also the first two vets thirty-five plus to finish, and the other category winners were forty plus, Sue Ogilvy with 86:50, forty-five/forty-nine, D. Phillips (Angels RC) 93:39; fifty/fifty-four, Diane Stares (Reading Roadrunners) 99:14; fifty-five/fifty-nine, Pat Bonner (Finch Coasters) 109:47, and sixty plus, Christine Usher (Reading Roadrunners) 99:02.

In the team competitions local teams were dominant, with Reading AC winning the male team event with just thirty-five points for the first time since their back-to-back wins in the first two years — (Tom Munt tenth, Andy Neatham twelfth and Dave Lancaster thirteenth). Reading Roadrunners were the runners-up with sixty-five points and they also provided the third, fifth, sixth and seventh teams. The veteran male team winners were Reading Roadrunners with 307 points, and the same club won the female team award with just eight points (Whiley, Hartney and Bowker). The outstanding feature of the women's race was that all six finishing teams were from the same club, Reading Roadrunners. The company team male went to Royal Mail, that was made up of their employees who were also members of the 'Green Vests' of Reading Roadrunners. The race was also used by the police as their Half Marathon Championship, and the winners were Sussex Police AC.

With all the technical support the race now had, it still had difficulty in producing the results for the presentations; a problem that persisted for several years, until they decided not to try and produce all the category winners immediately after the race.

The Reading Half Marathon 1997 moved a little earlier in the year, and this did produce a better entry with just over 3,600 finishers. There were no African runners in the men's race this year, and the winner in a comparatively slow time for the event of 64:50 was Spencer Duval (Cannock and Staffs AC). He was chased home by two Blackheath Harriers, Mark Steinle 64:55 and William Foster 64:58. The only Kenyan in the race, Lucia Subano, won the women's race in 75:44. Chris Madden took the wheelchair race with 58:13, which made up for his disappointment in 1996 when he had a puncture. I decided to run the race for the first time as I was nearly sixty-one years old, and I managed to finish in an official time of 1:57.58. My real time was a couple of minutes faster, but that did not matter, I had run the event that I started and it was very satisfying. I had run the full course several times in early years to check it out for problems from the runners' point of view.

In April I ran the London Marathon for the second time; this time wearing the SportsAid vest and raising money for that organisation. On this occasion I had the advantage of starting from the special start with the older runners, as I was over sixty years of age. This was a lot easier than the mass start, as there were a lot less runners to battle against, at least until the three various start groups merged after three miles. I knew I had not done enough training, but I had prepared with my limited time available and I did survive, although I was suffering towards the end, and finished in just about four hours thirty minutes, after reaching halfway in just under two hours. I vowed I would not put myself through it again, and to date I have not done so, but there might still be time. It is a marvellous event to take part in, and wherever or whenever you finish there is a feeling of satisfaction.

At the same time as I started with SportsAid in 1995, I also started writing a column for the *Reading Evening Post,* and this took me back to my early days as an athlete, when I used to write that column for the *Reading Standard* at £3 a time and that free portable typewriter. In the early years of the Half Marathon I also had a column in the weekly *Reading Chronicle*. I have always enjoyed putting words on paper, and I suppose this is why I have put this book together in my latter years.

I did work for a number of years, both in a voluntary and professional capacity for Disability Sport. I still think that working with disabled people in sport is very worthwhile, and I have not been able to completely let go of my involvement with them. I enjoyed organising the London Wheelchair Marathon in the early 1990s, even though it was not easy having to fight with Chris Brasher over certain aspects of the event. The most publicised battle was in 1992, when there was an attempt to put restrictions on the racers in wheelchairs. There was always a limit on slower competitors taking part, because it was thought that they could interfere with the runners in the latter stages of the race, but in this particular year there was an attempt to introduce a time limit the other way. Because the wheelchair athletes were getting very much faster (the world best was down to under 1:30), there was a fear that anyone getting round in under 1:45 would cause serious problems at places like the Tower of London. We were therefore given instructions that all wheelchair athletes should finish between three hours and 1:45, with a threat that anyone going faster could be pulled out! Imagine saying this to the leading runners in the race. I was furious at this crazy suggestion, and there was a lot of media coverage surrounding this dispute. I think I won that battle, but it did not matter anyway as there was no way the top wheelchair athletes were going to go that fast on the twisting, fairly difficult, London course with the Tower of London cobbles. In the end the restriction was lifted, although I have a feeling that even as late as 2001, there may still be attempts to restrict wheelchairs in some way.

I enjoyed fund raising for BSAD, and I liked attending their various sports events. I met a lot of interesting people, including the late Denis Howell (Lord Howell) the former Minister of Sport at an athletic meeting in Birmingham. He was a great man, dedicated to sport in general, and we had something in common; we were both diabetic. Sadly I only met him on this one occasion, because he was a fascinating man to talk to and his knowledge on sport was unsurpassed. On the same day I hosted the then Heritage Minister Chris Smith, but they conveniently did not meet, as I understood Denis Howell did not have much sympathy for New Labour and wanted [illegible] away from the stadium before the minister arrived.

Since my involvement with BSAD in 1983, I have remained very interested in sport for people with disabilities. From a voluntary role with BSAD, to a short time helping professionally with fund raising; a very interesting time. In 1990 I helped to set up an affinity credit card for the organisation. It was with a bank who at the time were the leaders in the field of credit cards for charities. The bank was the infamous BCCI, and although every check was made about their credibility, and we received written assurances from the senior man in the bank in this country about certain allegations that were floating around at the time, the full story did not emerge until after we had set up the card and put in a lot of work all over the country. There were some compensations, the offices in London were very swish and their hospitality there was always of the highest standard. They did of course eventually go into liquidation, which also led to court proceedings, but while we were working with them we did receive some much needed funds through the scheme, and it was not without its perks, as I attended a very nice dinner in the House of Lords as their guest. The card was launched in August 1990 at the BSAD National Swimming Championships in Darlington. The two people who had been selected to appear on the card were there to promote it. One was Duncan Goodhew, the Olympic Gold Medal swimmer, and the other was Julia Fernandez, a young disabled swimmer who was in a wheelchair. Shortly after she had appeared on our credit card, she joined the cast of the short-lived soap 'Eldorado'. Other work followed, and she has made a career in the media as a presenter.

I was involved in the setting up of the English Federation for Disability Sport in the Southern Region, as one of a small group of four who started the process which developed into the present organisation.

The whole question of sport for the disabled is very complex, and although I support the principles, I cannot always agree with the demands of some disabled sports people. Some disabled people can and do succeed very well at able-bodied sport, and it is right that they should be encouraged to do so.

In September 1997, while I was Chairman of the Board of Disability Sport England, I was privileged to have an invite to the funeral of the Princess of Wales. During my time with BSAD/DSE I had been present at several events, including one where she launched a swimming initiative for disabled youngsters. In her smart outfit she knelt at the edge of the pool, and was not in the slightest worried when they splashed her. Originally the invitation to the funeral was for just two people from our organisation, but very rapidly we were able to get this increased to about ten, so that I then had to find people, especially some of our disabled athletes, who could make it to London in time for a very early start.

I will never forget that day. An early start by train from Reading and there were just thousands of people making their way to London for the sad occasion. I saw a lot of people on the train that I knew, and most were just going to anywhere they could get to to see and pay their respects. I met with other representatives of the charity at our headquarters, and we then went by taxi to Westminster Bridge. We had our special passes and we were escorted by the police as we walked down the centre of the road towards Westminster Abbey. We saw and read the cards on some of the many flowers hanging from the railings around the abbey, and then arriving at the Great West Door, we queued along with the great and the good for about an hour, before the doors opened and we made our way into the abbey. We were not sitting together but scattered in various parts of the abbey. I remember sitting only a few seats away from the great Pavarotti and escorting ladies. The singing of 'Candle in the Wind' by Elton John and the applause that drifted into the abbey from those outside at its conclusion, caught the imagination of all those in the abbey who also started to applaud. It was a remarkable occasion and one that I will always remember.

I had in those frantic days before the funeral, to find some of our disabled athletes to take part in the procession to the abbey. I managed to fill our allocation with the help of one of the leading sports clubs for disabled people, Rushmoor Mallards in Hampshire and their chairman, Don Gilbert. One of those I was able to get to this special event was Peter Hull; the man who became a star after his first appearance in the Reading Half Marathon.

The next Reading Half was run on Sunday, 15th March 1998, again from Rivermead Leisure Centre beside the Thames. There were 4,622 finishers and the last one crossed the finish line in 3:29:32. This was two hours twenty-five minutes behind the winner James Karanja (Kenya), who made it to his finish in 63:59. It was again quite a close race at the front, and second-placed man Kassa Tadesse, was just three seconds behind, with Malcolm Price (Sunderland H and AC) third in 64:24. The celebrities in attendance were Uri Geller, the spoon bender, and Kelly Holmes. Although not the numbers that had taken part before, there was a reasonable entry from the wheelchair racers. The first four all got inside the hour, and the winner David Holding set a new record of 52:59. Tanni Grey was sixth overall, and first woman in 64:40. Again the standard in the women's race was not high, and the winner was a thirty-five plus vet, Maria Bradley in 76:08.

Bridgend again won the team race from Sunderland, with three local clubs taking the next three places; Bracknell AC, Reading Roadrunners and Newbury AC, in that order. The very comfortable winners of the women's team race were Reading Roadrunners, with nearly 3,000 points to spare over second team Basingstoke and Midhants. The Charity Fun team winners were Imperial Cancer with only 171 points, against the second team Avenue School with 2,289. The race was used as the South of England Championship for the distance. Brian Fozard (Reading AC) won the over sixty age group with 84:56. I ran again but had slowed considerably, and it took me 124:16. But it was almost forty years to the day since my greatest ever race in 1958.

On 14th March 1999 the last Reading Half Marathon of the century was held on a bright sunny day. It was not the best day to chose for the race, as it was Mothering Sunday, and two other major half marathons were on the same day; Portsmouth and Hastings. In my years of organising the event, Mothering Sunday was the one Sunday that the police always said the race could not be run, because there was more traffic on the road that day than any other day in the year. Amazing how they changed once the race was controlled by those who paid their wages. There was a good entry for the race, although the field lacked quality, except for the inclusion of two of the many Kenyans on the British running circuit.

The wheelchair race, which had been such an important part of the half marathon day, was a disaster. Several of the top names in wheelchair racing had entered, including David Holding the four times winner, and Tanni Grey; but they did not show, and just one unofficial wheelchair, propelled by a local lady who had multiple sclerosis, lined up for the start in front of the 4,000 plus runners.

The race organisers had brought a few gimmicks to the event, such as a musical warm up which a few of the runners took part in. Perhaps the best attraction of the day was the appearance of Sally Gunnell who spent all day at the event, and encouraged both the half marathon runners and the runners in the mini marathons.

The winner was Kenyan Sammy Nyangincha (Team Puma) in 64:18, from Carl Warren (Birchfield Harriers) 64:58, and Michael Kimitei (Kenya and Team Puma) 65:15. There was a very good run by a Berkshire runner who had a few years earlier won the Mini Marathon, Steve Smith (Newbury AC) was sixth in 66:52. It was an easy win for another overseas runner from Russia, Lyubov Belavina in 75:18. Local girl Lesley Whiley (Reading Roadrunners) was second in 81:56, which gave her the first over thirty-five vet prize, from Joy Noad 83:56, and Caroline Stevens (Reading AC) 84:38. Another local runner from Reading Roadrunners, Margaret Clark was first over forty-five years with 94:23. The category winners in the men were forty plus, Nick Sirs (Exeter Harriers) 70:03; fifty/fifty-four, John Exley (Oxford City AC) 73:59; fifty-five/fifty-nine, Keith Scudamore (Burnham Joggers) 83:10; sixty/sixty-four, Brian Fozard (Reading AC) 86:58; and sixty-five plus John Cullingham (Reading AC) 99:42.

The team race went to Sunderland H and AC, with Portsmouth second, Newbury AC third, Reading Roadrunners fourth, Advance Performance fifth, and Reading University sixth. Reading Roadrunners were easy winners in the women's race, from White Horse Harriers and Headington RRs. Imperial Cancer were the charity team winners.

Sadly the last race of the century had lost its magic. The fancy dress costumes had more or less disappeared, the wheelchairs had gone and the quality of the field was not very good. There was no Pasta Party the night before as in the early years, and the sponsors were more interested in their own publicity rather than the good of the event.

The event is now organised by people who are not athletes and not even fun runners, and they have no real feel for this huge event. It is run for profit by the local council, who do not produce any accounts of the event, which must be making a lot of money.

The organisation of the event did not get better in 2000. They were completely unable to give sensible information about entries to the media. In the early days I had regular spots on local radio, as well as news stories in the local papers, and some times even the nationals. We fed the media and they responded, but sadly the Reading Borough people do not have that level of enthusiasm and interest in the event.

Surprisingly the event did get the highest number of entries for a number of years, and around 5,300 finished the race on a very nice warm March day. There was a good race at the front, although the time was nothing special. The winner was another one of the many Kenyans domiciled in the UK, Sammy Bitok, in the best time for a number of years 62:56. A fellow member of Team Puma, Stephen Ariga was second in 63:04, with Morpeth Harrier, Ian Hudspith, next in 63:19. Eric Kiplagat, also Kenya, was fourth with 63:43. There was a good battle for first Reading runner, which was won by Richard Usher (Reading Roadrunners) taking thirty-third place in 73:48, just one place in front of Tom Munt (Reading AC) 73:49. In the closest and best ladies' race for years, Ethiopian now with Essex Ladies, Birhane Dagney, was first to finish in fortieth place with 74:23, chased home by Ukranian, Yelena Plastinina, in 74:36; Lynne

McDougall (City of Glasgow) 74:50. Local runner Lesley Whiley was seventh and beat the eighty minute barrier for the first time with 79:59. The age category winners were Men:— Vet forty/forty-nine, Peter Embleton (Chester Le Street) 70:03; fifty/fifty-four, Roy Treadwell (City of Oxford) 75:48; fifty-five/fifty-nine, Liam Hanna (Maidenhead AC) 79:39; sixty/sixty-four, a regular award winner from Reading AC, Brian Fozard with 85:21; and the sixty-five plus winner was Professor Norman Myers (Headington Road Runners) 88:32. Women, thirty-five/thirty-nine, Y. Plastinina; forty/forty-four, Joy Noad (Maidenhead AC) 84:58, from Carol Pagan (Reading Roadrunners) 86:25.

In the team race, Thames Hare and Hounds took the trophy from Highgate Harriers, with Advance Performance third, Reading Roadrunners fourth, Oxford City fifth, Reading University sixth, and Reading AC seventh. The team winners for the women, were Reading Roadrunners from White Horse Harriers and Herne Hill Harriers. The Company Team Trophy went to *Runners World Magazine* who just beat the sponsors Yellow Pages. The women's trophy went to London Solicitors Allen and Overy, who also beat Yellow Pages into second place. Another strong team from Imperial Cancer enabled them to take the Charity Trophy again.

The event did go off well, which despite my anger at the way I was dumped by the council, still gave me some satisfaction as the basis on which the race was built must have been sound, and much of what I had done in organising the race continued. The event deserves success on the basis of the work done by volunteers in setting it up, and running it for twelve years. Even as late as 2000 I was still receiving congratulatory letters about the event, but fortunately I do not get the complaints today. If it was being set up now by those that run it today, it would not have got past year one. One noticeable change was the total lack of police around the event. The volunteer marshals had to take full responsibility for the runners and traffic. That one big mystery remains though, and that is regarding the finances of the race. With over 7,000 people entered, and some paying £16 for the privilege of entering late, the cash income without sponsorship would have exceeded £80,000. Even after six years, no accounts are ever produced to show where the money goes, or more important where the profits go. It is certainly not like the early years when most of the income went to charity, especially the British Sports Association for the Disabled for whom the race was set up. My one big mistake was possibly not setting the event up as a charitable trust or foundation, so that money could continue to go to the charity. It would also have dissuaded Reading Council from getting too involved with the race.

After eighteen years of the event, it was interesting to find about twenty runners taking part who had run in all those eighteen Reading Half Marathons. Some may have struggled to be fit for 2001, but at the moment their 100% record is intact. These include Nicholette Sayer and Arthur

Abbott, two stalwarts of Reading Joggers, as well as some individuals; Mike Baldwin, a former orienteering expert; Roger Woolven-Allen, a tennis and table tennis player; Mick Sheehan, a local footballer; Brian Williams who took up running on the loss of his wife with cancer in 1982, to raise money for charities connected to cancer; David Wise, a local bookmaker; Gordon Crutchfield; Ken Carmichel, a company director and Group Scoutmaster; David Moseley, who was one of the founders of another local club, Wargrave Runners, as a result of that first half marathon; John Cullingham, a long-standing member of Reading AC, and others from Reading Roadrunners, including Andrew Breakspear; Martin Bush, a man who can rival marathon legend Ron Hill for the number of marathons run, and Patrick (Paddy) Phillips, who is seventy-three years old, and is another of those responsible for me putting all my life down on paper. All these runners ran in every Reading Half Marathon to date, and have raised a very large sum for a great list of charities. But it was a great disappointment that once again the event that first took wheelchairs had only one entry, and that was not an official racing wheelchair athlete, but a local lady who had run in the event before suffering from MS, and who was the sole entry in the previous year.

I am flattered that the race has continued to be a success, and I know that it was because it had very firm foundations, and had been developed by a lot of hard work by dedicated interested people. I do wonder how long it will survive without the enthusiasm of people interested in running? I believe its on-going success has partly been due to the fact that many people who still run the event, think that the original team are still running the race. I hope the record has now been put straight.

The lack of interest and enthusiasm by Reading Borough Council was highlighted again in 2001. Their own Leisure Services Mini Marathons for younger age groups, had in recent years been held on grass alongside the Thames, and it was obvious from November of 2000 that, with the excessive rain, it was not going to be possible to use that area for races in March. Instead of preparing to run the events on a road course or elsewhere, the organisers left it until three weeks to go before announcing that they were cancelling the Mini events for 2001.

It did appear that the main event, the half marathon, was going to be a great success, as a number of major events disappeared from the running calendar, so that even with their very poor promotion and advance publicity, the entry kept up. But on Friday, 2nd March, disaster struck the event just ten days before it was due to be run. The 'Foot and Mouth' outbreak was the alleged reason for the cancellation of the race, and so for the first time since 1983, there would be no Reading Half Marathon. The cancellation in its own way confirmed what I had always known, and that was that the council were not interested in the event itself, but only in making money from it. They put out a short announcement that the race was cancelled, and then started bleating about the cost of the cancellation. For the first time in seven years there were clues as to the money involved in the event. They talked loosely about the £120,000 event, which I would agree was about the total income from entry fees and sponsorship. The letter they sent to competitors was very cryptic. They explained the cancellation, and pointed out that on the entry form it had said there could be no refund. They then offered a refund, reluctantly to anyone applying by 6th April; just four weeks after the event. If a refund was not claimed they would keep the money, and there was no suggestion that the money would buy a place for the following year. They also claimed that most of the income had been spent before the event, and that any refunds would be at a loss to the organisers and sponsors. The only way that the large sum of £100,000 could have been used before the event, was if the fees charged by the council for staff and outside help was exorbitant. They commented that if they had to refund to everyone, they would lose in excess of £40,000. I could not sympathize with them as their actions a few years earlier had cost me at least that figure, and I had to pay out that money personally. Perhaps justice has been done.

Will the event continue? I have my suspicions that it will not happen again, but I hope I am wrong.

Chapter Nineteen

Statistics of the Reading Half Marathon

It is interesting looking at some statistics in the Reading Half Marathon, and these generally show a decline in performance over the years, which is surprising as many people in those early days had not been runners. The table below reflects on the general downturn in performance, and similar statistics from other races over the years would, I am sure, produce the same picture.

Year	Winner	10th	50th	100th	250th	500th	1000th
1983 —	67:45						
1984 —	64:39	68:25	73:23	75:36	80:30	84:24	89:34
1985 —	63:55	64:50	70:34	74:47	80:01	84:45	90:39
1986 —	62:39	65:04	71:71			83:29	89:08
1987 —	62:07	64:58	71:58	75:25		84:13	90:18
1988 —	63:16	64:51	73:27	76:13	81:08	85:56	91:52
1989 —	64:11	65:55	73:19	76:17	81:08	85:35	92:06
1990 —	63:32	66:47	73:16	76:40			
1991 —	64:28	66:58	74:04	77:29	83:05	88:14	94:53
1992 —	62:20	— Race Short — Therefore Times Not Accurate					
1993 —	61:38	67:03	75:42	79:05			
1994 —	66:46	73:47	80:47	84:58	90:10	96:40	106:05
1995 —	64:49	70:39	79:12	82:24	88:31	95:35	105:27
1996 —	63:31	73:33	78:36	81:55	88:16	93:55	103:09
1997 —	64:50	66:42	73:42	78:15	85:01	89:56	98:21
1998 —	63:59	66:55	76:08	79:51	85:00	90:08	97:35
1999 —	64:19	68:29	78:07	82:01	86:51	92:37	100:13
2000 —	62:56	67:29	75:38	80:50	86:57	92:21	99:45

It should be pointed out that if it were not for the many overseas, in particular Kenyan athletes, who have competed in recent years, the times of the leading places above would be very much worse.

Chapter Twenty

The Changing Image of Athletics

Over the years I have met many athletes, many of them outstanding, and sadly some have passed away a long time before their sell-by date. I know that many of my generation of distance runners could and would have held their own with the best around today, and I include the Kenyans and other African runners in this generation. The likes of Gordon Pirie, Derek Ibbotson, Martin Hyman, Bruce Tulloh, Frank Sando, Ken Norris, George Knight, Basil Heatley, Gerry North and John Merriman were dedicated runners, who in the main had to work for success alongside a regular job with very little financial support, but sport in those days was happy and none the less competitive. The likes of Dave Bedford and David Moorcroft followed on in that tradition in later years and were great athletes in any generation.

Much has gone wrong with the sport of athletics, and sport in the wider sense; money is at the root of all its problems, not because sport has become more professional, but because it has not been managed properly. I have often been asked if I regretted not being at the top of my running career today, instead of forty plus years ago. Yes, today I would have been a big earner from the sport, BUT I am sure I would not have enjoyed it as much.

When I got involved in bringing running to the masses in the late 1970s and 1980s, I was confident that not only would it be good for people's health, but it would help to create more good athletes; in particular distance runners, both male and female. I am sure that Chris Brasher, when he started the London Marathon, must have thought the same. How wrong we both were. Many people now enjoy running in a way not dreamed of perhaps thirty years ago, but it has not produced better runners. The standard in almost every distance event in this country has deteriorated at an alarming rate. The pyramid principle of a broad base creating a peak of talent, has not worked.

Some of the information in this book shows how performances have declined, not just since the middle of the 20th century, but even from as recent as the mid- 1980s. The reasons are many, and these must include the lack of initiative by the AAAs and succeeding governing bodies of athletics. They were so slow to react to the great enthusiasm of the late 1970s to 1980s. Those running the sport did not understand this great upsurge in interest in distance running. Their only reaction to it was to try and boost their funds by putting on a levy of 50p a runner, without giving anything back to the events or individuals. Below the top, the runners that run for fun do just that, and they do not appreciate how much enjoyment there can be in seeking excellence. There is another reason, and that is that the runners today are too well off, comfortable and well fed. I think that the success of the runners in the 1950s, 1960s and perhaps even the 1970s, was because the runners had been brought up in, or just after the war, when there was food rationing and food was basic with no frills. We were 'hungry' runners, and very much like the Kenyan and African runners in the year 2000. If we are to return to the days of success, particularly in distance running, athletes will have to forget fancy supplements, and have the discipline of sticking to good basic diet and much harder training. The 'Three Ds' — Discipline, Diet and Dedication are the key to success.

I recently found an old Berkshire Constabulary memo, dated 3/1/1960, which I had obviously used to make some notes on as preparation for a talk I was to give to some group or other forty years ago. My training tips from those notes were:—

Hard work and common sense.
Use different training methods.
Winter build up and Summer speed up.
Continuous regular training.
Do not train too much in groups.
Warming up before competition; very important.
Timed training and sprinting very important for all events.
Do not run directly after meals.

The last point I had put down is very basic, but all of these are still sensible training tips for today's athletes. There are plenty of runners from the successful years still around, they may not want to be fully involved in the administration of athletics or full-time coaching, but their experience could be used to help aspiring athletes today.

I spoke to one of these successful runners while in the final stages of putting this book to print, and although he was a runner some ten years younger than myself, his thoughts and views were the same as mine. Mike Hurd was a winner of the Reading Half Marathon and had also won the vet category in the race. His best time for the full marathon was 2:13, and for the half marathon just over sixty-three minutes. He was once asked about what supplements he took in his diet. His reply "None except fish and chips and Mars bars." He is not the first runner I have known to become very successful on what might be deemed by the purists to be unhealthy food. The important thing to remember is moderation in all things. As I have always said, and he made the same observation, there is only one thing that really helps a runner to improve; running; lots of it, and it must include quality running and not just going for a seven to ten mile run at even pace. Dedicated hard training is how most runners really succeed.

Chapter Twenty-One

Rotary International

An important change in my life came in 1977, when I was invited to speak to the Rotary Club of Caversham about my running experiences. Little did I know how that talk was going to change my life over the next twenty-four years, and probably beyond. After that talk to many of the key people in the commercial life of Reading at that time, I was invited to join the club and very quickly got involved in the work of Rotary. Within months I was producing the monthly magazine, a job which I kept for four years.

I chaired committees of the club, and this included organising a Polish evening where we had the attendance of the Polish Ambassador. It was at a time when there was a lot of suspicion between East and West, and I had problems to solve with the security people on both sides. I was later elected Junior Vice President, which took me through in two years to being President of the club in the year 1983 to 1984. If my promotion had been quick, Marion had made even quicker progress; having only joined the Inner Wheel Club of Reading in 1981, she was made President of that club in the same year as me.

It was a happy year, with one exception, and that was on Valentine's Day, 14th February 1984. While Marion was at her Inner Wheel meeting in Reading, I received a phone call from my brother to tell me that my mother had died suddenly. It was a bright winter day, and she was walking to the old people's club that she visited in Windsor, and collapsed in the street and died aged seventy-eight years. She had always been very active, and was still riding her bicycle around Windsor, although not on this occasion. It was a shock to all the family and her many friends, but one thing is certain, it was the way she would have chosen to leave this earth. It was a sad time, especially as she was the last of our parents; Marion having lost both of hers by the time she was thirty-two years of age, and my father having being dead ten years. But we both got on with our year as Presidents of our clubs, as well as running our sports business and bringing up our own family of five children; this kept us busy, but St Valentine's Day is never forgotten. There is another important family connection with 14th February now, as on that date in 1999, our eldest daughter Caroline had a son, Jack.

The main event of my Rotary year as President was an Oration held at the new Hexagon in Reading. The club had in previous years held such an event with many and varied top speakers, including Lord Boothby. I decided to hold this special event again in my year, and my Orator was Alistair Milne the Director General of the BBC at the time. It was a very grand evening with hundreds of guests, but the Director General's speech did not go down too well as it was very technical for the time, but it did get major publicity with it being quoted in the *Times* and other newspapers. On reflection it was probably quite earth shattering, as it was about the coming of Digital Television.

About this time I helped to establish interest in dyslexia in Berkshire. The subject was rather taboo and not accepted as a problem by most teachers at this time. With the help of one or two people who did understand the problem, I set up a seminar on the subject for head teachers and others. It was not well attended, but did sow the seeds with those that did come and listen to some established experts on the subject, and in particular a student who despite his dyslexia had gained a very good degree at Edinburgh University. It was a slow start, but I know it did start to change attitudes within my home county.

I took on the position of Youth Exchange Officer for our District, and was responsible for receiving and sending young people overseas for a year's education. For some years our Rotary District 109 had exchanges with another district in Denmark. This was no ordinary exchange, but was for disabled young people from both countries. In August 1986 I took nine young people with a multitude of disabilities to Denmark. We flew from Heathrow, and I was going to be in for a very busy fourteen days, as there were several wheelchair users as well as one blind lad.

At the end of the trip we were put on the plane to fly home, and the first thing that happened was a message from the captain that I was to be specially looked after by the crew, as I had been looking after the youngsters. I remember having a whisky or two at his invitation.

On the return trip with young people from Denmark, I remember the August day when they had been taken to Littlecote House at Hungerford in Berkshire. It was that terrible day in Hungerford when all those people were shot. Fortunately they were clear of the trouble, and did not get caught up in the tragedy.

Perhaps one of my most enjoyable and rewarding activities during my years as a Rotarian, was taking young people on a Rotary Young Leaders Award Course on three occasions in 1989, 1992 and 1996. All of these courses were held at the Berkshire Outdoor Centre at Rhos-Y-Gwaliau on Lake Bala in North Wales. I did things late in life that I had never experienced before. Going underground in a slate mine, abseiling, rock climbing, gorge walking and camping overnight in a bivouac made by my own hand out of brushwood and grasses. Plus an overnight expedition, sleeping under the stars and watching the satellites going across the Welsh sky. The overnight sleep in my bivouac in 1992 proved that I had not lost the ability to sleep any where in any conditions.

All on the course were taken to the forest in late evening and told to build our own shelter for the night. The weather forecast was not good, but we all completed our task and settled in for the night. By now it was raining hard, but I got into my shelter made from brush and reeds, etc., and after a little while of listening to the rain, I went to sleep.

Next morning, about 7 a.m., one of the instructors came walking through the forest and gave me a shout. I woke up and I was virtually an island with water flowing around me and quite a bit flowing through my shelter, which was nearly as wet inside as out. I got up and made my way back to the minibus, only to find that many of my young charges had either gone back to the centre or spent the night in the minibus. Only a few of us had braved the elements for the whole night. But like sleeping in phone boxes in the police, or on luggage racks on trains in my days of travel to races, I had no difficulty in getting my sleep.

In 1990 I had been elected to be the Governor of the District that covered Berks, Oxfordshire and parts of Middlesex and Buckinghamshire; and in February of 1992, I went off to Kansas City for the Rotary International Assembly, to learn about taking on this important post. It was a great experience, especially the meeting with 500 plus men holding the same office as myself in all parts of the world. Now of course this get-together of the officers of Rotary International includes women, as many are making it to the top in the organisation.

In July 1992, I became the District Governor of Rotary International District 1090; something that I could not have anticipated fifteen years earlier, when I accepted that invitation to join Rotary. I had many interesting events during my year, including my 'At Home' where I introduced many Rotarians to Wheelchair Basketball for the disabled, when we had some of the best wheelchair players from this country taking part in a tournament in Reading, as well as a team from France. Other memorable events during the year included a dinner in Windsor Guildhall, attended by HRH The Duke of Edinburgh; a weekend at Cliveden with the Rotary Club of Maidenhead on Twelfth Night; and dinner at Blenheim Palace with Woodstock Rotary Club. It was a 'black tie' event, and a member of my Rotary Club, Peter Belcher, was acting as my chauffeur for the evening. We arrived early and were walking around the grounds of the palace in our dinner suits, when a tourist came up and asked a question. He obviously thought one of us was the owner of the splendid palace, the Duke of Marlborough. I also had a very enjoyable evening at the Rotary Club of Faringdon and District, where I was a guest along with the late Jonny Morris. We got on well together, as we both suffered from diabetes, so were able to compare notes over more than one glass of wine, which we both enjoyed.

The big event was the annual conference in March 1993, which I took to Torquay for the first time. The star performer was Sir Ranulph Fiennes and the timing was perfect. He had just completed his latest exploration to the South Pole, and in fact a few days before he was due to speak we did not know if he would be back in the country in time. He did arrive with his frost-bitten feet, and when I introduced him to the audience in the Centre at Torquay, the place was packed with every seat taken and with many standing. I felt I had a little in common with him, although I could not compare. He was born, like me, in the Royal Borough of Windsor, and I think we have both done some crazy things; he with his expeditions and me with my long runs.

For a number of years from 1994, I was the main link between Rotary in Great Britain and Ireland and all the Scandinavian countries. This included chartering aircraft to fly up to 100 Rotarians and wives from this country to Billund (the home of Lego) in Denmark, and in the same aircraft flying back a similar number of Danish Rotarians, who would stay with their host clubs on the same weekend. Chartering an aircraft was a new experience for me, especially as I had to sign up to a bill of over £35,000, with the total responsibility to get sufficient money back on my shoulders. Eventually towards the end of the 1990s, the chartering ceased as the price of scheduled flights to Denmark became very much cheaper, and the charter price could not match these reduced prices.

One of my happiest and enjoyable experiences in Rotary, was when I had the honour to represent the International President of Rotary, Glen Kinross from Australia, at a Rotary Conference in Arundel, Norway. The Norwegians were so friendly and appreciative, even if they thought my accent when singing with them was more Swedish than Norwegian. I had to address the Conference a number of times, and fortunately the Norwegians do speak English, and when they were speaking in their own language there was always someone on hand to translate for me. One of their other main speakers addressed the problem of UK pollution hitting their country. I did not get a full translation of this speech, but it was quite hard hitting about the damage we do to their environment. It was a working weekend but it was very enjoyable.

I have enjoyed my association and membership of this great organisation. It has done much good work, largely unrecognised, in local and international communities. I do wonder what the future holds for such organisations in the new millennium. Do organisations like Rotary, the Lions, Round Table, Inner Wheel, have to change drastically to meet changing circumstances and conditions in society, or do they stick to their tried and trusted formula, principles and structure? Sadly society has changed, and until it changes back to being more caring and less selfish, and people realise the great satisfaction that can be derived by working together for the common good, such organisations are going to decline and so will the society we live in.

As far as Rotary is concerned, I think if it is to change, the changes may need to be quite drastic and far-reaching. The organisation is based on a club structure, and each individual belongs to a club. It may be in the future that Rotarians will not belong to a single club, but to the organisation with the same right as now, to attend any club anywhere. 'Cheque Book Rotary' has always been frowned upon by traditional long-standing members, but if individuals do not belong to a single club and cannot work on Service within that club area, perhaps money could be the answer.

I believe that Rotary has done, and still does, a great deal of good throughout the world, but I do have one major concern. I believe that like many similar organisations, it spends far too much time and money on its own pleasures. Socialising and fellowship is important, but the proportion of money spent on such activities is often disproportionate to moneys raised for charity and good causes. I believe in Rotary and the work it has done and continues to do, like being the driving force behind the immunization of millions to eradicate polio, and the tremendous support it gives to millions of local projects around the world. In 2005 it celebrates its centenary; it will be worth celebrating, but there is a big question mark over the future which is not entirely in its own hands.

In 1998 I had the responsibility for extension of Rotary in our District, and had the good fortune to be able to form three new clubs. These clubs attracted new, younger, forthright men and women from the modern business world, and it is they and those like them who will carry the torch in the future.

Chapter Twenty-Two

Matters of the Heart

Even as late in my life as 1996, I was called on as a celebrity for a special task. This was to launch the National Lottery Scratch Card in the Thames Valley. I had to go to a local garage who were the first to be 'switched on' to the new system for the Scratch Cards, and be photographed wearing a cap promoting the new gamble. The photographs were supposed to go out to all local papers to promote the start of the Scratch Card era. They did, but the PR fell a bit flat as the system did not work and people could not immediately buy their cards.

In May 1998, as a result of the money lost on the Reading Half Marathon, we decided to cut our losses and move from Reading where we had lived for forty-one years, and out of the county of Berkshire where I had lived for sixty-two years, to Didcot in Oxfordshire; a smaller town but very conveniently situated for wherever we might want to travel. The move has been good and not least because the medical attention I have received at the Radcliffe Infirmary, the John Radcliffe Hospital in Oxford and from my local GP, since moving counties has been excellent. Didcot is now our home, and we have found it a very pleasant place to live with the lovely countryside so close to hand.

My final 'real job' was from 1995 to 2000 with SportsAid Southern, 'The Charity for Sport', where I was the Regional Director. When I started with them in March 1995 they were in trouble, and not able to pay their way or meet their obligations. I agreed to work for a small fee of £500 a month, and rapidly helped to turn the organisation back into profitability. I enjoyed working again in a sporting organisation, but sadly even that organisation changed and it had an uncertain future. Over twenty-five years the regional organisation had raised money by its own efforts, and distributed over £400,000 to many up and coming and hopeful young sportsmen and sportswomen, some of whom have become household names in sport. In September 2000 I resigned from my post as Regional Director, as a stepping stone to retirement. SportsAid is another organisation that did a good job in a small way, with local help of volunteers, for many young people wanting to make their mark in sport, but in the new world of money in sport, I do not think it should or will have much relevance in the future. As one door closes another always opens, and even now that I have retired and reached OAP status, I wonder if there is yet one more career waiting for me around the corner.

Life was about to take another turn in early October 2000. I was feeling good having got back into running three times a week, which I hoped would start to reduce the weight I had put on since going onto insulin. My most recent run had been for forty-five minutes; the longest since I ran London in 1997, and I was looking forward to increasing the training because I felt quite confident I could run for an hour without a problem. I then went off to my six-monthly checkup at the Diabetic Clinic at the Radcliffe Infirmary in Oxford. Marion had accompanied me as she always did, and we parked the car at the Park and Ride and took the bus to the hospital. Everything was normal, and I then went in to see the doctor; a new one, as my old friend Dr Hisham Maksoud had moved on. He was not happy with something and sent me to have an immediate ECG. He then called me back in and took my pulse, which was reading around thirty per minute. He was not happy and said he would speak to the specialist at the John Radcliffe Cardiac Unit. After a short while he spoke to Marion and myself again, explaining that he thought I had a serious problem, and that I should go straight to the JR without returning home. I think we were both shocked, but I did ask what was the alternative, and his reply was "possible sudden death". I decided I had better take his advice and go straight to hospital.

We drove to the JR a short distance away, as his message was still ringing in our ears. I had been given a largish packet containing all my records and a letter, and I reported to the Cardiac Unit. The bed was ready for me, and I was immediately wired up so that they could monitor me at the nurses' station. Then I was attended by doctors and nurses, all asking questions and doing various things to me. I was then fitted up with a tape box to record my every heartbeat, and I looked like a bionic man with patches and wires all over me. At this stage I had been told I was booked in to have a pacemaker fitted the very next morning, so Marion was dispatched to fetch the usual requirements for a hospital stay from home. She returned and stayed a while before leaving me in the hands of the hospital. While she was there they gave me another ECG, and during this, one of the nurses came rushing in to say they had found the blip that had given the concern; they seemed quite excited. After she had left, another doctor came and examined and spoke to me at some length. He did not think I was a desperate case; that was the first bit of good news that day; but said he wanted to consult with a colleague before making a final judgement. He came back and said that he thought I would eventually need a pacemaker, and that as I was on the list, I could have one fitted on the next day as arranged, but he thought there might be some advantage in me going home with my 'black box' so that they could have a full twenty-four hour recording, which would clearly identify exactly what I would need. He left the choice to me, and looking around the ward at those much more desperate for treatment than me, I decided to go home.

I then tried to ring Marion, but had difficulty in reaching her as she was busy ringing the family to let them know what had happened. I did catch her off the phone, and within the hour I was back home complete with my wires, pad and 'black box'.

After all the publicity that had recently surrounded the Cardiac Unit at the John Radcliffe, and the press stories about the NHS, I was amazed at the superb and swift way I was dealt with.

Only a couple of weeks later I was back at the "JR" for a checkout; two days before I was to have a pacemaker inserted. I duly arrived at the appointed time of 9:30 a.m., and had various tests to ensure I was OK for the treatment. At about midday I was seeing the final person, a doctor, before going home. Just as we were finishing there was a knock at the door; it was the doctor who was carrying out the surgery of implants that day. "Mr Eldon, I am Dr .... We have a problem. A patient who should be here for his pacemaker today can't make it. Can we do yours today?" "Yes, why not." I then had to go and tell Marion that I was not going home.

A bed was ready for me, and after being looked at again, and my blood sugars being checked, I was prepared for the insert which was to be done at 2 p.m. For this little procedure there was no trolley or wheelchair to convey me to the theatre. I just walked there and climbed up onto the 'table'. A few minutes to 'lay me out' properly and set me up, and then it was "Light. Camera. Action" as the doctor said, and we were off. I could not see what was going on, but could hear everything and was having a conversation with the theatre nurse throughout. We had something in common, she was the partner of a well-known local veteran runner who I knew well. I was shown the pacemaker just before it was put in, and was amazed how small it was; not much larger than a fifty pence piece.

I did get a ride on a trolley from the theatre back to my bed, where I was confined for just two hours, except for a trip to have an X-ray by wheelchair. It was supposed to be bed rest, but there was not much of that, as various people descended on me to carry out various tests.

By 6:30 p.m., Marion was at the hospital, and I was dispatched home to Didcot. The staff at the John Radcliffe had done a very good job, and I was soon back to running again. I was very impressed with the NHS, but felt a little guilty about the speed I had been dealt with, bearing in mind some of the men I had met in hospital waiting for weeks, and not knowing whether their operation could be carried out in time to save their lives.

The pacemaker does its stuff now, and I have a faster and better heart beat, and I can still run; although I am not that happy with my speed or rather lack of speed, and feel that perhaps more long walks and even cycling could be the answer. The trouble is I do not know if my poor running is down to my weight, my pacemaker, the diabetes, or is it old age?

I am very concerned that, like me, many athletes of my generation appear to have developed heart and other medical problems such as diabetes in later life, which has in many cases brought lives to an end well before the "Seventy score years and ten". If it was more recent generations, then perhaps this could be put down to the misuse of drugs, but as far as I know this is certainly not the case in the generation I am referring to. In my own case, and that of others, the problem starts with the low heart rate that is essential to the distance runner. Training reduces that rate, but in later life it seems the heart gets even slower and irregular, which is where the problem starts. I believe it would make an interesting piece of research for a doctor with an interest in running. Even while I was writing this book deaths were occurring, including the thirty-nine-year-old brother of Steve Cram. I do not want to put people off running, and still believe that keeping physically fit is important, but I do believe that not enough research has been carried out to prevent the problems I have referred to.

I have now been "On the Run" for fifty-four years; that is nearly twice as long as Ronnie Biggs! I have always enjoyed running and I cannot visualize life without it. I have been very lucky having never suffered from injuries that can be associated with the activity. I have found running hard recently, and it is not quite as easy as it was. I do not know if it is the diabetes, the heart, or just old age; probably a combination of all three, but depending on how I feel, I will run up to three times a week for anything from twenty minutes to an hour. I must confess I have taken a few breaks of some weeks in between, but I always have the urge to get back to it. Many people have described running as being like a drug; an addiction; I cannot argue with that. I will 'keep on running' as the 1960's song said.

Chapter Twenty-Three

My Outlook on Sport Today

As I look back over more than fifty years of being involved with sport, I can see the many changes that have taken place. I have seen the changes in the popularity of different sports, and of course the change from amateur through shamateurism, to virtually full professionalism in most sports today.

In my early days there was no doubt that the big sports were athletics, boxing and cricket, with soccer some way behind. Over the years sports like squash have also had their day. I remember the big upsurge in that sport in the 1970s, and I nearly got involved with others in setting up squash clubs. The sales of squash rackets went up from about two a year to around fifteen a week in one shop, but the popularity did not remain, although the number of people playing did increase considerably from the very low figures prior to the boom. Cricket was hugely popular in the 1940s and 1950s, with the popular stars like Denis Compton and Bill Edrich. Athletics had a terrific following after the war, and I was lucky enough to be part of it. There were the great runners like Sydney Wooderson who were around both before and after the war. I remember seeing another great miler, Bill Nankerville (Bobby Davro's dad). He used to wear very bright purple satin shorts that glistened under floodlights, and I could not wait to get a pair like them. Yes I did, and in fact I had a whole set of different colours. Then of course there was the excitement in the early fifties, as athletes like Roger Bannister, John Landy (Australia) and Wes Santee (USA), chased what was thought at that time to be the ultimate athletic goal; the sub four-minute mile. There was the great Emil Zatopek, who won his three gold medals at the 1952 Olympics in Helsinki, and set eighteen world records; and later the great Hungarian athletes Tabori, Iharos and others.

The crowds drawn to the sport in those days were huge. The White City had a capacity of around 40,000 seated, but crowds could touch 60,000 with people standing in front of the stands. Even on a Friday night of the AAA's Championships, where there were only two finals, there could be a crowd of 30,000 to 40,000. Of course there was little television coverage of sport, but the radio was well used. Television has increased the number of 'couch potatoes', but it has been at the expense of genuine supporters attending some sports events. Even small events, like those at agricultural shows, fetes, carnivals and the Paignton Regatta Sports, the Devon Police Sports, the Air Ministry Sports, and the many handicap meetings in the north of England in particular, drew crowds of at least 5,000 people to see a few races run on grass tracks marked out around a cricket field, in those days of the 1950s and early 60s. Even as late as the 1970s some of these special events, like the Reading Gala of Sport, drew 5,000 to 6,000 people to a small stadium.

My sport of athletics has changed from those days of the 1950s and 60s. The fifteen shillings a day; the near enough genuine expenses; the maximum prize value of £7.7s (not money but goods to the value of); the underhand payment of perhaps £10 for a TV appearance; the odd £10 to £20 handed out by a grateful promoter; have all been replaced today with the commercial sponsorship; the £25,000 plus annual lottery grant; prize money; real money for TV appearances, and the chance to travel the world, not just to compete, but to train. But despite all this the sport has been ailing for some time, and the management of it at all levels has been very poor to say the least. It fought to stay as an amateur sport for far too long, and when it did find itself dragged into the professional era, it was slow to react and has still not got it right.

There are other differences, and these are perhaps more important, as they have contributed to the loss of public interest in the sport. In those good years there was a lot of competition, as there were so many good middle and long distance runners that you never knew who would be on top and going to win major races. There was real competition and people raced each other. I have not seen a decent race between our current or recent runners for a very long time. Most are frightened even by their own shadow, and modest performances give them a reasonable income. There are so few potentially good runners, and I think the present financial structure makes it harder for new talent to challenge the established runners. We do have sprinting talent, but how long does a 100 metres last; less than ten seconds; and is not therefore a great pull with spectators. The interesting events have to be from 800 metres upwards, and until we develop the talent in those areas, we will not draw the crowds or TV audiences back to the sport. I have always said that the way to encourage is not by handouts to the few, but by a sensible prize structure at all levels, so that if an up-and-coming beats an established star, he or she gets the big payday. This would then start them on the learning curve, and give them money to train and travel properly.

As I am writing this book, there is a lot of discussion about cutting down on the number of false starts allowed to only one, and reducing the number of throws and jumps down from six to three, to improve the excitement on television. I believe there is some merit in these proposals, as in most sports you only get one chance; there is no opportunity to have a rerun or second chance to win. I am not quite so sure about the one false start though, because I once did a false start in the Polytechnic Marathon that started in Windsor Castle and ran to Chiswick. Under the new proposed rules I would have been out!

There have been other missed opportunities for the sport, like the mass running boom of the late 70s and early 80s, which could have helped to fund the sport if properly handled. It has been content to rely on the goodwill and free services of a very aging and disappearing stock of athletics officials. While attending an athletic event in the last couple of years, I heard a conversation between some of these aging officials. The gist of it was that one day athletes would turn up to run in a meeting, and there would be no officials present because they would all have passed on.

Athletics is a complex sport; in fact it is a compendium of different sports. There are three main activities; cross-country, road running, and track and field, and the latter is the main problem, as it is not a single activity. There are all the different running events, as well as the throws and the jumps. All different disciplines demanding their own specialisation and specialist coaching. There are many in traditional clubs who criticise the setting up in recent years of the new road running specialist clubs. They think they have helped to destroy the long standing clubs, but I do not think this is true. In fact these single purpose clubs have probably helped to keep the sport going through the difficult years. In fact the way forward may be to have more, not less, specialist clubs. The way athletics is going now, there will be an elite set of clubs at the top level and other clubs, including some long-established clubs, will have to rethink their policy and structure to survive. The traditional club in most towns may have to be the feeder club for the top twenty clubs, which will mean strong junior and younger teams, but weaker senior sections. These clubs may have to depend on the veteran athletes that already make a valuable contribution to many clubs. With the problems in many parts of the country with running on public roads, I think that the number of road races will drop, and the sport will largely revert back to track and field and cross-country running. Maybe in the long term this will be good for the sport, and we will start to produce more and better track runners, especially in the distance events.

There are still hundreds of road running events around the country, but it is not just the standard of the runners that is declining, but the standard of race organisation. Many events have gone back to the 'bad old days' as far as organisation is concerned, with little imagination and just one thing in mind, to take as much money as possible off the runners, without giving a well-organised and professional event. Many events still do not know how to produce quick and accurate results; they have commentators who know nothing about the event, running or the runners; and the prize structure of these events is sometimes worse than fifty years ago. There are of course people around who do all these jobs very well, but there are far too many 'Micky Mouse' events run for the wrong purpose. What other sport allows all and sundry to organise a sporting event outside of that sport as long as the 'thirty pieces of silver' are handed over?

Athletics has been very slow as a sport to integrate the disabled into its events at all levels, although hopefully that is slowly being put right, but it is very slowly and I have heard all the excuses as to why clubs and others cannot take on this extra responsibility.

Today the major sport is football, which I am pleased to say has been integrating the disabled, but for how long will they remain the top sport? I believe that there will be further changes, and support will increase for other sports as people get bored with watching twenty-two men kick a round ball around a pitch. The football machine is huge, but it can and will come to a grinding halt; perhaps in five years or less. I believe that football supporters will come to their senses and stop paying the high price to watch their sport, and the high price of all the proliferates such as replica shirts. The 'powers that be' in the sport will also realise that they cannot keep adding more and more competitions into the already crowded calendar. Anyone who knows anything about fitness and the human body, knows that you cannot keep putting physical demands on the body week in, week out, especially with a contact sport.

What will take over where football leaves off? I hope that athletics makes a big comeback, but it is more likely that rugby will lead the way in the next few years. I believe that football can have a major role to play in helping other sports. Athletics struggles for money and a professional approach, and what a great contribution a club like Manchester United could make if they took over a Manchester Athletic Club, and had it as part of its big machine. Initially there would be a cost; perhaps one million pounds a year to get athletics onto a professional footing, but once set up, there would be great prestige and further income for the owning club. Sports clubs in other parts of the world are often multi-sport, and I believe this country could follow this example.

My hints earlier in this book might suggest that I am against modern professional sport, but I am not. I have always lived in the real world, and the days of the total amateur and shamateurism had to disappear at the top level. What I have a quarrel with, is the excesses of modern professional sport and the inequality of it. There is no need for footballers to be paid their £40 or £50,000 a week, and cricketers at the top level earning two per cent of that. There used to be a top wage in soccer of £20 a week; the time may be coming when they have to reintroduce a maximum wage, although a little higher than that £20 per week! I think it should be remembered what the definition of sport is "a source of diversion or recreation, a pastime, a physical activity engaged in for recreation". In other words sport is for fun and wellbeing.

I do not like the modern presentation of sport on TV. It should be about watching the action, and not be preceded by or followed by a load of waffle from so-called experts who are often not that expert, even if they have succeeded in their chosen sport. Perhaps the definition of expert sums this up. *'Ex'* needs no explanation, it means in any context 'past it'; *'Spurt'* (spert) is a drip of water under pressure. So by definition an *'expert'* is a little drip under pressure, who is past it. Keep them off our screens and let us get back to good professional commentators, if they can be found. The problem is probably caused by the 'experts' being paid so much that they have an inflated ego and want to have their face as well as their voice on the programme. The good commentators like, David Coleman and Ron Pickering, were in the main heard but not seen.

The funding of sport in various ways through the National Lottery Sports Fund, has made a tremendous difference to many sports and the individuals in those sports. The successes at the Sydney Olympics and Paralympics in 2000, is testimony to that. But there has also been a huge wasting of that precious resource by those who control it. Governments have made reports, set up committees and reviews, but have never really grasped the problems of sport in this country; which is that we have too many controlling bodies, and more than any other country, we promote every activity from kite flying to tiddlywinks, to sport status eventually.

I believe, and always have, that there needs to be a new body to replace that organisation that is supposed to be the voice of sport; what was the Sports Council, now Sport England and Sport UK. The only thing that it has ever been good at is producing masses of printed paper; most of which is never read. It has been allowed to grow like 'topsy' and has only ever been tweaked. It has never been seriously reviewed. I have worked closely with individuals within that organisation, and most of them do a great job within the structure, but any government that really wants to get to grips with sport and its management, would not just revamp this body but scrap it and start again. The best and most useful campaign run by them was the Sport for All, which was in my opinion what their work should really have been about, not concentrating on increasing sport participation by ethnic groups, women and other minorities. Their old slogan Sport for All covered all these groups.

Why do I think they should be scrapped? It is because they have been so wasteful of the resources given to them, and so much money has gone on so-called restructuring various bodies involved with sport and the management of sport. I think they have suffered too much from government interference and the whims of sports ministers. A post that is not treated seriously by prime ministers as was obvious when the best minister of sport for years, Kate Hoey, was sacked last year. In fact I wonder if there is really any need to have a so-called minister of sport at all. Sport is probably best left to those who know, appreciate and understand it.

Every now and again, as if to flex their muscles, Sport England works to disband and run down one organisation, and then pumps in a great deal of money to start up something very similar, and often with the same people involved. I have been involved with three organisations that have suffered from 'the treatment'. The first was Disability Sport England (formerly BSAD), the next was the English Federation of Disability Sport, and lastly SportsAid, both before and after it changed to a charity. In all of these organisations there has been a huge waste of money. Disability Sport England was a good organisation that slightly lost its way, and suffered from poor management and lack of control by their funders, Sport England. It did however continue to provide a sound structure for sports clubs for people with disabilities, and some very good regional and national events.

The whole question of the disabled and sport is very complex, and my view is that the theory cannot be matched by practical considerations. A great deal of work has been done to put disabled athletes into a classification system that levels the playing field when in competition with each other. Although the opportunities should be there for the disabled to compete in the sporting events of their choice, they should accept that there are limitations for them as there are for able-bodied sportsmen and sportswomen. A person who is five foot nothing, does not expect to compete seriously at the high jump. An eight-stone man does not compete in the shot or discus, nor does a fifteen-stone man or woman take up distance running. We cannot all take part in every activity; it is "horses for courses". The same restrictions in sport have to apply to the disabled, and this means that depending on the disability, they may not be able to take part in every athletic and sporting activity. In my association with disabled sport, I do not think this message has got across to the various Disability Sports Organisations and some individuals.

The English Federation of Disability Sport is making a brave attempt at pulling all these organisations together, so as to strengthen their arm in negotiating for more money and support. It is beginning to work, but some of the large cracks between different disability groups are still there, and may be getting wider. I do believe that there are very specific problems with all disabilities, and the best people to deal with them are the specific disability sports organisations with the support of EFDS and Sport England.

Chapter Twenty-Four

People I Admire

Somebody once said to me "How many really smart people have you ever met? I bet you could count them on one hand." I suppose this is true of any of us, but there are people that you admire for many different reasons.

My all-time sporting hero has to be a runner that I followed, Emil Zatopek. He was a great man, athlete, Olympian and example to all.

There are a number of people I know who have suffered either from ill health or disability, but have survived to lead full active lives. One of these would be my secretary of many years, Gladys Daly, who suffered from a number of very serious periods of cancer. She survived for a long time and was instrumental in getting me to a doctor in 1988, when my diabetes was diagnosed. She was also one of those people who said I should write this book.

I also had the pleasure of meeting another hero, Terry Waite, when he was the starter of the London Marathon in one of the years when I was in charge of the wheelchair racers. He met and spoke to all the competitors in wheelchairs before sending them on their way.

Another person I have already mentioned, my old next-door neighbour and the man who got me involved with the Nabisco Fun Runs, Mike Paxton OBE. He suffered from multiple sclerosis, cancer of the liver and heart attacks from the age of late fifties, but still carried on with many activities helping others.

In terms of survival and courage, Sir Ranulph Fiennes has to be in my list as a survivor and extraordinary explorer.

Then there is Philip Lewis MBE, the man who took me into disabled sport, and who was largely responsible for many of the special initiatives that have helped disabled people have the opportunities to take part in sport at all levels. He himself had been in a wheelchair for over thirty years, but had still been able to enjoy sport, both as a competitor and supporter.

It was through him that I met Peter Hull, the young man I first met while he was at school outside Reading, and who later competed in the Reading Half Marathon as well as the London Marathon. Peter is an example to anyone with a disability. He has no arms or legs, but he won

Paralympic medals for swimming, drives a car, and has a full-time responsible job. I suppose it is people like him that have kept me interested in sport for people with disabilities in spite of the politics that go with it.

I look back on a hard but enjoyable life with a number of careers; delivery grocers boy; policeman; soldier; salesman; sports writer; retailer; importer; event organiser; charity worker and administrator. I have never been wealthy but have always got by, even when income was virtually nil, I have never had to use State help, and have never been afraid to change direction, hence my multitude of careers. Life has been exciting, challenging and never boring. I have met many interesting people; some honest and hard-working, and some a little less than that, and I believe in maintaining standards, but I certainly have never had any time for snobbery whether connected with social standing, art, music or whatever. Sport has been my life, and all my careers have had sport as a major part of it, from the police through to charity work. I have been "On The Run" for fifty-four years, as a runner and with organising running events for others. I have the satisfaction of having a long happy marriage and our wedding in 1957 only seems a few years ago. We have five children and six grandchildren, although the family name will not be continued through to the next generations as our two grandsons are the families of our daughters. In general I have always been able to do the things that I have wanted to and enjoyed doing them all. I have only really had too much to drink about four times in my life, and one of them was on my fortieth birthday, when we had a big party at our old home on St Peter's Hill. I enjoy wine occasionally, but my main enjoyment is a glass of fine malt whisky. My musical tastes range from organ and church music, to brass and military bands, as well as classical music, in particular Handel. If I had my life over again what would I do? Would I make changes? I suppose if I was to have chosen a profession, it could have been as an accountant (it would use my talent for figures but oh so boring). I could have stayed in the police, where I was told I had a promising career, but I am not sure I could live with the politics of the job or all the other changes in recent years. I might have even entered the Church, but with a large family, I don't think I could have afforded that career. If computers had been around when I was younger, I would have enjoyed a career in that industry, as I have enjoyed working and using them now for over twenty years. On the whole I would not have changed very much, just a little tweak here and there, and perhaps I would rather like to have said I did compete in the Olympics in 1960! But *Life on the Run* continues.....

INDEX